Mediation in the Reflection of Law and Society

Global Trends in Dispute Resolution

VOLUME 10

Series Editor

Nadja Alexander is Director of the Singapore International Dispute Resolution Academy and Professor of Law at Singapore Management University. Professor Alexander is an award-winning author and educator in the field of negotiation and dispute resolution. She is known for the passion, energy and creativity she brings to her various roles as scholar, policy adviser, mediation practitioner and trainer. She has been identified by *Who's Who Legal* as a global thought leader in mediation.

Introduction

Global Trends in Dispute Resolution offers readers a garden rich in ideas and insights into contemporary dispute resolution principles, processes, and practices. The series leads the way in first-class debate and analysis of dispute resolution trends across our rapidly globalising world. More particularly, its volumes analyse dispute resolution developments in various geographical regions around the world and in relation to diverse transnational practice areas. These practice areas include not only well-established legal categories such as intellectual property, construction, and resources law, but also emerging dispute resolution trends ranging from dispute systems design to cross-border mediation in private and public law.

Objective

With a particular focus on new initiatives and dispute resolution practices, the *Global Trends in Dispute Resolution* series aims to provide practitioners, scholars, policymakers, and 'pracademics' (that elusive yet rapidly emerging category of practical academics and academically-oriented practitioners – you know who you are) with the resources both to cultivate the dispute resolution gardens of the world and to explore new paths within and beyond them.

Frequency of Publication

A volume is published whenever an interesting topic presents itself.

The titles published in this series are listed at the end of this volume.

Mediation in the Reflection of Law and Society

European Perspectives

Lenka Holá
Martina Urbanová
Miloš Večeřa
David Fiedor
Jan Holas

Wolters Kluwer

Published by:
Kluwer Law International B.V.
PO Box 316
2400 AH Alphen aan den Rijn
The Netherlands
E-mail: international-sales@wolterskluwer.com
Website: www.wolterskluwer.com/en/solutions/kluwerlawinternational

Sold and distributed by:
Wolters Kluwer Legal & Regulatory U.S.
7201 McKinney Circle
Frederick, MD 21704
United States of America
E-mail: customer.service@wolterskluwer.com

ISBN 978-94-035-4214-0

e-Book: ISBN 978-94-035-4292-8
web-PDF: ISBN 978-94-035-4293-5

The book was written under the research project of the Czech Science Foundation (GACR) 'Conditions of Mediation Performance in the Czech Republic under the Mediation Act', GA18-01417S.

About the Authors

Lenka Holá is an Associate Professor at the Department of Political and Social Sciences at the Faculty of Law of Palacký University in Olomouc, where she focuses on out-of-court dispute resolution and mediation. She completed her doctoral studies in sociology at the Faculty of Arts of Palacký University in Olomouc. Holá focuses on the quality of mediation, institutionalisation of mediation and professionalisation of mediators. She has participated in research on family mediation in the Czech Republic and the effectiveness of tools for resolving parental conflicts. She is the author and co-author of a number of publications, especially on the topic of mediation. At the same time, she has more than twenty years of experience as a practising mediator in the field of civil, family, criminal and consumer disputes. She served as a member of the advisory body of the Minister of Justice for alternative forms of judicial proceedings. She was actively involved in the legislative process during the adoption of the Czech Mediation Act and in the preparation of mediator examinations. Holá currently serves as the chair of the examination committee of the mediator and family mediation examinations, and is a member of the Working Group on Mediation of the Ministry of Justice of the Czech Republic. During 2018–2020, she was the principal investigator of a research grant from the Czech Academy of Sciences entitled 'Conditions for the exercise of mediation in the Czech Republic under the Mediation Act'.

Martina Urbanová is an Associate Professor of Sociology at the Faculty of Law, Masaryk University in Brno, Department of Legal Theory. She graduated from the Faculty of Arts of Masaryk University in Brno, majoring in Sociology, passed her Post-Master's examination in Sociology of politics and public opinion, and completed postgraduate studies in the doctoral programme Theory of State and Law and Philosophy of Law at the Faculty of Law of Masaryk University in Brno, Department of Legal Theory. Her teaching work focuses on teaching Sociology, Sociology of Law, Conflict Management and Resolution, Social Communication and Rhetoric. Her scientific expertise has long been focused on issues of social control, social deviance and mediation. She has authored and co-authored a number of publications mainly in the fields of sociology, sociology of law and social aspects of mediation. Urbanová is a member of the Working Group on Mediation of the Ministry of Justice of the Czech Republic, and a member of the Czech Society of Criminology, Czech Association for Legal and Social Philosophy IVR and Czech Sociological Society. During 2018–2020, she was a co-investigator of the research grant of the Czech Academy of Sciences 'Conditions for the exercise of mediation in the Czech Republic under the Mediation Act'.

Miloš Večeřa is Professor of Theory, Philosophy and Sociology of Law and Head of the Department of Legal Theory at the Faculty of Law of Masaryk University in Brno. He graduated from the Faculty of Arts and subsequently from the Faculty of Law of Masaryk University in Brno. In 1993, he received the Candidate of Sciences in Sociology; in 1997, he habilitated in the field of legal theory and in 2005, he was appointed professor in the field of theory, philosophy and sociology of law. During 1994–2014, he also served as an assistant to a judge of the Constitutional Court of the Czech Republic. His professional interests include the functioning of law in society, system of law, legal culture, globalisation and europeanisation of law, social and legal state, social and legal equality, legal justice and legal communication. He has published a number of monographs on these topics, in particular *Justice in Law*, as well as academic articles and university textbooks at both home and abroad. Prof. Večeřa is a member of the Czech Sociological Society and Vice-Chairman of the Czech Association for Legal and Social Philosophy. He presented a lecture on mediation in the perspective of law and social change at the international scientific conference MEDIATION 2019. He is the main author of *Intercultural Mediation in Sociological and Legal Context* (2017).

David Fiedor completed his PhD in Regional Geography and Regional Development at the Faculty of Science of Masaryk University in Brno in 2017. Since 2013, he has been working at the Department of Geography at Palacký University in Olomouc, and since 2016 also at the Department of Sociology, Andragogy and Cultural Anthropology at the same university, where he teaches courses focused on the use of quantitative research methods in the social sciences, research methodology and the basics of demography. His research focuses mainly on the spatial aspects of social phenomena, especially gambling, and on the use of statistical methods and spatial statistical methods in social-science research. In the field of gambling research, he has published several scientific studies in prestigious domestic and foreign journals, and in 2020 he published a separate monograph, *Gambling in the Czech Republic*. Fiedor was a member of the research team of the grant 'Conditions for the exercise of mediation in the Czech Republic under the Mediation Act' and a member of the research team of two applied-research projects focused on the identification of places of fear of crime in cities and indicators of municipal development.

Jan Holas graduated in 2017 with a degree in Law and Legal Science from the Faculty of Law of Masaryk University in Brno. He is currently working at the Department of Civil Procedure. In addition to civil procedural law, his professional activity focuses on the legal aspects of mediation. In the doctoral study programme Civil Law and Civil

Procedure, he is working on his dissertation on mediation and its place in the resolution of civil disputes. As a principal investigator, he was involved in a university research project on trends in amicable resolution of civil disputes and in a development project to introduce the teaching discipline Mediation in Theory and Practice. Since 2017, he is also serving as an assistant to the President of the Senate of the Supreme Court of the Czech Republic.

Summary of Contents

Table of Contents

Preface

The current wider use of out-of-court dispute resolution methods is related to the modernisation and democratisation of judicial systems, increasing citizens' access to justice, and efforts to make the dispute resolution process more efficient, shorter and cheaper and to put responsibility back in the hands of the parties. In Europe, the growing trend towards the use of mediation places greater demands on its formalisation, that is, on finding an appropriate place in the legal system of a given country, to some extent with regard to foreign legislation. In countries with different cultural and legal traditions, mediation takes different forms and differs in its particular organisational set-up, which is dependent on the justice system in question, the level of institutionalisation of mediation, the philosophy of the goals towards which mediation is directed, and the required competences of mediators or their expected practices, which depend on the area of mediation. The experience of countries where mediation has a longer history shows that there are two stages in its implementation. The first is to create a framework for mediation (e.g., legislative conditions, qualifications and accreditation of mediators), while the second is to achieve community acceptance and use of mediation.

The actual study of mediation then moves away from one-sided examinations of psychology and law in particular, and the development progresses towards a more comprehensive and multifaceted understanding. The present book also goes beyond the relatively narrow framework of legal-positivist analyses and psychological approaches to the mediation process. It is a multidisciplinary collective work whose main aim is, through the application of different methodological and conceptual approaches, to analyse the legal, cultural, social, systemic and spatial aspects of the use of mediation in the legal practice of the different countries of the European Union (EU) and, based on a spatiotemporal analysis and models of mediation in the EU, to identify the reasons for the fragmentation of its legal regulation and the possible impact on the low level of its use in practice.

Recent research on mediation has been responsive to societal developments and has focused on broader societal aspects. This, in the context of the European society's efforts to harmonise the conditions for the practice and wider application of mediation, also provides the framework for the focus of our research titled 'Conditions for the Practice of Mediation in the Czech Republic under the Mediation Act' (GA18-0141S). This book has been produced as part of that project, and it sets forth the results of research conducted from January 2018 to December 2020. It is a collective work and the authors are mainly members of the research team. These have been joined by other experts on the issues discussed. This was a necessary step if the book was to fulfil its stated aim.

The book is a unique combination of exploration of the theoretical determinants of mediation and an empirical study of the extent of its use in the European area, which will show how the phenomenon has changed over time. It also elaborates on the findings published in the monograph by Alexander et al.,[1] in particular by categorising jurisdictions and the legal anchoring of mediation in the systems of functioning of mediation within the EU, including aspects of their further development.

In the first part of the book, we discuss mediation from the perspective of law and social change. The mediation process takes place in a particular social setting and is closely linked to legal instruments. Therefore, we are concerned with the social context of mediation, the operation of law in contemporary late modern society and the interdependence of law and society against the broader background of the sociocultural system in which law and social relations are materialised. The legal system is viewed through a sociolegal lens, and the topic of mediation is set in the environment of the relationship between society and law. The text presents law as an institution of society and part of its sociocultural system, where culture conditions the form of law and the development of social relations. At the same time, law reflects culture and often comes into conflict with it. Attention is paid to the contemporary transformations of law in late modern society, linked to the processes of globalisation and europeanisation, so important for the development of mediation in the European context.

Law is also presented as a means of regulating social relations and as an important instrument of social change in late modern society. We seek to answer the question of to what extent law itself reflects the ongoing social change. In this context, the text seeks to trace the extent to which the legal embedding of mediation is an instrument of purposeful change or whether it merely reflects and confirms the social changes taking place in society. Related to this fundamental question is the need to identify the limits of law in promoting social change. The relationship between law and social change is presented using the examples of mediation and its legal anchoring.

The second part of the book focuses on an analysis of selected cultural, social and legal sources of introduction of mediation into the legal orders in the European environment. It approaches the topic from the sociocultural and legal-theoretical perspectives, in which the two approaches are interconnected by a discussion of the question of values in culture, society and law. We consider the values of justice and cooperation as central values in the context of the topic of mediation. Social behaviour is closely related to values and the norms derived from them. Mediation is also guided

1. Nadja M. Alexander, Sabine Walsh, Martin Svatoš (eds). *EU Mediation Law Handbook: Regulatory Robustness Ratings for Mediation Regimes* (Wolters Kluwer 2017).

by certain rules. From this, it can be deduced that it has values. Moreover, mediation itself is an instrument for mediating values. It allows participants to discover values for themselves, to experience them, to create new values. This, with all their 'intentionality', is an unrepeatable and creative act.

In exploring the cultural sources of mediation, we set out a research subquestion: in what cultures can we find sources for the introduction and development of mediation? We analyse the different dimensions of cultures according to Hofstede in terms of their potential for the development of mediation. We will use the aspects of cultural integration of Europe as a starting point for EU efforts in the field of mediation. In analysing the sources for implementing mediation into the legal systems of individual legal orders, we must not ignore the development of society and the social conditions of its members. This allows us to anchor mediation as promoting social functioning and also to find possible social sources of them in this concept. Finally, we identify the legal sources of mediation in the ideas of legal philosophy and theory of law. In the context of justice as a fundamental legal principle, we will analyse mediation from three perspectives – as a means of improving citizens' access to justice, as a means of applying social justice in society, and as a means of restorative justice.

This is followed up by the third part of the book, which deals with systems of approach to mediation in the EU. A system of approach to mediation is conceived as a set of measures, factors and their interrelations that determine the possibilities of approach to mediation in a particular country. The various measures and factors may be legal or non-legal in nature. They range from the imposition of an obligation to participate in mediation to, for example, informal provision of information about the possibility of attempting to resolve a dispute in mediation. With respect to the development and forms that systems of approach to mediation in the EU have taken, we first discuss the origins of mediation in Europe, the EU's efforts in this area and the path towards the incorporation of mediation into the legal systems of the Member States. Subsequently, the basic forms of systems of approach to mediation applied in the Member States are outlined. The systems usually consist of several types of models. Most often, these are the coercion-based model, the motivation-based model, and the model based on the provision of information on mediation. Each of these is discussed in more detail in the third part. We then take a closer look at the limits placed on coercion to use of mediation in the EU. Some systems of approach to mediation can be so invasive (e.g., in the form of mandatory mediation) that they can interfere with the natural functioning of mediation, access to court and civil proceedings. The aim of this part of the text is therefore to define the basic boundaries for the regulation of mediation in the European context.

Examples of how mediation systems are set up in selected EU countries then form a smooth transition to the fourth part of the book. The latter, unlike the previous parts of the book which are of a theoretical nature, is empirically oriented. On the basis of national data on mediation in each EU country, we analyse and compare the extent of use of mediation in each EU country, expressed as a proportion of disputes in which mediation has been recommended or used. Three main agendas will be analysed, namely, civil, family and criminal. Given the potentially low number of disputes in which mediation is applied, the period of the last three years (2017–2019) is analysed. We want to focus on the Visegrad Four (V4) countries in more detail as mediation was not used in them at all in the period before 1990. The cultural, political, economic and geographic proximity of these states could better shed light on the obstacles that prevent a wider use of mediation in litigation in the Central European area.

A spatiotemporal differentiation will show to what extent mediation is used in each country and how this phenomenon changes over time. Based on this, we will then identify states where mediation is used more and where it is used less. The research will provide one of the first comprehensive insights into the use of mediation in litigation in individual EU states. A spatiotemporal analysis of the extent of use of mediation in a region as spatially large and at the same time diverse as the EU has never been carried out before.

The book concludes with Part V (Chapter 10), which aims to outline the prospects for the further development of mediation in the EU. The chapter is mainly based on the interweaving of the theoretical analysis of the systems of approach to mediation (Part III) and the results from a spatiotemporal analysis of the rate of mediation use in individual EU countries (Part IV), which is examined especially in relation to the mediation success rate. Although we are aware that the issue of assessing the success rate of mediation is not addressed in the literature unambiguously, given the focus of this book on the exercise of mediation in the context of judicial dispute resolution and the nature of the data collected for the spatiotemporal analysis of mediation in the EU countries, we rely on a formal approach to success rate. Therefore, what we understand as success in mediation is the conclusion of a mediation agreement resolving the dispute or a subsequent conclusion of a court settlement. This final chapter, given its specific character, will also have a different approach than the previous sections. This is because this chapter itself will draw conclusions and formulate prospects for further development of mediation on the basis of the previous parts of the book.

How can we conclude this introduction to the book and open up the space for the reader? Surely by citing the very apt words of Professor Carrie Menkel-Meadow, a prominent figure in the field of alternative dispute resolution (ADR), and one who believes that the question of whether there are too many or too few court disputes is a question of what the most appropriate ways for people and society to access justice are. She believes that 'one size will not fit all'. The question of how much litigation is appropriate in any given legal culture depends on a variety of factors that go beyond simple counting.[2] It is in this multidisciplinary spirit that we have approached the subject of the present book. On behalf of the authors' team, we can only hope that the book will contribute to refining the arguments for the promotion of mediation and its development in theory, research and application practice, and not only in the European context.

Lenka Holá et al.

2. Carrie Menkel-Meadow, *What Is an Appropriate Measure of Litigation? Quantification, Qualification and Differentiation of Dispute Resolution*, 11 Oñati Socio-Legal Series 320–353 (2021).

Acknowledgements

The authors would like to thank the Ministry of Justice of the Czech Republic, the Ministry of Foreign Affairs of the Czech Republic, and the Probation and Mediation Service of the Czech Republic for their assistance in obtaining the necessary data. They also thank the Grant Agency of the Czech Republic for financial support of the research and publication of this book.

PART I

Mediation in the Perspective of Law and Social Change

Martina Urbanová & Miloš Večeřa

INTRODUCTION TO THE TOPIC

The aim of the first part of the present book is to look at law and mediation as part of the legal system from the perspective of sociology of law, focusing primarily on the impact of social influences. These are reflected in the legal system and influence the form of law, which in turn acts back on society.

Placing mediation in a social context and trying to contemplate it from the perspective of sociology of law is a topic that is still rather neglected. Yet, mediation cannot be understood without its social, cultural and legal context. Therefore, the authors place the topic of mediation within theoretical and legal concepts such as cultural systems, justice and legitimacy, trust in law and others, and subsequently focus on the topic of law and social change.

The authors define the interrelationship between mediation, which is part of the legal system, and society as a whole. In particular, they present the operation of law in contemporary late modern society and mechanisms by which law influences social relations and its effectiveness, which is directly reflected in the functioning of mediation and its procedures. Law is defined by the authors as an institution of society and part of its sociocultural system. The operation of law in society is expressed by its functions and roles in society, reflecting the fact that law represents one of the most important instruments of social control in late modern society. At the same time, law acts as a symbol of justice and is associated with the idea of fair law and fair decision-making. In order to achieve this goal, it is necessary to have trust in law, as well as in the alternative means of dispute resolution which have made their way into law, especially in late modern society. The notion of fair law and trust in law is undeniably reflected in the entire mediation process.

As far as methodology is concerned, the authors depart primarily from the interpretive paradigm, which states that social reality and law are socially constructed. Social reality is real for those involved because they perceive it as real. The human world and therefore also law including mediation exist in the form in which people understand and construct them. Cognition of social reality not only is cognition of social reality itself, where the laws of causality, determinism and purposiveness apply, but is also determined by the principles asserted in the social construction of reality by the individual, as pointed out in particular by Berger and Luckmann.[1] Key concepts, ideals and goals are constantly changing as people construct them in the process of social interaction. The social construction of reality and law necessarily depends on the intensity of public power that enters social discourse. Consistency between political and legal reality depends on reaching an informed consensus on a particular interpretation of social facts among participants in social discourse.

Mediation is a legal tool for peaceful resolution of disputes and contributes to the fulfilment of one of the main functions of law. It shares with law the social and cultural limits of its operation. The following definition of law as part of society and its culture and the analysis of the role of law can be fully applied to mediation too. The view of law as an instrument of social change in late modern society, along with an analysis of the extent to which law reflects social change in society, can be fully applied to the introduction of the institution of mediation into law and its operation in legal practice. The institution of mediation as an applied change in law confirms the traditional Poundian notion that law is primarily meant to serve as social engineering and can thus maintain social equilibrium.[2] It was Roscoe Pound, a representative of sociological jurisprudence and the founder of sociology of law in the USA, who as early as in 1906 in his paper 'The Causes of Popular Dissatisfaction with the Administration of Justice' pointed out that the judicial process is only one of many ways of resolving legal disputes and he highlighted the possibilities of alternative dispute resolution (ADR). Pound found the judicial process to be slow and archaic and primarily concerned with winning at all costs, not with seeking justice.[3]

The authors of the text therefore ask themselves whether law, of which mediation is a part, is an instrument of targeted social change in contemporary society or whether it merely reflects and confirms the social changes taking place in society. Related to this fundamental question is the issue of identifying the limits of law in promoting social change. The starting point for the authors of this text is the concept of the legal system as an open system where stimuli from outside enter and where mutual inputs and outputs between society and law take place. The theoretical conception of social reality as a system adopts the concept of the 'open system' that arose in the field of biology: a process of mutual exchange with the environment and surrounding systems.[4]

1. Peter L. Berger & Thomas Luckmann, *Sociální konstrukce reality. Pojednání o sociologii vědění* 11 (Centrum pro studium demokracie a kultury 1999).
2. Lenka Holá et al., Právní a sociální aspekty mediace v České republice 1–20 (Wolters Kluwer 2020).
3. Roscoe Pound, The Causes of Popular Dissatisfaction with the Administration of Justice (29 A.B.A. Rep., pt. I, 395–417, 1906), https://law.unl.edu/RoscoePound.pdf.
4. Talcott Parsons, *The Social System* 90–110 (The Free Press 1966).

In contrast, a closed system implies a gradual differentiation of individual social systems and a new type of link between them based on self-reference. The social system then becomes autonomous in the sense of *autopoiesis*. Autopoietic systems are systems that reproduce all the elementary units or wholes of which they are composed throughout a network of these elements and thus separate themselves from their environment. Within the open system we depart from, such a trigger was the need for more effective dispute resolution in the form of mediation. Law will therefore not be seen as a closed autopoietic system[5] in which law circles around itself and in which law refers back to law, but rather it will rather be seen as an attempt to capture the relationship between law and social change that is taking place in the emerging late modern society. From the perspective of these considerations, law should be seen primarily as a set of legal norms constituting a legal system and as the decision-making activity of legal institutions applying law. In doing so, it is important to respect the fact that there will always be a tension in law between its ideal, normative and factual aspects.[6] In this sense, Anleu stresses that it is not enough to associate law only with its normative content, the doctrine and procedures used by law, but rather legal institutions and representatives of the legal profession should also be associated with it.[7] These legal professions can be broadly understood to include mediators, whose activities are (also) linked to the judiciary and who themselves often have a legal background.

5. Jiří Přibáň, *Sociologie práva* 129–131 (Sociologické nakladatelství 1996).
6. Manfred Rehbinder, *Einführung in die Rechtssoziologie* 9 (Athenäum Verlag 1971).
7. Sharyn L. Roach Anleu, *Law and Social Change* 13 (SAGE Publications 2010).

CHAPTER 1

Law, Society and Mediation

Martina Urbanová & Miloš Večeřa

The following chapter focuses on the social and cultural context of law and mediation and the interaction between society and law, and attempts to sociologically reflect on mediation as part of the legal system.[8] Law is understood as a social phenomenon and a social institution operating within a particular sociocultural system. It represents an important area of social life, it co-creates the social world, it is one of the elements constituting culture and society. The following second chapter of this first part of the book will then focus on law as a means of regulation and social change in social relations.

§1.01 MEDIATION AS PART OF THE LEGAL SYSTEM

Mediation as a form of conflict resolution based on negotiation with the participation of a neutral third party using knowledge from psychology, social psychology, social work, sociology, law and other disciplines began to develop dynamically in the last decades of the twentieth century. The development of mediation is linked to the postmodern era, and the influence of social changes is evident. Behind every social change there is a change in social conditions. The interest in mediation, which has resulted in the legal regulation of this issue, is closely linked to society and the dynamic changes it has undergone since the second half of the twentieth century. Contemporary society, which has been described as late modern or postmodern approximately since the 1960s, is becoming less and less homogeneous, with growing ethnic, national, religious and cultural diversity. Postmodernity brings an increasing number of rules,

8. This chapter of the first part of the present book, dealing with the social and cultural contexts of law, is followed by the second part of the book, which identifies the cultural, social and legal sources of mediation.

which makes it more difficult to navigate in society. Social and technological developments have long since created a situation where there are several equally valid answers to every question, each with its own plausibility and legitimacy. This era is also associated with a growth of social tensions and social conflicts.[9] As Beck aptly notes, in contemporary postmodern society, there is a range of social conflicts that previous types of society had not experienced.[10] These are conflicts that arise in relation to addressing issues of quality of life and equality of rights in the context of emancipation of particular social groups, be they women, ethnic groups, people with different sexual orientation, different religious beliefs, specific demands, etc. Traditional formal institutions cannot handle resolution of disputes, which become long term, and the results do not lead to the satisfaction of the parties to the conflict. Mediation can also be seen as a reflection on the problematic efficiency of how the judicial system runs, related in particular to its overload.

Mediation is thus tied to the effect of social influences and is associated with the emergence of postmodern society, the world of networks, and deregulation leading to the search for alternative conflict solutions, which are based on looking for individual responsibility and active involvement in conflict resolution. Mediation is a way to deal with increasing conflicts in postmodern society and the dissatisfaction of conflict actors. It is a search for new ways to mutually understand the plurality of thinking, ways of acting, value systems and orientations.[11] Mediation also includes respect for human dignity as a value anchored in the very foundations of the entire system of fundamental rights contained in the constitutional order. It entails the right of every person to respect and recognition as a human being.[12]

Mediation places high demands on all parties involved. Active participation in conflict resolution presupposes social responsibility, which is related to the classical concept of individualism (IND) as encountered in Rousseau and expressed in the Declaration of the Rights of Man and of the Citizen (1789). IND has a similar meaning in the work of Alexis de Tocqueville, whose concept is based on the perception of IND as the willingness and ability to sacrifice part of one's own interests for the benefit of others.[13] Mediation involves building a spirit of community. As Etzioni puts it, in the absence of accountability, the public space becomes a battleground where there is no room for compromise and matter-of-fact agreement.[14] Isolated individuals are unstable, neurotic and prone to various deviations.

9. Martina Urbanová, *Mediace jako nástroj sociální kontroly v postmoderní společnosti – vybrané sociologické aspekty mediace* 289–304 (Lenka Holá et al., Grada Publishing 2013).
10. Ulrich Beck, *Riziková společnost: Na cestě k jiné moderně* 162 (Sociologické nakladatelství 2004).
11. Urbanová, *supra* n. 9, at 289–304.
12. Martina Urbanová, *Společnost a její normativní systémy, hodnoty v právu a mediaci* 19–32 (Lenka Holá & Michal Malacka et al., Leges 2014). *See* Carrie Menkel-Meadow, *The Future of Mediation Worldwide: Legal and Cultural Variations in the Uptake of or Resistance to Mediation* 29 (Ian Macduff ed., Kluwer Law International 2016).
13. Marcel Mečiar, *Alexis de Tocqueville a vztah jeho pojetí individualismu k současnosti. Člověk-dějiny-hodnoty jako filosofický, historický, sociálně politický a výchovný problém* 149 (Vysoká sˇkola báňská 2002).
14. Amitai Etzioni, *The Spirit of Community: The Reinvention of American Society* 9 (Touchstone 1994).

Mediation, which has become a part of the legal system and reflects the consequences of the changes that law is confronted with and undergoing, in its legal (and non-legal) form includes a response to the growing complexity of contemporary society, while at the same time incorporating the much-needed process of individualised dispute resolution. As Tomlinson argues,[15] mediators themselves contribute to the understanding of law and to the chance for people from lower classes to better navigate the bureaucratic system. Unlike traditional hearings, mediation is confidential and takes place in private between the two parties. The discussion between the participants is also much more open and flexible than it would be in court. The desire to incorporate the interests of the person at the forefront is evident in the Explanatory Memorandum to the Czech Government's 2012 Mediation Bill, where the reason given (in addition to meeting the obligation to implement the Mediation Directive) is also:

> the desire to enable all persons to resolve their conflicts in an alternative way by means of a quick and sophisticated out-of-court solution [...], to decongest the courts, to avoid litigation and to resolve conflicts without long waiting periods, without unnecessary financial costs and without prolonged psychological burden on the parties. [...][16]

However, let us return to the concept of law in the perspective of sociology of law, where law is understood as a social phenomenon.

§1.02 LAW AS A SOCIAL PHENOMENON AND AN INSTITUTION OF SOCIETY

The existence of social forms of human life has gradually forced the regulation of human behaviour by social norms in an attempt to exclude or restrict certain ways of behaviour and to enforce a certain social order. Respect for and adherence to the normative orders formed for this purpose, consisting of sets of social norms as generally binding and socially recognised patterns of behaviour, is confirmed and enforced by social sanctions. Social norms were first and foremost religious and moral in character. The gradual growth of social inequalities, giving rise to conflicts of interest, the deepening of the complexity of social life and the expansion of the social (public) character of interpersonal relations gradually forced a new organisation of public life, namely, the creation of public authority and the state as an institution of society. At the same time, at that stage of development, generally binding rules of behaviour regulating, under the pressure of public authority or state coercion, social relations in a particular territory were being formed. Therefore, the creation of public (state) power goes hand in hand with a gradual creation of a legal system to ensure

15. Elizabeth C. Tomlinson, *Mediation and Legal Literacy*, 2 Community Literacy Journal 71–100 (2010).
16. Poslanecká sněmovna, *Explanatory Memorandum to the Proposal of the Government on the Mediation Statute*, Sněmovní tisk no. 426/0, part no. 1/2 (2010), http://www.psp.cz/sqw/text/tiskt.sqw?O = 6&CT = 426&CT1 = 0.

relative social stability while applying a relatively equal standard to unequal subjects of law.

Law is a social phenomenon. The social nature of law is evident not only from its purpose and object but above all from the fact that law is, in terms of its origin, the result of social processes which it influences and frames but also from the fact that it is closely linked to social institutions, especially the state.[17] In Luhmann's view, law forms part of the social structure of society where law as a structure and society as a social system must be viewed and examined in interdependence.[18] Law is a social subsystem of society and performs important social functions in relation to the sociocultural system.[19] On the other hand, changes in the sociocultural system are also reflected in changes in the functions and role of law in society and determine the dynamics of its development. According to Luhmann, law directly or indirectly affects all areas of life and is therefore difficult to isolate empirically as a special phenomenon.[20]

Law is one of the most important means of stabilising social relations. The demands placed on law and the expectations associated with its existence and operation stem from the need to secure and reproduce existing social relations, to bring order to society and thus reduce the level of social entropy.[21] Law is therefore primarily not only an instrument of social control[22] but also a means of social integration and an instrument of social change.[23] All this characterises law as an important social institution.

The importance of the social essence (nature) of law is highlighted within legal science by the legal-sociological approach to law, which is an expression of the sociological concept of law as a social phenomenon. The sociological understanding of law as a specific social system expresses the fact that law is valid and operative in society and that it exists as a real social agent that influences the everyday life of society and its members. Therefore, legal norms structure and define the boundaries of the social world, co-create the reality of everyday life, and participate in the formation of social structures. Legal norms are mediators of values, '... values are affirmed and guaranteed by contemporary law and thus also highlighted and fixed in social consciousness, including legal, moral, etc. consciousness',[24] and this also applies fully to mediation.

The basis of the sociological approach to law is the claim that law is more than just a set of legal norms; it is an important area of social life alongside the economic, political, moral and other fundamental areas of society. This is referred to as a sociological approach in law. Law is studied not only as a normative system but also

17. *See* Pavel Maršálek, *Právo a společnost* 102 (Auditorium 2008).
18. Niklas Luhmann, *Sociological Theory of Law*, London–Boston 7 (Routledge & Kegan Paul 1985).
19. *See* Miloš Večeřa & Martina Urbanová, *Sociologie práva* 59–62 (Aleš Čeněk 2006).
20. Niklas Luhmann, *Rechtssociologie* 2 (Westdeutscher Verlag 1987).
21. *See also* Jiří Přibáň, *Sociologie práva: Systémově teoretický přístup k modernímu právu* 135 (Sociologické nakladatelství 1996).
22. *See* Martina Urbanová, *Systémy sociální kontroly a právo* 41 (Aleš Čeněk 2006).
23. Roger Cotterrell, *The Sociology of Law* 44 (Butterworths 1992).
24. Jaromír Harvánek et al., *Teorie práva* 89 (Aleš Čeněk 2008).

above all as a social phenomenon.[25] In addition to a set of legal norms, law as an area of social life also includes, in particular, legal acts and legal relations, legal consciousness of individuals, social groupings and society, legal communication, activities of institutions applying law, and other legal phenomena. The subject of sociology of law was aptly defined by the French legal sociologist Georges Gurvitch, according to whom sociology of law studies the fullness of the social reality of law.[26] Sociology of law, therefore, primarily studies how and to what extent law actually operates in society, and it analyses the functional interdependence of law and other social phenomena. The difference between positivistically cultivated legal science and legal sociology is thus to be seen primarily in contrast between the 'normative' science of law and the 'factual' sociology of law.

Sociologically oriented legal science emphasises the interconnectedness of the relationship between law on the one hand and society and social life and institutions on the other, where the ideals that people hold at a certain point in time, the social conditions in which they live, and the legislative outcomes are both the cause and effect of each other. Law as an area of social life develops in contact with other social areas, in particular politics, economics and morality. The continuity with these social subsystems, which represent decisive social impulses, creates a tendency to renew and reinterpret the content of law. Therefore, law as a structure and society as a social system must be viewed and studied in a relationship of mutual influence.[27]

§1.03 SOCIOCULTURAL SYSTEM AND LAW

Law is, as already mentioned, an important area of social life. At the same time, however, it is also one of the basic constituent elements of culture, forming part of individual sociocultural systems. It is impossible to capture, analyse and understand the social life of law, the interaction of law and social reality or the factuality of legal acts without thematising the sociocultural system.

Culture is closely tied to a particular society, and one can speak of a social and cultural determination of social behaviour. Conceptually, one can distinguish the terms 'society' and 'culture', but there is a very close connection between the two concepts. Culture refers to the way of life of the members of a given society, while society refers to the system of social interactions linking individuals sharing a common culture. The two terms cannot be separated; culture and society cannot exist in isolation.[28] Culture is not only the creation and expression of a particular social formation but also the condition from which that formation develops. We therefore often use the term 'sociocultural system' to refer to a specific culture linked to a particular social system.[29]

Culture is the creation and expression of a particular social formation (group, society) and, on the other hand, it is the condition in which this formation develops.

25. *See also*, e.g., Viktor Knapp, *Teorie práva* 6 (C. H. Beck 1995).
26. Georges Gurvitch, *Sociology of Law* 47 (Kegan Paul 1947).
27. Niklas Luhmann, *A Sociological Theory of Law* 7 (Routledge and Kegan Paul 1985).
28. Anthony Giddens, *Sociologie* 32 (Argo 1999).
29. Ruth Benedict, *Kulturní vzorce* 27 (Argo 1999).

Culture is the reference system to which the social processes of the social formation in question are related and in whose coordinates certain phenomena are considered socially valid, desirable and binding. These processes also apply to the creation and implementation of law and thus apply to mediation.

Culture cannot be associated narrowly only with aesthetics, that is, culture as art. The sociological concept of culture is broader and includes the totality of all material and spiritual results of human activity. Benedict considers the core of culture to be a certain complex of behavioural patterns (cultural patterns) as a system of learned behaviour representing the 'way of life' of a certain community (society). The real link between people is the ideas and standards they share. Culture is a way of explaining the world and allows a certain way of seeing the world to be transmitted. One of the ways of grasping the external world is law as part of human culture. Law can be seen as an institutionalised cultural agent whose actors (legislators, judges, mediators, state officials and the addressees of law themselves) set the meanings of social facts. In this sense, Geertz concludes that law is one of the ways in which we make sense of the world around us; it is a way of organising meanings, one of the essential ways we imagine reality.[30] Law co-creates the social world and cannot be separated from culture since it is also one of the elements that constitute culture and society.[31] Law shapes individual and group identities, social behaviour, and social processes and practices, including how to resolve disputes.[32]

It can be concluded that, in general, law reflects culture but at the same time comes into conflict with it. Mezey finds three different approaches to characterise the relationship between law and culture:[33] the first approach places law in terms of power above culture; the second approach emphasises that culture stands above law. The third approach assumes a state of unstable synthesis between the two, shaped by the continuous recycling and rearticulation of legal and cultural meanings. Law, as part of culture, expresses a certain way of life of a community, capturing human meanings and values, which law translates into requirements for human behaviour and the functioning of social institutions.

Here we come to the issue of the informational, value and attitudinal aspects of legal consciousness as a projection of the entire legal sphere (not only legal norms) into the consciousness of legal subjects.[34] In her study,[35] Kourilsky-Augeven concludes that the way we are introduced to law in childhood has a significant influence on later legal behaviour, attitudes towards law and beliefs about law. The crucial age is 13–14 years, which is considered to be something of a breaking point as it is usually at this age that

30. Clifford Geertz, *Local Knowledge: Further Essays in Interpretative Anthropology* 184 (Basic Books 1983).
31. Daniel Šmihula, *Evolúcia práva* 258 (Epos 2013).
32. Ronald Dworkin, *Ríša práva* 11 (Kalligram 2014).
33. Naomi Mezey, *Law As Culture,* 13 The Yale Journal of Law & the Humanities 38 (2001).
34. The issue of legal consciousness is dealt with in detail in Miloš Večeřa & Martina Urbanová, *Sociologie práva* 222 (Aleš Čeněk 2011) and Miloš Večeřa et al., *Právní vědomí v teoreticko-empirickém pohledu* 24–32 (Masarykova univerzita 2015).
35. Chantal Kourilsky-Augeven, *Legal Socialisation: From Compliance to Familiarisation Through Permeation,* 1(1) European Journal of Legal Studies (2007).

mindsets change. Kourilsky-Augeven points out differences in development between the two sexes; women try to resolve disputes in a non-confrontational manner and are generally more conforming to the rules they have learned. Men, on the other hand, are not reluctant to enter into conflict if they feel that individual rights are being violated, and they generally approach and evaluate rules more critically. This is confirmed in the Czech Republic, where, according to the list of registered mediators, the majority of mediators – three-quarters of them – are women.[36] However, this is not the case in other countries. As can be seen from surveys in the United Kingdom (UK),[37] Italy[38] or even Turkey,[39] in most countries, we can observe a balanced ratio of men and women, which falls on one side or the other depending on the type of mediation.[40] However, the ratio is visibly unbalanced in the area of international mediation. Only about 6% of female mediators have led peace processes, and 2% of female mediators have had the opportunity to lead the main peace processes.[41] Therefore, there is still a gender imbalance as is the case in the judiciary, with women more likely to be involved in the lower types of courts.

Legal communication plays an important role in the formation of legal consciousness of the addressee of law, as it mediates not only the information content but also the transmission of information concerning evaluative views of law. Hoecke stresses that the concept of legal communication is one of the important – and perhaps the most important – aspects of law. The concept of legal communication determines the extent to which psychological elements in law become important, especially in terms of the acceptance of law and its interpretation.[42] As far as the formation of evaluative aspects of legal consciousness (rational and emotional judgments and ideas) and attitudinal elements are concerned, the process of socialisation of an individual, of which legal socialisation is a part, plays a fundamental role. The purpose of legal socialisation is to reproduce legal rules of behaviour, ways of legal motivation, acts in legal relationships, and legal attitudes of the addressees of law. Based on empirical studies, Kohlberg showed the importance of the moral development of an individual in legal socialisation.[43] The stages of legal socialisation in relation to law translate significantly into

36. http://mediatori.justice.cz/MediatorPublic/Public/FR003_ZverejneniVybranychUdaju.
37. Grant Morris, *From Anecdote to Evidence: The New Zealand Commercial Mediation Market* p. 8, Faculty of Law, Victoria University of Wellington (31 Mar. 2016), https://papers.ssrn.com/sol3/papers.cfm?abstract_id=2923901.
38. List of registered mediators in Italy is available here *Albo dei Mediatori (giustizia.it)*.
39. Oguzhan Akyıldırım, Dilan Oran & Oguz Önel, *Project on Developing Mediation Practices in Civil Disputes in Turkey* str. 14, Council of Europe – Ministry of Justice, Mediation Department (6 Dec. 2017), *Microsoft Word – Mediation_Followup_V5.4_EN.docx (coe.int)*.
40. In family mediation, there is traditionally a greater representation of women, whereas in commercial mediation, for example, the proportion of men is over 70%.
41. Laura Davis, *EU Support to Women Mediators: Moving Beyond Stereotypes*, Civil Society Dialogue Network (2019), EPLO_CSDN_Background-Paper_EU-Support-to-Women-Mediators.pdf, *Facts and Figures: Women, Peace, and Security*, UN Women (2020), *Facts and Figures: Women, Peace, and Security | What We Do | UN Women – Headquarters*; Elisabeth Slåttum, *It Is Time for More Women Mediators*, GIWPS (Říjen 23, 2018), *It Is Time for More Women Mediators – GIWPS (georgetown.edu)*.
42. Mark Van Hoecke, *Law as Communication* 203 (Hart Publishing 2002).
43. Lawrence Kohlberg, *The Development of Children's Orientations Toward a Moral Order*, 6 Vita Humana 11–33 (1963).

legal attitudes and the level of legal consciousness. Therefore, efforts to bring law and mediation in particular into all types of education and to target individuals from the earliest age can be considered justified.

§1.04 FUNCTIONS AND ROLE OF LAW IN SOCIETY, LAW AS AN INSTRUMENT OF SOCIAL CONTROL

[A] Functions of Law in Society

The institution of mediation and its application must be understood in terms of the functions to which it is intended to contribute in social relations. The overall meaning of these functions may not be clear in the case of legal institutions. The functions of law and the regulation of a specific area cannot be reduced to the objectives of legal regulation alone; they are broader and, moreover, they relate to the entire legal sphere, including, in particular, the activities of legal institutions and the real form of legal relations. However, the overall sociocultural system and its elements, especially the influence of other social regulations, cannot be ignored. Therefore, the specification of the functions of law will necessarily be influenced by the form of the political system and its basic value bases, the structure of social relations (moral, economic, division of labour, etc.), the quality of the activities of the bodies applying the law, etc.

When analysing the functions of law (legal regulation), we usually distinguish between the function of law and the objective (purpose) of law. The objective of law (or of a specific legal norm, legal regulation) expresses what is wanted, what is to be, what is to be achieved, whereas the function of law emphasises the aspect of factuality, what law ensures, what it actually contributes to in the sociocultural system. In some analyses and opinions, the distinction between the objectives and functions of law is almost lost. This is especially so if we speak more generally of the purposes (objectives) of law, which in their generality will be close to the functions of law. Law performs primarily positive functions in society, and not only the creation of law but also the entire process of applying law is directed towards this end. The essential positive functions of law include the following:[44]

(1) Maintaining social order – public law in particular establishes the basic categories of prohibited and required behaviour of legal subjects. Within this function of law, law as an instrument of social control is most clearly manifested.
(2) Defining rights and obligations of legal subjects in social (legal) relations through interaction.
(3) Facilitating cooperative behaviour by promoting the conclusion and fulfilment of contractual obligations of cooperating legal subjects in the field of commercial and civil law.

44. Miloš Večeřa & Martina Urbanová, *Sociologie práva* 261–263 (Aleš Čeněk 2011).

(4) Resolving conflicts in social relations by determining who enjoys rights and who has obligations in a legal relationship. Here is potential space for the application of mediation procedures.
(5) Mediating the transmission of cultural patterns of behaviour and values. Law thus provides important information about the patterns of behaviour that are generally accepted, approved and expected by society and that are rational, utilitarian and desirable.
(6) Lending legitimacy to the exercise of public functions. Law determines the ways in which public offices are filled and how public power is exercised in society.

In addition to the positive functions, some negative functions of law are also manifested, which escalate during crisis periods of social development. These include mainly preservation of the status quo, an instrument of oppression, justification of the use of violence, and strengthening of the power of the state.[45] Among the functions of the state mentioned above, the role of the state in maintaining the social order is significant, with law acting as a basic instrument of social control.

[B] Mediation as an Instrument of Social Control

Mediation is currently one of the tools of social control helping to deal with growing conflicts and dissatisfaction of the actors of the conflicts with their resolution. It is a search for new ways to mutually understand the plurality of thinking, ways of acting, value systems and orientations.

The sociolegal approach we take can be understood as a series of reflections on the topic of lost control. It is this definition that allows us to approach mediation in a sociologising way and thus to emphasise the social influences that have contributed to its expansion and transformation. It is thus possible to contemplate mediation from a less conventional perspective. It is the sociological approach that 'allows us to see in a new light the same world in which we have lived all our lives'.[46] Conflict and mediation associated with its resolution can be conceived as a social phenomenon and explained in terms of other social phenomena and the nature of reality itself. Therefore, it will not be, in the words of the theoretical context, a kind of closed (autopoietic) system having an immanent nature and circling only around itself. Rather, it will be an open system with complex relationships where we see the social system as persons and organisations acting in mutual interaction and striving for the greatest satisfaction of their needs. In doing so, actors adapt their actions to the conditions dictated by the external environment.

Law undeniably represents one of the most important instruments of social control in late modern society. The notion of social control encompasses a set of all

45. David O. Friedrichs, *Law in Our Lives* 8 (Roxbury Publishing 2003).
46. Peter L. Berger, *Pozvání do sociologie: Humanistická perspektiva* (Barrister & Principal 2017).

means, social institutions and processes existing in a social unit by which the social unit ensures conformity to accepted values, goals, needs and norms.

The concept of social control is understood by sociology not only as a technical characteristic of certain specific 'tools' by which society is influenced but also above all as a certain social process by which certain standards and social patterns of behaviour are transmitted to people. Social control is a collective term for all the mechanisms that ensure the order and stability of society. The meaning of the term 'social control' is close to that associated with the term 'power', that is, the ability to control people. The term 'control' can be understood in the sense of governing, directing, regulating, not only checking and supervising, etc.[47] Control is therefore considered as the governing of the actions of others. It then becomes the extent to which the group regulates the actions of individuals who function as members of the group.

During social interactions, the real behaviour of an individual or group is constantly confronted with collectively shared values and norms. Social control is the principle through which the behaviour of individuals or groups is detected, and it is ensured that this behaviour does not deviate further from these norms and values. However, social control does not only act as a retrospective assessment of whether social behaviour is acceptable or appropriate, for it also serves as a baseline of what is desirable. 'It is thus not only a regulatory but also a normative mechanism in the social process.'[48]

It is clear, therefore, that law also needs to interact with other normative systems and conventions to strengthen its power. Social control occurs in normal everyday activities and social interactions, very often unintentionally and spontaneously. Social groups exert social control over their members, from whom they expect appropriate behaviour. Individuals internalise social norms and values, form opinions of themselves, and establish a psychological mechanism of self-control. They thus acquire permanent responsibility for their behaviour, and this is one of the main objectives of social control.

Mediation is based on responsibility for the consequences of one's behaviour and actions, especially if they take the form of negative social deviations. The postmodern situation, however, places increased demands on the actors, especially demands related to the nature of today's ever-changing society, a society that creates considerable uncertainty and unpredictability.

Law as an instrument of control, according to Pound, whom we used to introduce this section and who can be credited with the development of mediation, channels the individualistic instinct in favour of the social instinct, and this is because otherwise the aggressive instinct would override the social tendency to cooperate and the end of civilisation would occur.[49]

Law as an instrument of social control is also mentioned by the contemporary German legal sociologist Manfred Rehbinder, who sees law as a means of social control

47. Urbanová, *supra* n. 22, at 191.
48. Hana Maříková et al., *Velký sociologický slovník I, II* 1627 (Karolinum 1996).
49. Roscoe Pound, *An Introduction to the Philosophy of Law* (Yale University Press 1922).

that directs and corrects social life.[50] This role of law can only be fulfilled if group behaviour is fixed. It fails when legal norms do not meet the expectations of the group, in which case law loses its role, that is, the role of an instrument of social control. Law therefore depends on social life and its changes.

§1.05 LAW AS A SYMBOL OF JUSTICE, TRUST IN LAW AS A BASIS FOR TRUST IN MEDIATION

[A] Justice and the Legitimacy of Law

Evaluation by means of justice criteria represents one of the basic evaluative approaches of human beings to social reality, to human behaviour, to social relations, processes and institutions. One of the compelling arguments for the application of mediation is the sense of injustice that people feel in the context of court proceedings. Each of the parties to a dispute often sees its approach as the only possible and fair one. The words 'justice' and 'injustice' have become a common part of our everyday language. It is an anthropological fact[51] that humans perceive these contexts through a culturally shaped sense of justice that has not only a rational component but also an irrational and emotional one. It is inherent in our everyday thinking and evaluation as a very convincing argument, and it is irrelevant whether the acting subject is explicitly aware of the principles of justice and consciously and intentionally applies them, or whether they are immanent to their actions and are implemented completely intuitively and spontaneously.

Law plays an important role in finding and administering justice, but it is not a privileged domain of justice as lawyers often tend to absolutise. Justice is not exhausted by law as Aristotle already observed by stating that justice has an overarching character over law. In the *Nicomachean Ethics*, he thus distinguished between ethical justice and legal justice.[52] Similarly, Knapp recalls the distinction between legal, moral (ethical), historical and social justice, which can hardly be reduced to a common denominator.[53] In addition to these basic areas of evaluation by means of justice criteria, the political, economic, transcendental (divine), historical, environmental and other areas cannot be ignored. Therefore, a decision according to law may appear unfair according to other areas of evaluation by means of justice criteria, for example, moral justice considerations.

The plurality of evaluation by means of justice criteria necessarily makes it difficult to provide a universal, all-encompassing definition of justice. Justice can be characterised as a value or principle expressing a good organisation of interpersonal relations, a desirable mode and outcome of the distribution of values, and an optimal

50. Manfred Rehbinder, *Einführung in die Rechtssoziologie* 4 (Athenäum Verlag 1971).
51. Ota Weinberger, *Norma a Instituce: Úvod do teorie práva* 193 (Masarykova univerzita 1995).
52. *See* Aristotelés. *Etika Nikomachova* 104 (J. Laichter 1937).
53. Knapp, *supra* n. 25, at 82.

organisation of society.[54] The category of justice can also be understood as the absence or presence of injustice.[55]

Questions of justice in law can be broken down into two basic thematic areas. The first area is the question of the justice of law itself, that is, what is fair law? Traditional liberals departed from the idea that justice is a value or idea that precedes law and should therefore be expressed in law. Similarly, the natural-law theory conditioned the justice of law on conformity to natural-law principles. The second area of justice in law is the question of legal justice, that is, the justice of interpreting and deciding according to law and on the basis of law, where in this case we depart from the a priori assumption of fair law. In particular, this concerns the entire area of interpretation and application of law, that is, the issue of justice of the decision-making activity of judicial and administrative authorities, in terms of both fair procedure and the fairness of the decision itself. Issues of fair decision-making under law also touch very closely on the mediation process.

The issue of fair decision-making concerns two levels of justice: formal justice and substantive justice. From the perspective of legal justice, the requirements of formal justice are a prerequisite for achieving substantive justice. This primarily concerns equality before the law. It can be characterised as a principle that under the same relevant conditions, the same legal consequences occur in all the cases under consideration, and the relevant legal order determines what conditions are relevant and what legal consequences are to occur. That is, all identical (equal) persons must be treated equally in the same relevant circumstances. The fulfilment of formal fairness in the application of law is essentially conditional on respect for the requirements of procedural fairness not only in the procedure before courts and other state bodies but also in the procedure before a mediator. Procedural fairness creates the conditions for a fair evaluation of a given case.

Requirements for the substantive aspect of justice consist mainly in working with a legal text and subsequent finding of law and justice in a particular case. In their decision-making, judges are bound by laws, international treaties and European law. In most cases, the linguistic method of interpreting a legal text alone is not sufficient to meet the requirement of substantive fairness in decision-making. Judges shape law by their interpretive and decision-making activity, applying other methods of interpretation and considering the issue of the limits of the certainty of law, interpretation of vague concepts, space for judicial discretion, etc.

The fulfilment of the formal and substantive requirements for fair decision-making in specific cases constitutes the basis for the legitimacy of the exercise of judicial decision-making, operation of the judicial system and mediation. Procedural fairness in judicial decision-making emerges as an important basis not only for the perceived legitimacy of judicial decision-making and its quality but also for the legitimacy of law itself.

54. *See* Miloš Večeřa, *Spravedlnost v právu* 16 (Masarykova univerzita 1997).
55. For comparison *see also* Vladimír Zoubek, *Postmoderní právověda a státověda* 54 (Aleš Čeněk 2016).

[B] Trust in Law

For the field of mediation to be part of the legal system, trust in the system is essential. If people do not trust law, trust in mediation cannot be expected. Law is not only what is written in books but also what people have in their consciousness.[56] For this reason, we shall examine this subject in more detail. Even trust in law undergoes changes as we will demonstrate through the example of a number of research studies.

[1] Trust as a Basis for Social Coexistence

Trust can be considered a basic condition of social coexistence, whether it be traditional, modern or postmodern society. Although the principle of trust remains the same, the forms that trust take change with the nature of society.[57] Whether this concerned Émile Durkheim's organic solidarity,[58] which replaced mechanical solidarity or Ferdinand Tönnies' post-community society,[59] trust in non-kin relations always emerges in more advanced stages of society. Trust implies that others will be trustworthy, that is, that their behaviour in the future will exhibit combinations of some of the following characteristics: regularity, efficiency, reliability, representativeness, fairness, responsibility and benevolence.[60] Trust can be characterised as a social phenomenon that links the micro and macro lines at different social levels.[61]

Trust is crucial to culture and democracy and is linked to the formal rationality of modernity. In order to trust others, we need to know the principles that others observe. True democracy is based on trust. When we trust, we assume that others are capable of thinking about our welfare and the welfare of the entire community. In contemporary society, we are often forced to place our trust in people we do not know and in systems that we often do not even understand well and that are only guaranteed by the authority of rules. Theories of modern social systems are based on high division of labour and their functioning is conditional on trust in others. We trust the doctor to treat us, the teacher to teach us, the lawyer to defend our interests, the judge to do justice, and the mediator to help us peacefully resolve a dispute and reach an agreement. We believe that modern social systems are based on rational foundations, with the aim of creating a harmonious democratic society and eliminating the greatest social inequalities.

56. Vojtěch Cepl, *Prameny práva – Nejpraktičtější jsou dobré teorie. Centrum pro ekonomiku a politiku*, Centrum pro ekonomiku a politiku (6 Jun. 2020), http://cepin.cz/cze/prednaska.php?ID=70.
57. Markéta Sedláčková, *Důvěra v demokracii* 23 (Sociologické nakladatelství 2012).
58. Émile Durkheim, *Společenská dělba práce* 375 (Centrum pro studium demokracie a kultury 2004).
59. Ferdinand Tönnies, *Community and Society* (Transnation Publishers 1988).
60. Silvia Capíková, *Sociology* 24–71 (Michaela Kostičová et al., Comenius University in Bratislava 2015).
61. Lenka Holá, Martina Urbanová et al., *Mediace v praxi optikou empirického výzkumu* 76–94 (Wolters Kluwer 2020).

The issue of trust focuses our attention on the quality of social relationships between people and institutions and on the obligations associated with these relationships.[62] Giddens[63] speaks of personal trust and abstract trust. In relationships that are based on personal trust, people will assume that they can rely on others. Abstract trust is not based on personal relationships and corresponds to the fact that in contemporary society, people are forced to place their trust in abstract (impersonal) systems of knowledge, technology, bureaucracy or law. Abstract trust relies on the expertise and competence of others. It is based on the impersonal belief that a member of a particular group of experts or institution will ordinarily act according to certain principles, obligations and requirements, which also take the form of professional and ethical codes, rather than according to their own personal interests.[64] These abstract systems depend directly on trust, which is related to the belief in the correctness of the principles and values on which these abstract systems operate.

Sztompka[65] sees trust as a key cultural resource and a useful tool for the future. In some respects, the natural and social environment presents threats and risks to human beings to which they are forced to respond and adapt. Trust in an active environment is confronted with the constructed social aspects of the future. We always face the risk that other people will choose to harm us or otherwise behave in ways that are disadvantageous to us. The risk continues to grow as our social circle expands and the group of potential partners becomes more diverse and more distant from us - in short, as we penetrate more complex environments.

Capíková[66] presents contemporary society as unpredictable, uncertain and socially differentiated, where people are no longer able to passively apply trust, but rather must actively take risks and consider whether to trust or not. Trust is thus always linked to the notion of risk.

Sztompka warns that if there is a decline in trust in society, something like a 'culture of distrust' will emerge. Distrust of the environment and of others leads to the creation of ghettos, building of impenetrable walls and buildings protected by private security agencies, and one is cut off from the outside world. An important role is also played by the mass media, presenting negative phenomena in the legal and political spheres more often than positive ones as well as the mentality of a social group accustomed to complaining rather than praising. A systematic effort to shape perceptions and knowledge in order to achieve a response that is in line with the desired intention is called propaganda.[67] In a narrower sense, propaganda is seen as 'manipulation of large collectives of people by power elites or political groups'[68] and it can greatly affect trust in the political and legal system.

62. Michal Vašečka, *Sociologické aspekty korupcie* 23 (Transparency International Slovensko 2007).
63. Anthony Giddens, *The Consequences of Modernity* 70–78 (Polity Press 1991).
64. Capíková, *supra* n. 58, at 24–71.
65. Piotr Sztompka, *Mistrusting Civility: Predicament of a Post-Communist Society* 191–210 (SAGE 1998).
66. Capíková, *supra* n. 45, at 64–67.
67. Garth S. Jowett & Victoria O'Donnell, *Propaganda and Persuasion* 2 (SAGE, Thousand Oaks 2006).
68. Alina Wróbel, *Výchova a manipulace* 105 (Grada Publishing 2008).

[2] Trust in Law

Trust in the legal system is associated with legal consciousness, which is the psychological manifestation of the projection of the legal domain into the consciousness of the addressees of law. It includes not only the rational but also the emotional component of attitudes towards law, which includes expectations, beliefs, evaluative judgments and beliefs in relation to law. It reflects the strong need of every person to believe that they live in a fair world where everyone gets what they deserve (what is due to them). A person's need for justice is the same as their need for truth. Trust in legal institutions therefore presupposes not only knowledge but also, more importantly, an opinion about those institutions.[69] As Sedláčková writes, 'in examining trust, one must first realize that trust is always a relationship formed by two parties. In our case, the degree of trust in institutions therefore depends, on the one hand, on the credibility of the institutions themselves – their reputation and performance – and, on the other hand, on people's general willingness to trust'.[70]

In law, it is trust that allows a person to meet strangers without automatically fearing that they have hostile intentions. In order for people to trust the law, there must be rules, approved by the majority, that apply to all members of society. Trust in others is thus often the result of a psychological mechanism of self-projection. Trust implies the possibility of relying on others, on social institutions and organisational forms, and ultimately on society and the state. Trust in law can then be understood as reliance on law as an area of legal life. Trust in law can be seen as a fundamental prerequisite for fulfilling the main purpose of law, which can be seen in ensuring peaceful coexistence of people through legal rules. Citizens' trust in law is the basis for the functionality, effectiveness and legitimacy of law and legal institutions in a state governed by the rule of law. The principle of trust in law is closely linked to the principle of legal certainty, which in turn forms the basis and component of trust in law. Legal certainty is usually understood as the fact that everyone receives effective protection of their rights from the state; they may exercise their rights and, in the event of a breach of a legal norm, only a sanction envisaged by a legal norm can be imposed. Legal certainty generally means the possibility of anticipating the actions of state authorities and the exclusion of randomness and arbitrariness, which creates certainty in a citizen's legal position and the basis for that citizen's confidence in the law. Legal certainty may also include stability of law, ensuring the continuity of law, and the aspect of the creation of fair law.[71] According to Evan, the basic pillars of trust in law include the degree of knowledge of law, expression of the value consensus of society in legal norms, the

---

69. There is no doubt that the media, opinion leaders and the groups a person is part of have a great influence on the formation of opinions about law. Socialisation, of which legal socialisation is a component, plays an important role in the willingness to trust.
70. Markéta Sedláčková, *Důvěra v instituce*, Socioweb (4 Jan. 2020) http://www.socioweb.cz/index.php?disp=teorie&shw=103&lst=106.
71. Jana Čechová Náplavová, *Krátce k principu právní jistoty ve světle aktuální judikatury*, epravo.cz (20 Jun. 2020), https://www.epravo.cz/top/clanky/kratce-k-principu-pravni-jistoty-ve-svetle-aktualni-judikatury-93342.html.

degree of severity of legal sanctions and their inevitability, enforceability of law, and equal approach in law enforcement.[72]

[3] Trust in Law in Empirical Studies

The European Values Study (EVS) has been conducted steadily since 1980 in many European countries. The Czech Republic joined data collection in 1991 and participated in the latest wave in 2017. We consider it necessary to recall at this point that the EVS processes data at regular intervals, always in seven-year cycles. Therefore, the most recent findings to date are represented by the 2017 data. The EVS contains a questionnaire on human values, attitudes and opinions, which can then be compared across socio-demographic groups and across countries. In addition to the possibility of placing the Czech findings in an international context, the temporal dimension of the EVS is also valuable as many questions are asked repeatedly and we can thus track the developments over time. The EVS in all countries uses representative samples based on random or quota sampling with a minimum of thousand respondents per country. For example, in the Czech Republic, respondents are selected in three stages of random sampling, namely, electoral districts, households and individuals within households.[73] In all countries, this survey was based on face-to-face interviews in households conducted in paper and later digital form. In 2017, some countries included the option of responding through an online or postal questionnaire, which is still being done experimentally under strict quality and data-comparability control.[74] The EVS can thus be considered a credible source of international data with the possibility of comparison over time.

In all waves, the EVS questionnaire included a battery of questions: 'Please tell me, for each item listed, how much confidence you have in them, is it a great deal, quite a lot, not very much or none at all?', which also included 'judicial system'. In the presentation of the results, we have again merged the two values, 'a great deal' and 'quite a lot', and show their representation in each country.

In Figure 1.1, we can see the rates of representation as a percentage for all European countries that participated in the last survey in 2017 and had published their data by the time this book was prepared for publication. For clarity, the large number of countries are grouped into the four regions Post-Communist, Southern European, Nordic and Western European countries, within which they are listed alphabetically. This overview makes a division between Post-Communist and Southern European countries with relatively lower trust in the legal system in contrast to higher trust in Nordic and Western European countries. The absolute highest level of trust (around

72. William M. Evan, *Social Structure and Law: Theoretical and Empirical Perspectives* 66 (SAGE Publications 1990).
73. European Values Study, *EVS 2008 Method Report: Country Report – Czech Republic*, Technical Report 2010 8–9 (3 Jul. 2020), https://dbk.gesis.org/dbksearch/sdesc2.asp?no=4770&db=e&doi=10.4232/1.10165.
74. European Values Study, *Method Report EVS2017*, Technical Report 2018 15 (3 Jul. 2020), https://dbk.gesis.org/dbksearch/sdesc2.asp?no=7500&db=e&doi=10.4232/1.13090.

80%) was found among the inhabitants of the four Nordic countries, with only Iceland, which underwent a significant political and constitutional crisis between 2009 and 2012, standing out in the group. The Western European countries are relatively homogeneous, with between 60% and 70% of the population trusting the legal system. The least represented region in the dataset is Southern Europe, represented by Italy and Spain, where the level of trust is around 45%. In contrast, the countries of the former socialist bloc are the most represented in the data, and this group is also characterised by the most significant differences. In addition to values above 60% for Estonia and Belarus, there are very low confidence levels close to 10% for Croatia and Bulgaria. Living standards may play an important role in explaining the overall picture, in addition to the perhaps even more important long democratic tradition and stable legal institutions of the Nordic and Western European countries, which may be related to higher levels of trust as well as its greater stability over time. While we are not able to identify the most important reasons for differences between countries from the available data, we can assess the stability of trust over time.

Figure 1.1 Trust in the Legal System in European Countries in 2017

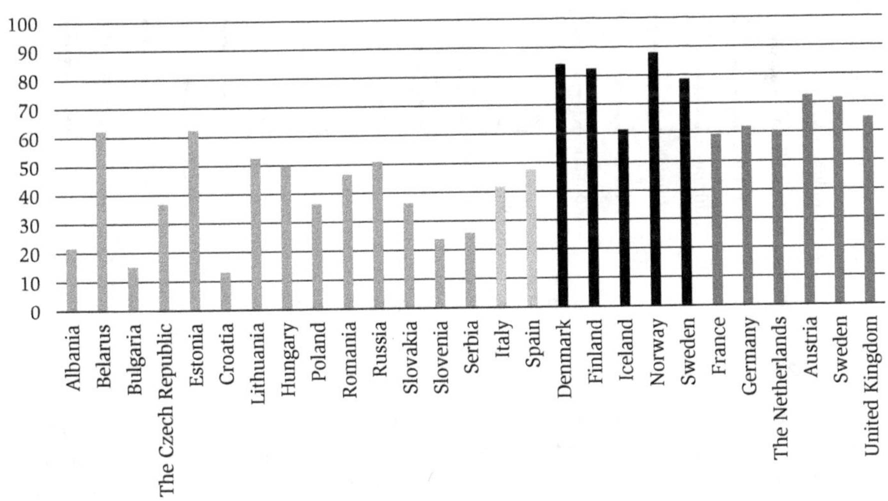

Source: EVS 2017, own data analysis.

Note: Shades distinguish Post-Communist, Southern European, Nordic and Western European countries.

The EVS conducts repeated data collection, so it also allows one to follow the evolution of international comparisons over time. The following analysis works with the last four waves of data collection held in 1991, 1999, 2008 and 2017. Figure 1.2 includes all countries present in these four waves, supplemented by Russia, not a participant in 1991, which we nevertheless consider an important case. We can draw several conclusions from this information-rich figure. First, the level of trust does not differ diametrically across countries, so we can observe at least some degree of stability at the country level. Second, we again see regional differences, with the highest trust in the Nordic countries and the lowest trust in the Post-Communist and Southern European countries, corresponding to the differences described in Figure 1.1. Regional differences are also quite stable over time. The degree of stability of trust also varies as greater fluctuations between years can be observed in the former communist-bloc countries. Third, the individual developments over time show different tendencies from a steady increase (Estonia, Russia, Finland and Sweden), to minor or irregular fluctuations (most countries), to a steady decline (Bulgaria and Poland).

Figure 1.2 Development of Trust in the Legal System in Selected Countries 1991–2017

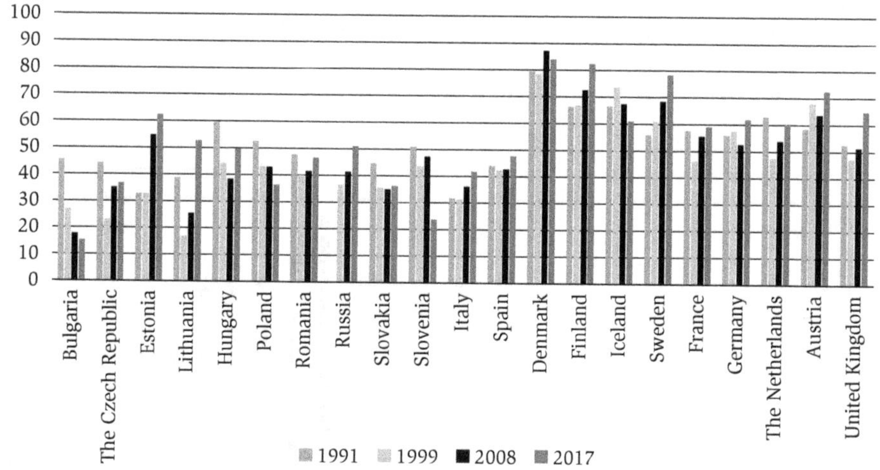

Source: EVS 2017, own data analysis.

The EVS further allows us to examine differences between educational groups. This entails however two methodological problems. First, education systems and their levels vary across countries, which can be partly compensated for, for example, by using the International Standard Classification of Education (ISCED) scale. Second, the data for the ISCED scale do not look entirely plausible for some countries and are completely missing for entire waves of data collection. Therefore, for the entire analysis, we use the second type of education information in the data – age at completion – which is categorised into three assumed levels of education, although we are aware of the inaccuracies associated with this approach. To obtain a single indication of the effect of education for each country, we subtracted the level of trust in the legal system for respondents with tertiary education from the level of trust for respondents with primary education.

The result of the described procedure is shown in Figure 1.3, which again groups European countries into four groups. Positive values indicate by how many more percentage points people with tertiary education trust the legal system, whereas negative values identify the degree of higher trust among respondents with primary education. For example, for the Czech Republic, we see a value of 12 percentage points, which means that among respondents with tertiary education, the number of respondents who declared trust was 12 percentage points higher than among respondents with primary education. A similar positive effect of education on trust in the legal system can be found in the vast majority of countries, with the highest the Netherlands and the UK. When comparing European regions, we see that, especially in the group of Post-Communist and Southern European countries, this effect of education was often not present or was in the opposite direction with higher levels of trust in primary education. Citizens with primary education have significantly higher trust in the legal system, especially in Serbia, Albania, Hungary, Croatia, Spain, and Slovakia. The Nordic and Western European countries can again be contrasted with the variability of the observed relationship. In these two regions, trust in the legal system increases with higher educational level for all countries studied. Even in the Nordic and Western European countries, the positive relationship between education and trust is somewhere stronger (the aforementioned 20 percentage points in the Netherlands, the UK and Germany) and somewhere weaker (around 5 percentage points in Norway, Finland and Switzerland). However, compared to Post-Communist and Southern European countries, the situation in these regions is again more homogeneous and predictable.

Figure 1.3 Differences in Trust in the Legal System in European Countries in 2017 Based on Educational Level

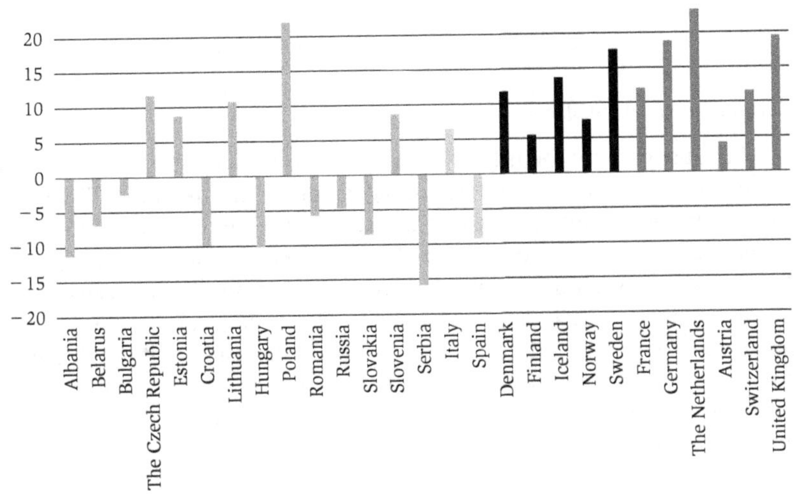

Source: EVS 2017, own data analysis.

Note: Education is measured by the ISCED scale, and shades distinguish Post-Communist, Southern European, Nordic, and Western European countries.

For comparison with the evolution of trust in the legal system over time according to EVS data, we also present Figure 1.4 based on Eurostat data (current as of 8 February 2021), which we created from available data. It is the only source on the basis of which we can observe how the situation is developing after a year of the coronavirus crisis. The decline in trust in the legal system can be, among other things, an indicator of trust in various legal institutions and their use in resolving legal disputes. Data from 2021 are added to the figure to highlight the most recent development of trust in the legal system after the year of the pandemic.

Figure 1.4 Development of Trust in the Legal System in Selected Countries 2016–2021

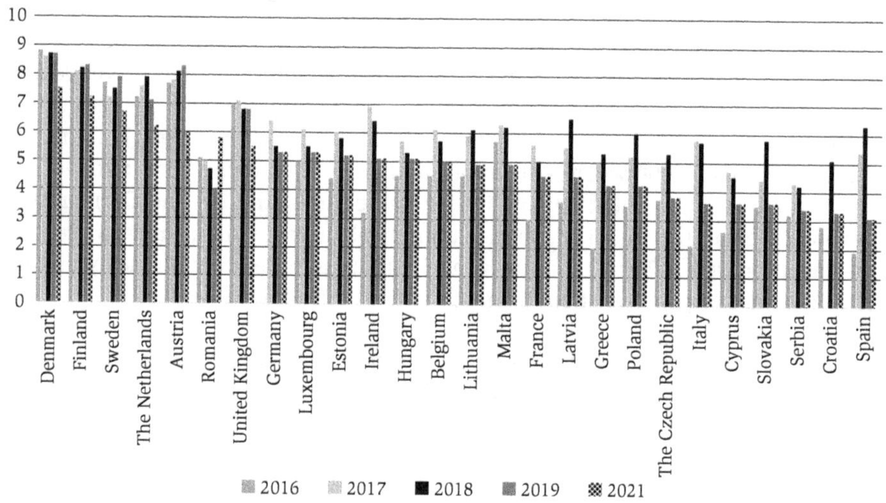

Source: Eurostat, own data analysis.

The EU Justice Scoreboards, which come from the European Commission, include, *inter alia*, promotion and encouragement of the use of ADR in civil and commercial disputes, labour disputes, consumer disputes and administrative disputes. The data between 2016 and 2020 show that the trend of increased use, or at least promotion, of ADR is steadily increasing. An increasing number of cases where ADR has been recommended by courts to resolve legal disputes can be observed in most countries in the data collected by the European Commission. Although statistics or surveys on mediation are extremely rare, not only because of the lack of activity on the part of Member States, this comparison at least offers some insight into the issue of mediation and other ADR methods.

The figures in Figure 1.5 indicate the percentage of court proceedings (labour, consumer, civil and commercial) where ADR was recommended as an ADR. Figure 1.5 shows an increasing trend in the promotion of ADR in civil, commercial, consumer and labour court proceedings.

Figure 1.5 Promotion and Encouragement of ADR in EU Countries 2015–2019

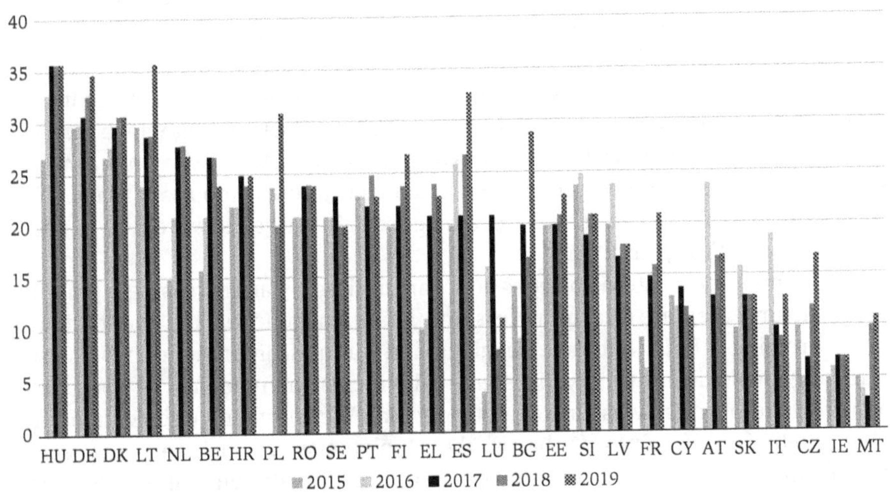

Source: European Union, EU Justice Scoreboards 2015–2019.

While the data sources used in this section do not directly provide information on mediation, they do place trust in the courts and the legal system in a broader temporal and geographical context. In international comparison, it appears that trust in Post-Communist countries is rather low. Therefore, mediation can, among other things, be a tool to reduce inequalities in society if it is a credible tool that creates an environment for a more equal form of negotiation than litigation. As can be seen from the trend illustrated in particular in the last graph, there is an increasing frequency of cases where ADR, and therefore mediation, is proposed as a possible solution to a dispute.

§1.06 TRANSFORMATIONS OF LAW IN MODERN AND LATE MODERN SOCIETY, THE PROCESS OF GLOBALISATION AND EUROPEANISATION

Law as an institution of society, as well as the institution of mediation, cannot be separated from the time in which it operates. The temporal nature of law cannot be understood in abstraction from a given sociopolitical, ideological and legal environment, which is also a fundamental theme of a normative universalist understanding of law.[75]

Society and law have undergone significant changes since the last quarter of the previous century.[76] Despite differences of opinion on the extent and nature of these changes, a number of social phenomena and processes can be specified that go beyond the characteristics of modern society and modern law. Moreover, their manifestations have a pan-European and partly global dimension. These changes are collectively referred to as the transition from modern (industrial) society to late modern (post-industrial, postmodern) society.

In late modern society, what changes in particular is the role of law and its social functions. Modernity has assigned to law its basic functions, among which resolution of conflicts in social relations, transmission of cultural patterns of behaviour and values and facilitation (enabling) of cooperative actions occupy an important place. Therefore, law in modern society can be characterised, in Kelsen's words, as a specific technique of social organisation.[77]

Contemporary Western societies are characterised by an increasingly pluralising social structure; they are becoming less and less homogeneous and monolithic, not only by growing ethnic, national, religious and cultural differentiation but also by progressing ideological diversity. This gradually increasing tendency towards pluralisation and heterogeneity was already noted by Max Weber when he spoke figuratively of the 'polytheism of values',[78] that is, their 'polytheism', anticipating the fact that today we are confronted with a number of substantially different value orders, social projects, lifestyles, cultural preferences, beliefs, ideas and functional systems of society, including normative systems, none of which can be ignored and all of which seem to be equally binding. Fragmentation, segmentation, particularisation, privatisation and deregulation of these functional systems of society make it difficult for them to interact and cooperate socially, which is particularly true of normative orders, including law. Therefore, the term 'society' should currently be understood as a plurality of subcommunities characterised by their own normative and value orientation. The pluralisation of society limits the achievement of a general value and normative consensus.

The absence of a broader value and normative consensus in late modern society may to a limited degree be substituted only by a generally binding legal order. Law thus ultimately enables us to understand the nature of society, its life and changes, and the British legal sociologist Roger Cotterrell[79] has termed society 'law's community' in this sense. It is such a law's community that can integrate an ideologically and socially plural society into a single, albeit heterogeneous, whole. The regulatory, integrative

75. Miloš Večeřa & Martina Urbanová, *Právo a recentní sociální změna* 455–467, Právny obzor. Veda 98, 5 (2015).
76. Miloš Večeřa & Martina Urbanová, *Sociologie práva* 117–125 (Aleš Čeněk 2011).
77. Hans Kelsen, *General Theory of Law and State* 5 (Russell and Russell 1961).
78. Max Weber, *Zwischen zwei Gesetzen* 145 (Universitas Verlag 1980).
79. Roger Cotterrell, *Law's Community: Legal Theory in Sociological Perspective* 19–22 (Clarendon Press 2005).

and innovative function of law thus becomes an existential necessity in late modern society. In this context, what seems an essential question is to what extent law is and will continue to be able to fulfil this increasingly difficult integrative social function, to what extent it can respond to, correct and initiate social change, while freeing itself from political, economic and other powerful influences.

In this regard, Cotterrell[80] asks to what extent law has become independent of its social and cultural roots and sources and whether it can independently influence social relations and affect social change in Western societies in the late twentieth and early twenty-first centuries. He notes that the overall ideological climate of societies has changed since the time of Friedrich Savigny and William Sumner.[81] As Luhmann[82] adds, law is no longer the 'good old law' whose validity was derived from its immutability based on the past and symbolised by its unalterability. Today's law cannot be seen merely as an aspect of society but increasingly as an instrument of public power. Law today derives its effectiveness not only from conformity to the normative systems of a value-wise, ideologically and culturally plural society, but also increasingly from political power represented not only by the state.

Legal science reflects the law of late modern society with the concept of legal pluralism, which describes the shift of law towards a plurality of its sources and the retreat of the nation state from the position of the exclusive lawmaker. The legal order of a state takes the form of a multicentric legal order with a dominant position of international and European law in the process of globalisation and Europeanisation of law.

The globalisation of law as one of the spheres of globalisation is a process of internationalisation of national law aimed at creating uniform or at least harmonised rules that would apply regardless of national borders and would replace national legal regulations. As a necessary means of stabilising transnational legal relations, the globalisation of law proceeds in principle along four paths:[83]

(1) national acceptance of foreign law, consisting in the adoption of the law of countries that have had or retained significant political influence on the national legal environment;
(2) globalisation of law through public and private international law;
(3) supranationalisation of law through the formation of certain regional groupings (for the Czech Republic, this is typically the EU);
(4) spontaneous process of legal globalisation in the form of spontaneous law-making practices (e.g., *lex mercatoria* establishing itself in international commercial relations).

80. Roger Cotterrell, *The Sociology of Law* 46 (Butterworths 1992).
81. Friedrich Carl von Savigny was an important representative of the German historical-legal school of the second half of the nineteenth century. William Graham Sumner, the first professor of sociology at Yale University, was also active at the same time.
82. Niklas A. Luhmann, *Sociological Theory of Law* 268 (Routledge and Kegan Paul 1985).
83. Viz Miloš Večeřa & Tatiana Machalová, *Evropeizace práva v právně teoretickém kontextu: výklad základních pojmů* 66–69 (Masarykova univerzita 2010).

Closely related to the process of globalisation of law is the process of Europeanisation of law. It consists not only in the implementation of European law but also in the Europeanisation of the sources of law, the concept of human rights and the rule of law, judicial activity, interpretation of law, legal procedures and methods, and ultimately in the Europeanisation of the way of legal thinking, at both the European and national levels. The process of Europeanisation of law is thus manifesting itself throughout European Union (EU) and national law, modifying the European and national legal environment. For the countries of Central and Eastern Europe, the process of Europeanisation takes on even other aspects. For them, Europeanisation is significantly linked to the process of transition to democracy, democratic rule of law, democratic standards, and the values of Western European democratic society.

The globalisation and Europeanisation of law contribute to the progression of legal pluralism, with multiple legal systems operating within a country. In addition to national, international and European law, spontaneously emerging quasi-legal systems of a global nature (*lex mercatoria, ius humanitis*, etc.) and quasi-legal systems of religious and ethnic minorities (e.g., Islamic law) are emerging in a plural society. At the same time, the relationship between parallel legal systems does not have to be precisely defined by constitutional documents, and the actual solution is left to judicial decision-making, political decisions or their spontaneous course. Even more serious are situations referred to as conflicts of law, where parallel quasi-legal systems exist without mutual recognition and acceptance by the state authority.

Postmodernity brings about an accumulation of a large number of changes in relatively short periods of time. The process of postmodernisation of law is usually characterised as a deconstruction of law, which usually means the revelation of hidden organisational principles or metaphysical assumptions of law, but in turn implies a certain loss of the symbolic value of law.[84] However, demythicised law devoid of symbolism loses the glories of a meta-institution. The deconstruction of the system of law is manifested as a loss of the systemicity of law and giving up on law often associated with a cynicism of legal practice. The legal system loses much of its substantive and partly formal unity and is overwhelmed by legislative overproduction. Frequent changes in legislation lead not only to a loss of the ability to navigate the law but also to a tendency towards ever more specific legislation, which creates the need for further detailed regulation.[85]

The postmodern situation places limits on the ability to promote significant social change in the public interest through law. This is mainly due to the following:

- weakening of the nation state from the outside (processes of Europeanisation and globalisation) and from the inside (tendencies towards privatisation, segmentation and deregulation of public power);
- difficulty of achieving social consensus in a highly pluralised society; law becomes a means of political struggle;

84. Brendan Edgeworth, *Law, Modernity, Postmodernity: Legal Change in the Contracting State* 223 (Ashgate 2003).
85. Pavel Holländer, *Soumrak moderního*, 1 Právník 1–28 (2013).

- giving up on the role of the state and the law as representatives of the public interest;
- influence of interest groups to promote private interests in decision-making processes through practices known as lobbying;
- privileging of economic considerations and practices over legal ones in the public sphere;
- absence of a unifying factor in promoting the public interest in lawmaking.

In addition to these more general limitations, there is the specific situation of Post-Communist societies in Eastern Europe, where the following limitations are manifested:

- reception of the measures resulting from international and European law is limited by the specifically different social and legal reality of these states, as even if the terms are translated correctly, they express a factually different meaning;
- the rule of law is often understood in a purely formalistic way in a state governed by the rule of law, that is, not as a rule constrained by law but as a pure power of the state to enforce law;[86]
- there is a reluctance of courts to directly apply constitutional laws (including the Charter of Fundamental Rights and Freedoms), which are seen as mere political declarations, not as legal texts to be applied;
- persistence of legal formalism in legislation, judicial decision-making and legal science.

Contemporary late modern society is characterised by increasing complexity, that is, society's complicatedness and multiformity, which can bring greater freedom on the one hand, but more uncertainty stemming from an ever-changing and less predictable social world on the other. The postmodern interpretive paradigm is reflected in the way of seeing social reality and necessarily also in the form, causes, contexts and ways of solving social problems, including the implementation of legal instruments in regulating social relations and promoting social change.

In a society becoming increasingly plural in terms of values and ideas, the culturally uniform normative order of society is breaking down. Law, after all, appears to be the only normative system of general binding force at the level of which society can be integrated, since it provides relatively reliable mechanisms of control and represents a system of normative regulation that is most strongly formalised, rationally constructed and exhibits a high degree of division of labour and purpose orientation.[87] However, law provides too narrow a consensus base, which needs to be broadened by seeking a wider common discourse, for example, by debating the appropriateness and effectiveness of a particular legal regulation. Also, for these reasons, the law has

86. Siniša Rodin, *Diskurz a autorita v evropské a postkomunistické právní kultuře*, 8 Právník 873–892 (2006).
87. Jiří Přibáň, *Několik poznámek k sociologii práva*, 6 Sociologický časopis 770–781 (1992); Martina Urbanová, *Systémy sociální kontroly a právo* 7–9 (Aleš Čeněk 1996).

deliberately regulated mediation only as a framework so that the informality of the mediation process can be preserved. It is only on the basis of practical knowledge about the functioning of mediation, captured through empirical research, that the law can then be modified or expanded and possibly amended.

The postmodern situation means increasing demands on law, from both society and the state. Thus, with the process of postmodernisation, law not only reflects and confirms social changes in society but also becomes an increasingly important instrument of social change. It comes into play as *ultima ratio* when the entropy of interests in society increases beyond a tolerable level.[88]

We are witnessing increasing demands on law and expectations associated with it, from the part of both society and the state. Late modern society has seen a decline in respect for authorities. This vacuum of authorities is, in some ways, sought to be filled by legal mechanisms that help to hold a diverse society together. Increasingly, law is replacing informal social mechanisms for dispute resolution, and the growing number of social conflicts sooner or later spills over into the legal sphere. What the local priest, mayor or teacher used to be able to resolve without much difficulty is now referred to the courts for decision. Broad space for the application of mediation procedures is also opening here.

Moreover, in multicultural Western societies, law is increasingly subjected to a difficult-to-implement requirement to respect certain value and normative principles and claims of particular cultures and ethnicities and to take into account their version of justice. A certain starting point is the search for a minimum common value consensus, which is primarily the concept of fundamental human rights and freedoms. However, in a highly pluralistic society, this is too narrow a consensus base, which needs to be broadened by seeking a common discourse, for example, by debating the appropriateness of certain legislation. Law thus becomes a normative system that is supposed to ensure a minimum integrity of social behaviour, namely, integrity related to:

- the breadth of activities of an individual social entity; and
- to the creation of a value and normative framework of the legal order.

Law thus becomes the most important means for stabilising social relations, bringing order to society and reducing the level of social entropy. This overuse of legal forms in promoting values and interests becomes part of the postmodernity of social life. It is, in fact, a kind of way out of a situation where no other possible paths are offered. However, law cannot substitute well enough for the sphere of moral, political, or generally human responsibility and culture, nor can it casuistically remember all future social situations and conflicts by creating a detailed and all-encompassing world of legal prohibitions and commands. It is, after all, an *ex post* means, addressing only the consequences of social actions. It can never sufficiently replace the preventive and motivational function of the other receding functional systems of society. This also sets its fundamental limits and boundaries.

88. Viktor Knapp, *Člověk, občan a právo* 1–15, Právník y. 131, no. 1 (1992).

The transformations of law in late modern society touch upon the situation of the individual, whose orientational uncertainty is growing and whose actions are situated in an indeterminately defined social world with a changing role of law. It cannot be overlooked that in the context of the postmodern situation, there are potential tendencies towards respect for and legitimacy of every opinion, even if it is a different one, and towards emphasis of a right (entitlement) of everyone to be different. There is a growing emphasis on approaches based on cultural pluralism and the elimination of any discrimination. The postmodern era thus brings a tendency towards democratic approaches because the basis of democracy is the assumption that in society, there are and can be different, equally legitimate yet ultimately irreconcilable opinions, claims and approaches. Democracy can thus fully assert itself precisely in the conditions of the postmodern world, while on the other hand, the postmodern situation can develop successfully only under democratic conditions, that is, not under authoritarian or totalitarian political systems.

§1.07 PARTIAL CONCLUSION

Mediation, as part of the legal system, takes place within a given society and its sociocultural order. To understand law, it is therefore necessary to consider its social and cultural context. Law acts as an institution of society and reflects its culture, while at the same time, it is one of the elements that constitute culture and society. The role of law in society is characterised by its functions, of which the fact that law is becoming one of the most important instruments of social control is becoming increasingly important in the increasingly plural late modern society. The issue of fairness of the law and fairness of decision-making under law is the basis for law's legitimacy and trust in it, which also affects trust in mediation as part of the legal system. The establishment of the values and norms of society and adherence to them contribute to it. If this is not the case, chaos, confusion and a state of anomie emerge, leading to a sense of loneliness, fear and deviant behaviour. This is a socially pathological state, a state of distrust of others.

In late modern society, law has become the most important means of stabilising social relations and contributing to the resolution of social conflicts and tensions. Mediation procedures, the success of which depends on trust and willingness to cooperate, should contribute to this. Where this trust and willingness to cooperate are lacking, mediation cannot thrive. Mediation, like the entire legal system, will always struggle to hold people's trust. In order to increase trust in mediation, it is therefore necessary to increase citizens' trust in the legal system, which, especially in the current coronavirus era, will be a difficult task.

Without the public's trust that a judge's actions will be fair and respect high moral standards, the judiciary cannot function properly. The *public's trust in the judiciary* is the most precious thing this power possesses, and that trust is one of the most precious things that any citizen of a state can have. In the words of Honoré de Balzac, 'to distrust the judiciary marks the beginning of the end of society'. However, the public's trust is not given a priori but must be built. It is easier to lose it than to retain it. That trust should be based on understanding because that makes it more lasting and stronger than trust based on fear and forced reverence. Trust is also promoted by open and direct argumentation, where it is clear why certain measures have been taken, and by all involved in settling disputes observing high moral standards.

CHAPTER 2

Mediation Through the Lens of Social Change

Martina Urbanová & Miloš Večeřa

When the institution of mediation was anchored in the legal system in many post-socialist countries, this constituted promotion of social change through law. The importance of law as a tool for innovation of social relations can be practically demonstrated in the example of mediation. This chapter thus shows law not only as a means of regulating social relations but also as a tool for targeted social change. This innovative role of law is enhanced as late modern society progresses. Late modern society is characterised by increasing differentiation, diversity and antagonisms. The consequence of the increasing ethnic, national, cultural and religious plurality of the social structure of society is a progressing ideological diversity of value and normative orders, ideas and social projects in society and their particularisation. In this situation, it is not possible to integrate social life in any other way than through the legal order. In late modern society, law is the only normative system with a universal binding character, and it is the basis of a minimum common value consensus. As postmodernisation progresses, law not only reflects and confirms social change in society but also becomes an increasingly important tool for social change.

The authors present law as a means of regulating social relations and at the same time as a tool for social change. In addition, they ask to what extent law itself reflects the social changes taking place in society. Is law a tool for purposeful change or does it merely reflect and confirm social change? Related to this fundamental question is the need to identify the limits of law in promoting social change and to assess the effectiveness of law as a tool for such change. Answering these questions allows us to understand difficulties in the process of introducing mediation into the legal system and especially its use in practice. Despite foreign experience that mediation procedures can be beneficial in resolving conflict situations in social relations, they are being promoted only slowly.

§2.01 LAW AS A MEANS OF REGULATING SOCIAL RELATIONS AND MEDIATION

Since the first forms of human communities arose, mechanisms to direct, coordinate and control the social behaviour of social subjects have been taking shape in these communities. All human communities that have been formed historically have had to respond to the fact that their members live 'side by side', which necessarily limits the freedom of possible action of individuals and groups. The needs and interests of individuals and social groups inevitably place them in reciprocal relationships and lead to the creation of social relations that are not only relations of cooperation or competition but also relations of mutual confrontation and conflict. In the wide range of possible forms and modes of social behaviour, it is necessary to unify the limitlessness of these forms and modes of behaviour into a narrower range of possible variations of behaviour.

Society and social life always involve a certain element of organisation (a certain form of social order), which is necessary for the predictability of the social world. Society reproduces on the assumption that people respect the existence of a certain social order and thus create society through their everyday actions. Among the instruments of systemic management and direction of social life and social relations, in addition to the legal instruments addressed by this text, the following are particularly applicable:

- economic instruments (systems of economic incentives and sanctions);
- public media (capable of exerting a major influence on social consciousness and public opinion);
- forms of use of power (application of political instruments in decision-making, especially by executive power);
- education systems (targeted action in public education and upbringing).

Legal instruments are normative tools for regulating social behaviour and social relations. However, they are not the only normative system in society; there are many other systems of social norms at work, but these are not formally institutionalised.

The social life of society is regulated by norms of a dual nature: social norms, which arise spontaneously and put 'soft' social pressure on the actions of individuals, and legal norms, whose hard social pressure is created by sanctions and institutions.[1] The share of these two types of social norms varies among societies and is related to the dynamics of social life. The 'soft' social norms are a manifestation of spontaneous social life and exert their pressure on individual behaviour in a relatively spontaneous way. In contrast, legal norms are the result of a formal institutional act of public authority, and that public authority also enforces them.

1. Petr Sak & Karolína Kolesárová, *Faktory ovlivňující dynamiku sociálních jevů, právních norem a kriminality ve vztahu ke společnosti*, INSOMA.cz (2020), http://www.insoma.cz/Faktory_ovliv%C5%88uj%C3%ADc%C3%AD_dynamiku_Sak.pdf.

Social norms create the normative order of society, which forms the core of social regulations within the sociocultural system. The normative order represents a wide range of binding rules and expectations of behaviour which touch on all areas of social life, be it modes of dress, diet, aesthetic habits, modes of work, forms of leisure, modes of speech, principles of hygiene, relation to self, modes of behaviour towards other social subjects and the relevant social unit, relation to divine authorities, etc.

The social norm can be understood in three shades of meaning:

(1) a norm is what is customary and proven (summarises experience and rationality of action);
(2) a norm is what is permissible (emphasis on the normative aspect);
(3) a norm is what is right and desirable (expresses evaluation).[2]

Social norms are never precise guidelines for action. Rather, they define certain boundaries or limits to action. These are rules, schemes of behaviour that are supra-individual in character, undergo a process of becoming objective and exist and apply 'objectively', in the group (social) consciousness, independently of the individual manifestations of social subjects. Given their relative stability in time and content, the existence of norms allows for the predictability of social behaviour and the formation of social roles. However, there is no single pattern of behaviour for a given situation, no single solution to the situation. In a decision-making process, the actor has the possibility to choose from a number of variants of action. Social norms are thus the basis for the organisation of meaningful action by social actors in social interaction. Social norms, representing the constituent elements of the normative system of society, can be characterised as abstract patterns that define certain boundaries of social behaviour or as a standard shared by members of a social unit enforced by positive and negative sanctions. The diversity of social norms shows the difficulty of defining their essential features. In addition to legal norms, other social norms worth mentioning are moral, religious, customary (etiquette, customs, etc.), political, economic, aesthetic, artistic and other norms.

Despite the different nature of social norms, the following basic (defining) characteristics of social norms can be identified, which are also essential for legal norms and will facilitate their definition:[3]

(1) generality – a norm applies to a relatively indeterminate (unspecified, unlimited) number of social subjects and cases;
(2) normativity – a norm expresses a normative requirement on human behaviour; it establishes what 'ought to be', the required way of behaviour;
(3) social acceptability – it is a rule of behaviour accepted, approved and shared by a social unit;

2. *See* Miloš Večeřa & Martina Urbanová, *Sociologie práva* 148 (Aleš Čeněk 2011).
3. *See* Večeřa & Urbanová, *supra* n. 2, 149.

(4) sanctionability – the binding nature of a rule of conduct is confirmed by a sanction.

Based on the above-mentioned features of social norms, the essential features of legal norms can be summarised:

(1) generality – legal norms have a general character in relation to the object of legal regulation and to the subjects of a legal norm. They apply, like other social norms, to an indefinite number of social subjects and cases;
(2) bindingness – they normatively oblige a certain behaviour or refraining from a certain action or provide the possibility of a certain action (authorisation);
(3) form recognised or established by the state – the state establishes the content of legal norms or recognises a certain norm as a legal norm (commercial practices, international conventions, etc.);
(4) enforceability by state power – this takes place when a legal norm is not adhered to or violated.[4]

The conceptual features of legal norms can be used to define law as a comprehensive system of legal norms. The difficulty of defining law is due to the diversity of conditions of social life, where every aspect of social life can be the object of legal regulation or judicial decision. Therefore, law is more than a sum of valid legal norms, legal principles, legal values and legal ideas. It also represents an essential area of social life that includes the legal consciousness of individuals and social groups and society, legal communication, the area of legal motivation, a complex of legal actions, the area of legal relations, the activities of institutions implementing and applying law and the area of lawmaking.[5] In this sense, law becomes just one of many social structures that emerge and change in response to the change and development of society.[6] In this respect, Luhmann understands law as a social system where law and society must be viewed and examined in a relationship of interdependence.[7] Legal theory must therefore be understood as part of the theory of society.[8] Mediation is thus not only its legal regulation but also its actual operation in the life of society, which must be focused on and investigated by sociolegal methods.

Legal norms are also an important tool for social change in social relations, activities of social institutions, the course of social processes and the occurrence of social phenomena. They manifest themselves simultaneously as a conservative aspect of law and an innovative effect of law on social reality.

The systemic management and organisational effect of law can be illustrated in the example of the Czech Republic. A legal institution enshrined in section 100(2) of

4. Jaromír Harvánek et al., *Právní teorie* 29 (Aleš Čeněk 2013).
5. Sally Falk Moore, *Law and Social Change: The Semi-Autonomous Social Field as an Appropriate Subject of Study*, 7 Law & Society Review 719–749 (1973).
6. Jiří Přibáň, *Sociologie práva* 129–131 (Sociologické nakladatelství 1996).
7. Niklas Luhmann, *A Sociological Theory of Law* 7 (Routledge and Kegan Paul 1985).
8. Denis J. Galligan, *Law in Modern Society* 26 (Oxford University Press 2007).

Act No. 99/1963 Coll., the Civil Procedure Code, as amended, gives courts the possibility (if it is expedient and appropriate) to order the parties to the proceedings to have an initial meeting with a mediator registered in the list of mediators maintained by the Ministry of Justice of the Czech Republic for a maximum of three hours. This is a procedural tool which enables courts to guide the parties towards an amicable solution to their conflict. According to the European Commission, the main problem with the mediation system is the general public's lack of knowledge of the institution of mediation and the lack of trust in this method of dispute resolution due to 'cultural habits'.[9] The Commission subsequently concludes that the Member States need to increase their efforts to promote and encourage mediation by the most appropriate means, which also include increasing the use of mediation by having courts order the parties to the dispute to hold an informational meeting with a mediator as seen, for example, in the Czech Republic and Hungary.[10]

In connection with the lack of knowledge of law, Fuller points out that the requirement that all legal regulations be properly published does not, however, presuppose that 'a conscientious citizen will sit down and read them all'.[11] Rather, addressees of legal norms learn about the applicable law indirectly from the media, from other people, from their own experience or simply by imitating what others do. Nevertheless, mediation itself can be a tool for increasing legal knowledge as Tomlinson argues in her essay *Mediation and Legal Literacy*. There, she examines the process of mediation with a focus on the acquisition of legal literacy in the context of the United States (US). The author asks how mediators contribute to legal literacy, which may ultimately increase the chances of people from lower classes to better navigate the bureaucratic system. Unlike traditional hearings, mediation is confidential and takes place in private between the two parties. The discussion between the participants is also much more open and flexible than it would be in court. On the other hand, however, just as in court, the parties must follow certain rules and requirements set by the mediators. Even if it is a shorter process than a court hearing, the parties will still meet several times before the mediator, and each time they will have a demonstrably better understanding of which legal paths are open to them and which legal remedies they can use, thereby increasing their own legal literacy. The mediation participants themselves report that they are better able to understand legal terms as a result of their participation in mediation. Legal education of the participants takes place even during traditional court hearings, but there the process is much more depersonalised.[12]

9. *Zpráva Komise Evropskému parlamentu, Radě a Evropskému sociálnímu a hospodářskému výboru o provádění směrnice Evropského parlamentu a Rady 2008/52/ES o některých aspektech mediace v občanských a obchodních věcech*, Komise Evropské unie (9 Sep. 2019), https://ec.europa.eu/transparency/regdoc/rep/1/2016/CS/1-2016-542-CS-F1-1.PDF.
10. *See* §6.05.
11. Lon L. Fuller, *Morálka práva* 52 (Oikoymenh 1988).
12. Elizabeth C. Tomlinson, *Mediation and legal literacy*, 2 Community Literacy Journal 75–100 (2010).

§2.02 MEDIATION, LAW AND SOCIAL CHANGE

Implementation of mediation in the legal system can undoubtedly be described as social change. Social change can be characterised as a transformation of elements of culture and social institutions over time.[13] The basis of social change is generally adaptation to changing conditions. Social change is the result of a number of factors, and social scientists, particularly in the last two centuries, have been striving to develop a general theory that can provide a universalistic account of the causes and process of social change. Giddens has aptly summarised the stimuli contributing to social change into three main categories. He included the physical environment, political organisation and cultural factors among the major agents of social change. The physical environment encompasses not only the environmental conditions of life in the broad sense but also the material conditions of production systems and economic influences. Political organisation and political decision-making support and direct social change today far more than in earlier periods, both externally and internally. Cultural factors include, in particular, developments of science and technology, modes of communication and ways of thinking and feeling that also include social ideals.[14] In the context of our considerations, one of the significant cultural factors of social change is law, whose role is increasing in the context of late modern society and the rule of law.

Friedman reminds us that some established social rules determine the direction of behaviour with great inertia and can determine expected behaviour in the long run. It used to be taken for granted that women were housewives and had no right to vote or hold office, racial segregation was considered perfectly normal, etc. These ruts, based on established mindsets and social norms, have implicitly perpetuated, for example, gender or ethnic inequality and thus impede the enforcement of legal changes. Legislated change is therefore not smooth because established patterns of thought are not always easy to overcome.[15]

The cause-and-effect relationship between law and social change is often difficult to identify because the ability of law to induce change is probabilistic, contingent and consequential. While some social changes may be achieved, other factors influence their effectiveness and time horizon. Factors of a spiritual nature, such as the morals and values of society, play a separate role. A certain degree of social consensus needs to be reached, especially on issues that are not so fundamental. To achieve social change, there should be social support for it, which is, however, not easy in case of morally sensitive issues such as same-sex marriage, euthanasia, surrogacy or the decriminalisation of marijuana. Some sociologists credit social movements inspired by disaffected members of society with playing a major role in bringing about some social changes.[16]

13. Sheryl J. Grana et al., *The Social Context of Law* 157 (Prentice Hall 2002).
14. Anthony Giddens, *Sociologie* 33 (Argo 1999).
15. Lawrence M. Friedman & Grant M. Hayden, *American Law: An Introduction* 265 (Oxford University Press 2017).
16. Devorah Kalekin-Fishman & Ann B. Denis, *The Shape of Sociology for the 21st Century: Tradition and Renewal* 81–100 (SAGE Publications 2012).

Laws can only impose normative requirements on behaviour, not values, morals and attitudes. They therefore change external behaviour with some probability, which is in turn followed by changes in attitudes, values and morals. External manifestations in behaviour then translate to some extent into personal attitudes and preferences. An example is the laws promoting equality for African Americans in the US, which the white population has been unwilling to accept for many generations. One such landmark in the area of civil rights and employment law in the USA was the Civil Rights Act, passed in 1964, which prohibited discrimination on the grounds of race, colour, religion, sex or nationality. The Act required a change in behaviour and gradually changed the attitudes of the majority society. Laws can thus change the values and moral attitudes of society under certain conditions.

In social practice, law is often attacked not only for not playing an important role in promoting social change but also for doing more harm than good.[17] Law in itself is no guarantee of social development or its direction. Even the success of law as a regulator of social processes, a means of conflict resolution and an instrument of social control is problematic.[18] It turns out that the most 'successful' changes through law have rested either on the disintegration of social groups or on their strict control.[19] The fact that change will be enforced by strong social control is evident, after all, also in the context of the coronavirus pandemic.

For many decades, legal scholars have sought to explain the relationship between legal and social change in the context of the evolution of legal institutions. In their reflections, we encounter a view of law as both an independent and a dependent variable, law as a cause and as a consequence of social change. They uniformly emphasised the interdependence of law and other social systems. Their views, however, often categorically diverged. The British legal philosopher and reformer Jeremy Bentham expected legal reforms to play a significant role in the process of industrialisation and urbanisation and therefore to respond quickly to new social needs and to restructure society.[20] This led him to recommend legal reforms to the leaders of the French Revolution because he believed that France, at that stage of economic development, needed such legal reforms to solve common problems. Paradoxically, the Revolution did not break out when social evils were at their worst but when reform was beginning. In contrast, Friedrich Carl von Savigny, a German lawyer and a representative of the historical-legal school, held that legal change can only come from the legal tradition of a given country, from legal customs, which are the basis for codification of only national circumstances, not universal ones.[21]

In support of Bentham's views, a number of examples can be cited where legal change has brought about fundamental social change. One can mention various decrees that changed the social situation of large numbers of people in the seventeenth

17. David Friedrichs, *Law in Our Lives: An Introduction* 254 (Roxbury Publishing 2005).
18. Silvia Capíková, *Medzi poriadkom a chaosom: právo v post-komunistickej transformacii na Slovensku*, 4 Sociologický časopis 617–640 (2005).
19. Andras Sajó, *New Legalism in East Central Europe: Law as an Instrument of Social Transformation*, 3 Journal of Law and Society 329–344 (1990).
20. Renata Rázková, *Dějiny právní filozofie* 183–185 (Masarykova univerzita 1997).
21. Alexander Bröstl, *Frontisterion* 190–191 (Kalligram 2009).

and eighteenth centuries, such as the abolition of restrictions on freedom of movement or the abolition of serfdom and indentured servitude. In more recent times, the 'legal two-year plan', as the period 1948–1950 is called, was the time when all the fundamental branches of law in Czechoslovakia were recodified with the aim of recasting the entire existing legal order. The new socialist law was to serve the people and express the will of the working class, to strengthen protection against the enemies of socialism and to create a new concept of socialist property. During the 'legal two-year plan', codifications of civil, criminal, family and administrative criminal law (especially misdemeanour law) were adopted.

There may thus be two fundamentally different perspectives on the relationship between legal and social change:

(1) law is determined by the legal and moral sentiment and sense of justice of the population of a given territory and will influence their behaviour as long as law is consistent with prevailing social norms;
(2) law is a tool to promote programmed social change. This is, however, true mainly for economically developed industrialised countries and less so for traditional agrarian societies.

The positive role of law is often associated with the expansion of social rights in the 1960s and 1970s with the development of the welfare state. According to Pound,[22] the main role of law is to maintain social equilibrium. Law is an instrument of social engineering; lawyers are social engineers because they act on the complex interplay of diverse social interests and seek to eliminate friction, conflict, and harm within society. The engineering character of law, in Pound's view, lies in the fact that legislative decisions and legal constructions can be (figuratively speaking) technical and engineering means to induce specific social relations.

Social engineering thus understood is in fact a special kind of legal policy that seeks to implement certain objectives in the public interest by means of legal instruments. Even mediation can deal with disputes involving public interests and, in the case of mediation in the field of administrative law, the public interest will receive increased protection. The concept of law as social engineering also corresponds to the process of europeanisation of law,[23] which seeks to promote changes in national law to achieve objectives that go beyond the national interests of the Member States. With globalisation, the study of the role of law in bringing about social change also focuses on the transnational level, as the role of transnational institutions and transnational law is growing.

The fundamental role of law in the organisation of society and its social change is attributed to law in particular by the evolutionist approach to the development of law and society. Giddens[24] considers social evolutionism to be one of the most influential general approaches to explaining social change. The evolutionist approach in law

22. Roscoe Pound, *An Introduction to the Philosophy of Law* 64–65 (Yale University Press 1922).
23. William L. Twining, *Globalisation and Legal Theory* 50 (Cambridge University Press 2006).
24. Giddens, *supra* n. 14, at 33.

considers the legal system as one of the most essential components of the model of organisation of society. Law has an impact on the operational efficiency of any society and its social change, and the mechanism of evolutionary selection is fully applicable to the legal system itself. Law determines in a fundamental way whether a given society and its model of organisation will succeed in historical development.[25]

In addition to their regulatory function, legal norms play an important role in many areas of social conduct and social relations by steering activities in a particular direction or by enforcing or preventing certain courses of action. Therefore, according to Friedman, they often act as hidden persuaders of human action.[26] Here, law influences the achievement of certain social changes by stipulating that certain behaviours will be rewarded and other behaviours will be disadvantaged or sanctioned. Law also contains a number of indirect persuaders that covertly direct human behaviour. These hidden persuaders should also play a role in promoting the use of mediation as a way of resolving disputes and conflicts peacefully.

Galanter emphasises the need to measure the effect of changes in law as an independent variable on social reality. However, a change in law is not only a change in legal norms but also a change in the number, organisation or working style of lawyers and a change in legal doctrine. These other changes can sometimes be more significant than the change in the law itself.[27] In addition to legislative instruments, social change can be triggered by groundbreaking or highly publicised judicial decisions. On the other hand, jurisprudence itself reflects social change, and sometimes even invokes social change and thus legitimises it to some extent. It is also possible to infer the feedback of judicial decisions on the further development of law and legal relations.

Law acts not only as an independent but also as a dependent variable of social change in society, as it also represents a consequence of such changes. In considering the role of social change on the change in law, the speed of social change must be considered. Social change has to be sufficiently slow to become a source of law. Therefore, what has gradually become the main source of law is legal customs. Law responded to social changes that lasted decades or even centuries. The speed of social change changed fundamentally with the transition to modern society, and even more so to late modern society. Many social institutions ceased to perform some of their social functions during this period as seen, for example, in some functions of the family or village community. New areas of criminality and new social needs were emerging. Social changes thus triggered the need for legal change.

Every significant change in social behaviour and social relations has its reflection in the legal sphere, in legislation or in the decision-making of courts and administrative authorities with a certain time lag. Conversely, a change in law will gradually be reflected in social change. In this context, the American crisis of medical practice is

25. Daniel Šmihula, *Evolúcia práva* 258 (Epos 2013).
26. Friedman & Hayden, *supra* n. 15, at 264.
27. Marc Galanter, *Conceptualizing Legal Change and Its Effects*, 2 The Journal of Law Economics, and Organization 236 (1987).

often cited as an illustration.[28] On the surface, this crisis appears to be merely a crisis of law, litigation and legal doctrines. However, it is a complicated interplay between patients, doctors and insurance companies. The late twentieth century saw a large number of lawsuits in which patients successfully sued doctors and hospitals for damages for incorrectly performed medical procedures. This had a significant impact on insurance companies, which had to pay large damages. As a result, insurance companies radically increased the premiums that doctors paid. Doctors then pushed through provision of legal protection from prosecution for medical malpractice. All these actions and stakeholder reactions changed the legal framework of medical care, the structure and cost of medical care, insurance practices and fees, and the relationship between doctors and patients. Legal and social changes intersected.

The Belgian legal philosophers van de Kerchove and Ost summarised possible variations of the relationship between legal change and social change, which express possible states of mutual influence and disregard.[29] Inspired by their reflections, we can recapitulate the following cases from the testing of the situations that have arisen:

(1) Legal change is accompanied by social change – the effect sought by the legislator has been achieved.
(2) Legal change does not lead to the expected social change – several situational variants may occur here. Leaving aside poor quality legislation, there may be a situation where legal change was implemented only to formally satisfy social pressure (symbolic satisfaction) or certain social groups managed to prevent an actual social change.
(3) Social change has subsequently caused legal change; that is, a change in the social situation has enforced new legal regulation.
(4) Social change remained without influence on the legal order – the legislator retained its autonomy and ignored pressure from social groups, movements or society.

If we try to place mediation into the above summary, we can make the following recapitulation using the example of the Czech Republic:

(1) Legal change is accompanied by social change. ADR is increasingly used in practice. Individual responsibility for conflict resolution is coming to the fore. Society's values and its preferred methods of resolving conflicts through reconciliation are changing. If we take data from the Ministry of Justice of the Czech Republic and compare the total number of cases resolved in 2018, which was 415,647, and the number of cases concluded by conciliation, which was 9,978, the ratio of these cases is 2.4%. Compared to previous

28. Friedman & Hayden, *supra* n. 15, at 289.
29. Michel van de Kerchove & Francois Ost, *Legal System between Order and Disorder* 121–122 (Clarendon Press Oxford 1994).

years, these figures signal a move towards amicable dispute resolution, facilitated by alternative methods of conflict resolution.[30]

(2) Legal change did not lead to the expected social change. Legal change has led to social change but not to the extent expected. The rate of use of cooperative practices is still very low despite what was in point (1) above. Despite the proven benefits of mediation, it is used in less than 1% of cases across Europe.[31] Therefore, on the one hand, out-of-court dispute resolution procedures are institutionalised and supported by the European Community and at the national level, but on the other hand, their wider use is still hampered by obstacles that have not yet been sufficiently identified by research.[32]

(3) Social change has subsequently caused legal change; that is, a change in the social situation has enforced new legal regulation. As already mentioned, the development of mediation is linked to the postmodern era and is closely related to society and its dynamic changes since the second half of the twentieth century. Social change has undeniably triggered the development of mediation in other countries as well, as Cholensky shows in the example of the USA, where serious social problems put pressure on the US Congress, which passed the Civil Rights Act in 1964 and this led to the creation of the Office of Community Relations. The mission of this agency was to recruit and train personnel who could spread the use of mediation in their respective areas.[33]

(4) Social change remained without influence on the legal order. This variant has not been confirmed, but we can observe a certain lag of legal changes behind social changes. If we look again at the example of the Czech Republic, we can conclude that social change has subsequently triggered legal change, as we argued in point 3, but with a considerable delay. Mediation was first anchored in the Czech Republic in the area of criminal conflict resolution (Act No. 257/2000 Coll., on the Probation and Mediation Service), and the Czech Republic was one of the first post-socialist countries to introduce this restorative element into the resolution of criminal cases. This happened more than ten years after the revolutionary change of the political regime in 1989. In civil cases, the adoption of Act No. 202/2012 Coll., on Mediation and on the Amendments to Certain Acts, and Decree No. 277/2012 Coll., on the Examinations and Remuneration of Mediators, took place more than twenty years after the change of the political regime. To a large extent, this happened on the basis of the requirement to implement the EU Mediation Directive, which obliged the Member States to make legal changes by 21 May 2011 at the latest. The Czech Republic presented information on the legitimacy of mediation and

30. *See Statistika a výkaznictví*, Justice.cz (9 Sep. 2019), https://cslav.justice.cz/InfoData/prehledy-statistickych-listu.html.
31. Evropský Parlament, *supra* n. 9.
32. Lenka Holá, David Fiedor & Martina Urbanová, *První setkání se zapsaným mediátorem na základě prostorové analýzy míry jeho využívání v České republice*, 9 Právník 876–886 (2019).
33. Robert Cholenský, *Praktický průvodce mediací podle nové právní úpravy* 75 (Linde 2013).

committed to supporting it only in 2012. It is therefore clear that legal changes in many cases lag significantly behind social changes.

§2.03 MEDIATION AND EFFECTIVENESS OF LAW AS A TOOL FOR SOCIAL CHANGE

Legal norms are enacted to have an effect on social reality and to be reflected in actual legal relations and in human behaviour. The effectiveness of the law expresses the degree to which the legal system is able to achieve the objectives that are associated with legal regulation. The effectiveness of legal regulation is also closely related to the issue of mediation.

The objectives of legal regulation and the results achieved by legal regulation can be verified on the basis of empirical material, in particular by analysing the following legal phenomena:[34]

- the actual behaviour of addressees of law and the activities of state authorities (e.g., by analysing commercial contracts concluded, the way courts decide in the given area, etc.);
- the extent of conflicts and disputes that arise in the area of the legal regulation in question;
- the side effects of legal regulation;
- the shortcomings of legal regulations (loopholes in law, difficulties of interpretation, number and reasons for decisions of a public authority overturned by a higher authority, etc.).

The question that needs to be asked in this context concerns the requirements that need to be in place to ensure that law is likely to be an effective instrument of social change. The eminent American legal sociologist William Evan notes a requirement for the interaction of the following seven conditions:[35]

(1) Law comes from an authoritative and prestigious source.
(2) Law must be rational in terms of the use of intelligible concepts and compatible with existing values.
(3) Proponents of new legal regulation should show that it also works in other countries.
(4) New legal regulation should be applied and required immediately after it comes into effect.
(5) Advocates of new legislation must support it and commit themselves to the change.
(6) Enforcement should include positive and/or negative sanctions.
(7) Law should treat its violators equally because this is enforcement of law.

34. *See* Večeřa & Urbanová, *supra* n. 2, 215–216.
35. William M. Evan, *Law as an Instrument of Social Change* 554–562 (William M. Evan ed., The Free Press 1980).

Works in the field of sociology of law specify the obstacles that block the achievement of change through law. Manifestations of resistance to change induced by law are mainly due to psychological, social, economic and cultural factors.[36] The effect of these factors manifests itself in mutual combinations and in different intensities.

Psychological blockages include tendencies towards psychological stability of personality manifested in the area of legal perception, legal motivation, the achieved stage of legal socialisation, the level of moral development, and personality habitus. Social factors of legal effectiveness include group interests, ideological attitudes, moral sentiments, and organised opposition platforms and movements.[37] Economic barriers are due to the limited economic resources in society, which is particularly evident in the context of the exercise of social rights within a receding welfare state. Such economic barriers include limited access to information resources. For the addressees of a legal norm to find their way around the legal order, access to information technology is required. A long-promised access to an information system containing the full text of legislation in the form of an electronic Collection of Laws should increase the accessibility, clarity and comprehensibility of existing law.[38] Cultural factors that limit the possibilities of enforcing legal changes include prevailing values and moral institutions of society, ethnocentrism of certain social groups and classes, prejudices, and incompatibility of cultural patterns of minorities in a pluralising society.

Law as a tool for social change involves two interrelated processes: institutionalisation and internalisation of behavioural patterns. Institutionalisation of a legal norm as a pattern of behaviour refers to the establishment of a norm with its enforcement, while internalisation of a pattern of behaviour refers to the internal acceptance of the value or values implicit in the legal norm by the addressees of law and society and in the belief of the persons concerned that a given legal regulation is appropriate and necessary.

A law is binding because most people in society consider it binding. The requirement of its observance is achieved if at least some of those to whom it applies recognise it. Even if, in some cases, laws come into conflict with accepted morality and majority values, they are still usually obeyed. In this context, the Nuremberg Laws are often cited as an example, which legalised the hunt for Jews and were ultimately intended to lead to the final solution of the Jewish question. The extermination of more than six million Jews in Nazi Germany, which is clearly the most extreme case of crimes against humanity, involved thousands of people in the name of obedience to law. Absolute obedience to authority can have disastrous consequences, as shown by the experiment of Stanley Milgram at Yale University. According to Milgram, the division of labour causes that 'a person does not get to see the whole situation but only a small part of it, and is thus unable to act without some kind of over-all directions. He

36. Steven Vago, *Law and Society* 241–247 (Prentice Hall 1988).
37. Grana et al., *supra* n. 13, at 4.
38. The launch of a free online electronic Collection of Laws keeps being postponed in the Czech Republic. According to the latest information, it is not expected to be available until 1 Jan. 2023. It is clear that without the possibility of using these systems, it is no longer possible to navigate the legal system.

yields to authority but in doing so is alienated from his own actions ... Thus, there is fragmentation of the total human act; no one man decides to carry out the evil act and is confronted with consequences. The person who assumes full responsibility for the act has evaporated. Perhaps this is the most common characteristic of socially organized evil in modern society'.[39] These experiments confirmed that under certain conditions most people are willing to submit to authority and thus to laws contrary to moral principles and principles of justice.

§2.04 LIMITS OF LAW IN ACHIEVING SOCIAL CHANGE

The extent of social change brought about by legal instruments depends on the sociopolitical context, especially in the event of major political changes. In the countries of Eastern Europe, the fall of the totalitarian political system was one such fundamental change. The area of extension of the protection of fundamental rights and freedoms, the development of the welfare state and the need to regulate new phenomena in society (e.g., changes in property rights, new types of crime, changes in medicine, etc.) have played a significant role in these fundamental changes. It is clear from the above that law often necessarily reacts to the dynamics of sociopolitical changes in society (such as changes in tax laws when political representation changes).

The question is how far the law can go in its innovative effect. Lawyers in particular but also many laymen hold to the idea of omnipotence of law, which can thus determine the functioning of social life, intervene in essentially any area of social life, and promote arbitrary social change.[40] This legislative optimism (also referred to as legislative naivism or legislative utopianism) is related to the 'professional blindness' of some lawyers, who see the world only in a dichotomous polarisation of what is and is not allowed under the law, and perceive only the normative dimension of the social world. It is characterised by the belief that by promulgating something into legislation, the regulation of certain legal relations is resolved. Therefore, the rule of law is replaced by rule by law. The notion of the omnipotence of law corresponds with the views of laymen blaming imperfect law for all the shortcomings of the world. At the opposite extreme is the idea that legal regulation can go no further than sanctioning the current (existing) state of affairs. That is, law can only conserve the state of society, it cannot change established ways of behaviour and social life, and it cannot reshape social relations to bring about deliberate social change. The real possibilities of law are broader and lie on a continuum between the omnipotence of law to change social life and the inability of law to change established ways of behaviour and the life of society, depending on the nature of the area of social relations regulated by law and the content of the chosen legal regulation.

The above-mentioned question of the limits of legal regulation cannot be ignored even by legal-positivist approaches. Determining the limits of law directs attention to the legal-political aspects of law, the level of legal policy and the quality of the

39. Stanley Milgram, *Obedience to Authority: An Experimental View* 11 (Tavistock 1974).
40. Roger Cotterrell, *The Sociology of Law* 63–65 (Butterworths 1992).

lawmaking activity of the personified legislator. Answers to questions that can be used in relation to the regulation of mediation can be an indicator of the effectiveness of legal regulation promoting social change:

(1) To what extent does (or will) a given legal regulation influence people's actual actions and produce the intended legal effects?
(2) Can the actions of the addressees of the law be sufficiently monitored by the available means and can any deviations from the requirement of the legal norm be detected?
(3) Can legal sanctions be used to effectively and adequately punish (or compensate for) violations of legal norms by the addressees of the law?
(4) Does the legal regulation in question produce unintended negative side effects?

The limits of law in achieving social change are also determined by the quality of legal communication. Law is fundamentally based on communication. Legal communication involves targeted and purposeful handling of legal information, and creating purposeful social contacts, interactions and social relationships. By selecting the legal information provided, for example, by picking out certain information, by targeted selection of communicants, by public dissemination of only selected information, by withholding certain information and its possible falsification, it is possible not only to deliberately influence the legal consciousness of legal subjects and the public but also to influence the decision-making activity of courts. This is necessarily reflected in the impact of law on social reality.

An example of a potential misuse of legal communication is the practices and procedures of public relations in the USA in recent decades. In the business sphere, public relations serve to create targeted communication to the public and to influence that public, especially potential customers and competitors. Their new application in the legal sphere also shows that it is effective to influence legal institutions and participants in legal relations with tools that influence their opinions and attitudes as well as public opinion and the legal consciousness of society. The term 'litigation public relations' has been coined for the application of public relations in the context of court proceedings. This is understood as a targeted influence on the public, public opinion, legal awareness and judicial institutions in connection with the consideration and adjudication of litigation. It is the 'management of the communication process during the litigation or adjudication process of a court so as to achieve a given result or effect favourable to the client's overall reputation'.[41] The practices of litigation public relations provide a wide space particularly in legally complex cases where the decision depends largely on judicial assessment. The outcome of the dispute thus largely depends on the way the communication is conducted, whether the litigation occurs and what the result is or whether the dispute is resolved out of court. In the legal practice

41. *See* James Haggerty, *In the Court of Public Opinion: Winning Your Case with Public Relations* 2 (John Wiley & Sons 2003).

in the US, and gradually in Europe as well, it is increasingly common to see law firms using the assistance of public-relations consultants and advisers as part of a targeted strategy to influence the public and the judge who is part of it.

Determining whether law is the cause or the effect of social change is increasingly difficult in the postmodern situation, as economic, ideological, political and legal elements form a tight conglomerate of interacting and intertwining relationships. Moreover, the lack of transparency of manifest and latent influences on law is potentiated by the globalisation and europeanisation of law, which give a new quantitative and qualitative dimension to the process of social change. Identifying who is the creator of social change and who is served by the change in law is thus difficult.

§2.05 PARTIAL CONCLUSION

The legal landscape in late modern society has gradually become characterised by application of laws to achieve targeted social change. In making these changes, law goes beyond mere reflection on the change in social relations and promotes change in these relations on the basis of certain social values, needs and interests. The law thus often shapes practices and standards that compete and come into confrontation with established practices and procedures.

The postmodern situation places increased demands on law, from the part of both society and the state. Law not only reflects and confirms social change in society but also becomes an increasingly important tool for such change. The relationship between law and social change takes the form of a number of possible variations expressing mutual influence as well as forms of negation and disregard, which is also evident in the changing relationship between mediation and law. The process of mediation can be seen as social change, the course of which is limited not only by the quality of the legislation itself but also by the attitudes of the persons involved, legal institutions and the public. It can be concluded that in the case of mediation, a change in law is accompanied by an expected social change, particularly in terms of the beneficial effects in the area of the practical use of mediation. Mediation has become part not only of the legal system but also of today's society and the culture from which it draws.

PART II

An Analysis of Selected Cultural, Social and Legal Sources of Mediation Introduction

Lenka Holá

INTRODUCTION TO THE TOPIC

Although formal application of out-of-court methods of dispute resolution dates back to the late 1970s – the era of a social and legal movement in the US that called for new and more effective forms of dispute resolution – amicable procedures, which are the underlying principle, are thousands of years old.[1] The oldest ways of resolving interpersonal conflict are built on voluntariness. However, with increasing organisation, society is exercising its power in dispute resolution through its institutions (e.g., courts). Judicial dispute resolution has gradually become a standard. A fundamental tool is law enforcement. This places high financial and organisational demands on the state, which can lead to a decline in the effectiveness of dispute resolution. We have therefore gradually begun to return to the original, natural, cooperative and amicable ways of resolving disputes.[2]

Although mediation as an approach and the idea of conflict resolution with the help of an independent third party has existed in many communities for centuries, there is still no single, universally accepted definition of mediation. In its modern conception, it is most often still defined as an intervention, an entry into a conflict

1. The basic philosophical questions we face now in dispute resolution, for example, were already addressed in the time of the rabbis and Hebrew sages two thousand years ago. This is illustrated by Lipner in his discussion of debates in the Talmud. Seth E. Lipner, *Dispute Resolution: From Torah to Talmud to Today*, 16 Review of International Arbitration 315–322 (2007).
2. Přemysl Raban, *Alternativní řešení sporů, arbitráž a rozhodci v České a Slovenské republice a zahraničí* 1 (C. H. Beck 2004).

situation by a third party – a mediator – who assists the parties in managing or resolving their dispute. The word 'help' or its synonyms (facilitation, assistance, resolution) are the most frequent in definitions of mediation. At the same time, definitions of mediation vary according to the values they emphasise, the areas of application, the professional background and conceptual apparatus of the author and, since approximately the mid-1990s, the approach to mediation. The conception of mediation, which is based on different theoretical backgrounds in different mediation approaches, is diverse. Many authors have attempted to categorise them, for example, according to the role of the mediator, the goal of mediation or the stages of mediation.[3] Therefore, today we can say with much less certainty what mediation is. It would be easier to define what mediation is not.

As far as terminological clarification is concerned, in addition to 'mediation', in this part of the book we work with the terms 'amicable dispute resolution procedures', 'constructive dispute resolution methods', 'consensual dispute resolution methods' or 'alternative dispute resolution'. We consider the term 'amicable dispute resolution procedures' to be superior to the term 'mediation'. Both are based on the same values and ideals and build on some common principle, but the term 'amicable dispute resolution procedures' is broader as it includes other procedures and methods besides mediation.

Amicable dispute resolution procedures are sometimes also referred to as 'out-of-court dispute resolution', very often as 'alternative dispute resolution' (ADR). Most often, these procedures are conceived as an alternative to judicial resolution and are defined more or less by what makes them different.[4] However, there is no terminological consensus on the concept of 'alternative'. Generally, an alternative is understood as a choice between two or more mutually exclusive options (from Latin alter 'one of two'). However, the literature views the alternatives of these processes through several prisms:[5]

(1) One perspective on what makes ADR an alternative is that it represents methods implemented by entities other than the courts. However, this is somewhat simplistic or even misleading. There are countries where the court

3. *See*, e.g., Robert A. Bush & Joseph P. Folger, *The Promise of Mediation: Responding to Conflict Through Empowerment and Recognition* (Jossey-Bass 1994); Howard H. Irving, Michael Benjamin, *Family Mediation: Contemporary Issues* (SAGE 1995); Leonard Riskin, *Understanding Mediators' Orientations, Strategies & Techniques: A Grid for the Perplexed*, 1 Harvard Negotiation Law Review 7-51 (1996); Vlado Labath, *Individuální styl mediátora* ch. 2 (Lenka Holá et al. eds., 2013).
4. *See*, e.g., Linda Mulcahy, *The Collective Interest in Private Dispute Resolution*, 33 Oxford Journal of Legal Studies 59-80 (2013); Eva Storskrubb, *Alternative Dispute Resolution in the EU: Regulatory Challenges*, 24 European Review of Private Law 7-31 (2016); Dorothy W. Nelson, *The Immediate Future of Alternative Dispute Resolution*, 14 Pepperdine Law Review 777-780 (2013); Brian Pappas, *Med-Arb and the Legalization of Alternative Dispute Resolution*, 20 Harvard Negotiation Law Review 157-203 (2015).
5. Lenka Holá, *K pojmu konciliace v řešení spotřebitelských sporů*, 2 Obchodněprávní revue 47 (2017).

itself applies one of the ADR methods (e.g., mediation) in the course of court proceedings.

(2) The second view is based on the fact that the standard procedure for dispute resolution is judicial resolution. Any other options are considered an alternative to it. The limitation of this approach is that it implies that alternative methods are secondary, second-rate. It is for this reason that the label 'alternative dispute resolution methods' is now increasingly being replaced by 'out-of-court' or 'amicable' dispute resolution methods'.

(3) The third approach to the term 'alternative' takes as its distinguishing feature the nature of the process. That is, whether the resolution of a dispute is produced by an authority (in the case of adversarial adjudication, this is the authority of the judge) or by the cooperation of the parties. According to this criterion, we can distinguish between authoritative and collaborative methods of dispute resolution. Collaborative methods are then considered alternative. Collaborative methods are sometimes referred to as 'consensual methods'[6] and the abbreviation ADR is interpreted as 'amicable dispute resolution'. This emphasises their alternative to adversarial, competitive dispute resolution.

(4) Last but not least, there is a distinction according to the degree of state guarantee, where 'alternative' means that the methods are alternative to the forms of dispute resolution guaranteed by the state through public power.[7] In other words, alternative methods are not guaranteed by the state. However, in this sense, the most noticeable development in the EU is that mediation, in addition to judicial dispute resolution, is also guaranteed by the Member States through separate laws.

We believe that the terminological inconsistency outlined above can become a 'mere' terminological richness if we focus on the value essence of processes and differences rather than on their characteristics.

The aim of the second part of the book is to analyse selected cultural, social and legal sources of introduction of amicable dispute resolution practices, among which we primarily focus on mediation. By amicable dispute resolution practices, we mean all processes that build on the values of togetherness, natural human bonds, reciprocity, respect, justice, dialogue and cooperation. We analyse the topic from a cultural-social and legal-theoretical perspective, in which the two approaches are interconnected by a discussion of the question of values in culture, society and law. We consider the values of justice and cooperation as central values in the context of amicable practices. These categories of sources (cultural, social and legal) are treated in separate chapters for clarity. The theoretical analysis thus carried out should contribute to a deeper understanding of the starting points of mediation and lay the theoretical basis for the

6. However, the term 'consensual methods' lacks the dimension of cooperation between the parties in the search for a solution and usually only reflects the outcome, which is consensus.
7. Naděžda Rozehnalová, *Rozhodčí řízení v mezinárodním a vnitrostátním obchodním styku* 13 (Wolters Kluwer 3d ed. 2013).

subsequent parts of the book, which will deal with the question of integration of mediation into the legal systems of individual EU countries and the extent of its use.

If we talk about amicable practices as a philosophy, an approach to conflict resolution based on cooperation, reciprocity and reconciliation, they can be considered a kind of a moral ideal, a value. Another argument for explaining their processes and relationships through values is due to their interrelationship. Social behaviour is closely related to (moral) values and the (moral and social) norms derived from them. The various institutions of amicable dispute resolution are also governed by certain norms. This implies that they have values. Moreover, these procedures are themselves, in our view, instruments of mediation of values. They are an influence towards values through values. They allow participants to discover values for themselves, to experience them, to create new values. This, with all their 'intentionality', is an unrepeatable and creative act. Therefore, the mission of amicable practices in the lives of clients is more serious than it might seem at first glance. They touch, or more accurately, can touch, on the very essence of human existence. For it is not indifferent what one believes, what one devotes one's strength and energy to. The participants in dispute resolution thus question the essence and nature of man, his needs, possibilities, ideals and perspectives.

From the perspective of sociological research, the relationship between values and culture and culture and society forms a separate part of the text. Already the founder of modern sociology, Emil Durkheim, was convinced that it is impossible to observe cultural reality without considering its value-boundedness. In his view, values are one of the basic elements necessary for the existence of society. Culture is made up of values that the members of a society hold. What follows is the fact that the values that are recognised by the individual members of a society somehow become norms. This brings us closer to the legal concept of values. Legal norms are mediators of values, '... values are confirmed and guaranteed by contemporary law and thus also highlighted and fixed in social consciousness, including legal and moral consciousness'.[8] Therefore, in anchoring amicable resolution of disputes in law, we have drawn on ideas from legal philosophy and legal theory, where the typical value-based argumentation is argumentation by legal principles. Among the basic legal principles, justice, legal certainty and human freedom are cited. We have focused on the principle of justice, which we consider to be a guiding principle in law and also relevant to amicable procedures. In connection with these, however, we are not directed towards the legal concept of justice (in the sense of legitimate claims) but towards justice as a social and value-based idea.

In analysing the sources for implementing amicable procedures into the legal systems of individual countries, it is therefore impossible to ignore the development of society and the social conditions of its members. In agreement with other authors, we conclude that contemporary social sciences are seeking effective ways to respond to changing social conditions while contributing to the social functioning of individuals, social groups and society as a whole. One modern concept that is a theoretical

8. Jaromír Havránek, *Teorie práva* 89 (Aleš Čeněk 2008).

prerequisite for such responses is the concept of participation and empowerment. It is understood as empowering individuals, groups and communities to be more capable of managing or constructively shaping their life situation through their own activities. A practical way of putting it into practice is through amicable procedures in conflict resolution between people.

Because of our long-standing interest in mediation, our focus among amicable procedures is on it. Mediation is generally conceived as a method of constructive, participatory conflict resolution with the help of a mediator, with the aim of reaching a mutually acceptable agreement to resolve the problem. We understand mediation as a method which focuses on the individual themselves, on their needs and interests, and through which that individual's untapped resources are activated to resolve their life situation. The basic principles of such an approach are participation and empowerment: participating in decision-making, taking the responsibility, being active has a much broader context than purely legal. Participation is not a universal tool to direct everything, but it determines the basic direction for further setting the rules for dealing with life situations in the long term. However, no participation can be exercised out of coercion. We cannot construct the process as an obligation or a necessity. At that point, it would lose its value. Reconciliation and agreement can be achieved in dispute resolution when civic values are applied. It is manifested in the way individuals balance their own needs with the needs of the whole. If, in accordance with amicable procedures, we want to create the reciprocity that conditions cooperative relations and, ultimately, a civil society, there should be shared values to which individual societies subscribe, also through their legal norms.

CHAPTER 3

Cultural Sources for Introduction of Mediation: Changes in Shared Identity

Lenka Holá

Societal development and social change can subsequently trigger legal change and vice versa. Therefore, a change in the social situation will force a new legal regulation. This fact, as argued in the second chapter of our book, is also reflected in the introduction of mediation into the legal systems of individual countries. Law must be rational in terms of the use of intelligible concepts and compatible with existing values. Therefore, cultural factors, which are an integral part of society, can also support or limit the possibilities of enforcing legal change. Sociologist of law Steven Vago, the author of *Law and Society*, includes among the cultural factors of legal change the prevailing values and moral institutions of a society, ethnocentrism of certain social groups and classes, and prejudice and incompatibility of cultural patterns of minorities in a pluralising society.[9] The cultural and social background of conflicts and their resolution are closely related to the values of a society and its preferred practices. Let us therefore take a closer look at the cultural factors for introduction of mediation.

§3.01 CULTURAL ASPECTS OF CONFLICT RESOLUTION

In discussing the cultural aspects of implementing mediation, let us begin with the broader issue of cultural aspects of conflict resolution. In this context, we obviously cannot do without the terms 'nation' and 'culture'. In the European tradition, the prevailing notion is that modern nations have evolved from their respective ethnicities, and these nations have their own states. On the basis of sociological theories, we can then define a nation as '... a distinctive and conscious cultural and political community whose formation is to the greatest extent influenced by a common history and a

9. Steven Vago, *Law and Society* 241–247 (Routledge 10h ed. 2016).

common territory'.[10] At the same time, three types of criteria for the identification of a nation are given: cultural criteria (common language, religion or historical experience), political existence criteria (nations have their own state or an autonomous unit within a state) and psychological criteria (the consciousness of belonging to a particular nation shared by individuals). Culture is therefore of key importance in this respect. The people of different countries live in more or less distinct cultures characterised by specific systems of shared values, social norms, ideas, traditions, experiences, customs and communication rituals. The characteristics of culture and its different types are discussed in more detail in Chapter 1. However, it is necessary to state, in line with Avruch, that culture remains one of the most elusive concepts in the social sciences, so much so that no simple, universally accepted definition of it has yet been arrived at.[11] Let us therefore focus on the characteristics that we believe play a role in conflict resolution.

The characteristics of individual cultures are described in sociology and cultural anthropology. Some sources state that there are up to 5,000 different nations in the world. More precise data on the nations of the world are provided by the description of 739 nations published by the Czech ethnographers Hubinger, Honzák and Polišenský.[12] Although there are various ethnological archives and databases, we cannot say with certainty exactly how many cultures live in the world today. The world and its cultural composition have changed significantly over the last twenty years. Therefore, we can only note with certainty the multicultural reality of the contemporary world. A typology of national cultures makes it possible to discern more detailed features of approaches to conflict resolution. In order to understand the typology, it is necessary to accept the initial idea that '... culture is always a collective phenomenon since it is always shared, at least in part, by people who have lived or are living in the same social environment in which they have acquired culture. It is the collective programming of the mind that distinguishes members of one group or category of people from another'.[13]

If we look at this issue on the basis of the sociological dichotomy of relativism and absolutism, it is obvious how difficult it is to understand different cultures.[14] Cultural relativism is an approach to cultural phenomena based on the assumption that different cultures represent unique and non-repeatable sociocultural systems that can only be understood in the context of their own values, norms and ideas.[15] Relativism may represent an extremely permissive way of understanding things, but it does not offer criteria for judging what is good and bad, true or false. In contrast, cultural absolutism contains undeniable notions of true and false, right and wrong and good and evil, but it is not open to negotiation. This brings us closer to the cultural aspects

10. Jan Průcha, *Interkulturní psychologie* 54 (Portál 2004).
11. Kevin Avruch, *Culture and Conflict Resolution* (U.S. Institute of Peace 1998).
12. Václav Hubinger et al., *Národy celého světa* (Mladá fronta 1985).
13. Geert Hofstede et al., *Cultures and Organizations: Software of the Mind – Intercultural Cooperation and Its Importance for Survival* 14 (McGraw-Hill 3d ed. 2010).
14. Miloš Večeřa et al., *Interkulturní mediace v sociologickém a právním kontextu* 14 (Masarykova univerzita 2017).
15. Lenka Holá: Václav Soukup, *Velký sociologický slovník* 920 (Jiří Linhart ed., Karolinum 1996).

of conflict resolution. In this context, we can examine them in the context of social culture and political culture. Both are reflected in conflict resolution. Social culture promotes joint interactions between members of a culture by creating a set of shared values and ideals that guide their behaviour. Therefore, members of different cultures can be expected to assign different meanings to conflict situations and to respond differently to each other's signals.[16] The more complex and differentiated the social system, the greater the number of potentially influential sources of each cultural attribute.[17]

Social culture is therefore personally connected to the participants in a conflict. The fact that socio-cultural differences are reflected in the different perceptions between parties and their approaches to conflict resolution has been demonstrated in many research studies.[18] Cohen adds convincingly that '... in international conflicts, the "rules" simply cannot be known, and significant cultural differences between adversaries can exacerbate conflict and complicate its resolution'.[19] Although his research is about 25 years old, even the current findings support Cohen's conclusions. For example, Leng and Regan examined the relationship between the cultural characteristics of rival countries and mediation outcomes in militarised disputes. In doing so, they distinguished between social culture, which is defined primarily in terms of religious identity, and political culture, defined by a country's political system. Having analysed 752 mediations in militarised disputes between 1945 and 1995, they concluded that mediation is more likely to be successful when countries share democratic political cultures.[20] Therefore, for mediation to be effective, they recommend that it be conducted in a global diplomatic culture in these disputes. They believe that cultural and political differences should not play any role in a mediation thus conducted.[21] The problem occurs in the actual application. The difficulties that arise in peaceful attempts at resolution, according to Avruch, stem not from poor communication or cultural differences but are the result of the irreconcilable competing interests of the countries in conflict.[22] Huntington comes to similar conclusions, stating that the main cultural obstacles do not come from communication factors but from religious affiliation.[23] The

16. Under the influence of this, culture is defined even more generally by some social anthropologists as a 'derivative of individual experience'.
17. Raymond Cohen, *Negotiating Across Cultures: International Communication in an Interdependent World* 11–13 (U.S. Institute of Peace 1997).
18. *See*, e.g., Raphael Patai, *The Arab Mind* (Scribners 1977); Stella Ting-Toomey et al., *Culture, France Maintenance, and Style of Handling Interpersonal Conflict: A Study of Five Cultures*, 2 International Journal of Conflict Management 275–296 (1991); James A. Wall, Jr. & Michael Blum, *Community Mediation in the People's Republic of China*, 35 Journal of Conflict Resolution 3–20 (1991); Kamil M. Kozan & Canan Ergin, *Preference for Third Party Help in Conflict Management in the United States and Turkey: An Experimental Study*, 29 Journal of Cross-Cultural Psychology 525–540 (1998).
19. Raymond Cohen, *Cultural Aspects of Mediation* 108 (Jacob Bercovitch ed., Lynne Rienner Publishers 1996).
20. Russell J. Leng, Patrick M. Regan, *Social and Political Cultural Effects on the Outcomes of Mediation in Militarized Interstate Disputes*, 47 International Studies Quarterly 431–452 (2003).
21. *Ibid.*, 437.
22. Kevin Avruch, *supra* n. 11, at 55.
23. Samuel Huntington, *The Clash of Civilizations and the Remaking of World Order* 41 (Simon & Schuster 1996).

latter is profound and immutable, which is why religious conflict resolution is not open to compromise. Huntington's thesis was later challenged, mainly for ignoring variations in cultural influences on individuals and their evolution over time,[24] yet it remains one of the most important theses on the influence of culture in international conflicts and a logical starting point for examining cultural aspects in mediation.

The second cultural attribute in conflict resolution, political culture, refers to the perspectives, values and patterns of behaviour that are generated by the political system. Political culture is a term that is used in different ways. In political science, it is used especially by comparativists to describe the civic attributes that influence the functioning of different political systems.[25] For example, Russett argues that democratic political culture, based on the norm of peaceful resolution of disputes through democratic processes, has contributed to the absence of war among democracies.[26] Leng and Regan come to similar conclusions as we noted above. Therefore, the cultural argument for the democratic peace proposal is that every democratic government is aware of the other side's propensity to settle disputes through negotiation and consensus.[27]

In short, both aspects of culture operate simultaneously in conflict situations: social culture at the interaction and communication level, political culture as an external social system. They condition each other and they mutually combine. This is not to deny other potentially important cultural influences, of course, but with a large degree of generalisation it would probably be possible to subordinate these two aspects of culture to these two aspects.

In this context, interesting research has been conducted by Inman et al. They focused on interactions between states and how cultural factors influence individual and group behaviour in different contexts. Specifically, they examined how culture influences the course of crises between states, how states interact with each other, and their willingness to resolve these crises through mediation. They conducted their analysis at the level of international systems and cross-cultural psychology. At the level of international systems, the study found that cultural differences between states affect whether or not mediation occurs during an international crisis but do not affect the reduction of tensions between states. At the level of internal actors, the authors found through psychological investigation that there are certain aspects of cultural identity that make members of a society more or less inclined to use mediation to resolve an international crisis, but even these cultural aspects have no effect on the actual reduction of tensions between countries.[28]

---

24. *See*, e.g., Errol A. Henderson & Richard Tucker, *Clear and Present Strangers: The Clash of Civilizations and International Conflict*, 45 International Studies Quarterly 317–338 (2001).
25. *See*, e.g., Ronald Inglehart, *The Renaissance of Political Culture*, 82 American Political Science Review 1203–1230 (1988); Robert D. Putnam, *Making Democracy Work: Civic Traditions in Modern Italy* (Princeton University Press 1993).
26. Bruce M. Russett, *Grasping the Democratic Peace: Principles for a Post–Cold War World* 31 (Princeton University Press 1993).
27. Russell J. Leng & Patrick M. Regan, *supra* n. 20, at 434.
28. Molly Inman et al., *Cultural Influences on Mediation in International Crises*, 58 The Journal of Conflict Resolution 685–712 (2014).

As is evident, the intersection of the personal and social levels in the issue of conflict resolution is permanent. Interactions between actors are influenced by both personal and cultural values.

§3.02 CULTURAL SOURCES FOR INTRODUCTION OF MEDIATION

In order to analyse the cultural sources for introduction of mediation, the cultural typology of Geert Hofstede, a Dutch sociologist and psychologist, who studied the interactions between and differences between different national and organisational cultures, serves as a theoretical starting point. Hofstede identified five universal cultural dimensions that can be used to characterise national, regional, community, organisational and also class cultures. The theory applies to several dozen countries, so it is a powerful tool that allows for comparisons between regions to identify the underlying cultural aspects that determine the behaviour of members of these cultures. In the introduction to his book *Cultures and Organizations*,[29] the author quotes a scene from the American film *12 Angry Men* (1957). In it, one of the jurors irritates the other juror, who is not inherently polite, with his politeness. He angrily asks his fellow juror why he is so polite. The first juror replies that it is exactly why the second is not – because his parents brought him up that way. The world is full of confrontations between people, groups and nations that think, feel and behave differently. At the same time, like the situation in the film, they are faced with common problems that require them to work together in order to solve them.

Hofstede sees culture as a mental program in the sense of computer terminology and refers to it as 'software of the mind'. In his view, from childhood onwards, people acquire the social environment in which they grow up and the patterns of how to think, experience and act as certain mental programs. Culture can then be understood as the collective programming of the mind that distinguishes members of one group from others. The author believes that there is a strong relationship between the mindset of an individual and the behaviour of the collective. According to Hofstede, the core of culture also consists of values concerning the dichotomy of good and evil, clean and dirty, beautiful and ugly, natural and unnatural, normal and abnormal, logical and paradoxical, rational and irrational. Cultural differences are manifested by four concepts: values, rituals, heroes and symbols. These form the layers of manifestations of culture. They can be imagined as the layers of an onion, with values hidden deepest in its core. They are visible to outside observers through actions.

When one searches for the meaning of cultural sources for the introduction of mediation, Hofstede's concept is an inspiring theoretical starting point, as it deals with the consequences of culture in the functioning of society, groups and individuals within these groups. Within this framework, he also works with the cultural conditioning of behaving in a conflict situation, controlling aggression or expressing feelings.[30] This is something that is crucial for mediation. Hofstede identified five

29. Geert Hofstede et al., *supra* n. 13.
30. *Ibid.*, 3–18.

universal cultural dimensions that can be used to characterise national, regional, community, organisational and also class cultures. Four of these – power distance (PDI), IND, masculinity (MAS) and uncertainty avoidance (UAI) – were discovered through surveys among IBM employees. The fifth – long-term orientation (LTO) – was obtained from a Chinese study on values. All dimensions are bipolar, measured by indices that can take values between 0 and 100.

To meet the objectives of this chapter, we now set a research subquestion, namely, in which cultures can we find sources for the introduction and development of amicable conflict resolution practices, specifically mediation? The methodological tool will be the different dimensions of cultures according to Hofstede, which we analyse in terms of their potential for the development of mediation.

[A] Power Distance

This dimension measures the degree of inequality that is expected, accepted and preferred in a given society. In societies that prefer a large PDI, inequalities are considered natural and useful, and are expected and desired. There is great differentiation of income, and accumulation of privilege and ostentatious presentation of high status are expected. Boundaries between social classes are rigid, respected and not very permeable, so social mobility is very weak. Organisations are strictly hierarchical and authorities are revered. Children are brought up to respect elders, parents and teachers. Hofstede also points out the strong need for dependency. Conversely, in societies that prefer a small PDI, there is an emphasis on equality and equal opportunity for all. Very often there is a redistribution of wealth to reduce inequalities. Inequality is seen as unfair and undesirable. In these societies, formal status is usually not very important and people have weaker relationships with regard to authorities. The need for dependency is low; on the contrary, there is a strong tendency towards decentralisation. Any accumulation of power is considered harmful. Children are brought up to be independent.

Partial conclusion: According to the characteristics and principles of mediation, it can be assumed that cultures that prefer a small PDI have a greater potential for the development of mediation.

[B] Uncertainty Avoidance

This dimension focuses on society's treatment of uncertainty, responses to uncertainty and danger, and interpretation of the future. It examines how willing different cultures are to tolerate uncertainty and their need to prevent and avoid situations that create uncertainty. Societies with a high value of this index have a low willingness to operate with uncertainty. Such cultures have a need to create a large number of relatively strict rules; there are many laws, control mechanisms and taboos, both formal and informal. People prefer stable social relationships and fixed norms because the stability of structure greatly reduces uncertainty. These societies are more conservative, with a distrust of innovation, are more anxious, so there is more stress. On the other hand, it is acceptable to show emotions in them.

Societies with the opposite relationship to uncertainty, with low index values, are more competitive. Conflict is accepted as a normal part of life and is generally accepted. People are more tolerant of differences, accept change more readily and are more willing to take risks. Emotions are kept hidden. There is less stress in these societies because uncertainty and ambiguity are accepted as a normal part of life. Rules and laws tend to be general in nature and do not attempt to cover every single situation that may arise.

Partial conclusion: In this respect, we believe that the sources for mediation lie more in cultures that do not shy away from uncertainty and take it as a normal part of life.

[C] Individualism

The dimension of IND (or collectivism) captures the extent to which people in a given culture act as independent individuals or as members of social groups. In collectivist cultures, the sense of belonging to a group is predominant. They integrate individuals into strong and cohesive groups from birth and place great emphasis on the extended family concept. These groups are willing to protect and support individuals in exchange for their loyalty. Not only do people act in ways that do not harm their group but also they take responsibility for other members of the group. There is an interest in the welfare of the whole. Harmony and consensus are important. In these societies, the family with strong ties between relatives plays a strong role. In individualistic cultures, the values of personal freedom and independent decision-making play a more important role. Here people tend to form a greater number of relatively weak ties. Relationships are more flexible and less binding. Task accomplishment and efficiency take precedence over them. Individualistic cultures are characterised by very loose social and family ties, with the individual expected to be primarily concerned with his or her own welfare or that of his or her family.

Partial conclusion: In the individualism dimension, the decision on sources for mediation is not as clear-cut as in the other dimensions. We assume that sources are more likely in collectivistic cultures with a need for harmony, consensus and concern for the well-being of the whole. However, in terms of the degree of taking personal responsibility, individualistic cultures are more conducive to mediation.[31]

[D] Masculinity

The MAS and femininity dimensions focus on general values in society, general goals and the meaning of life. Masculine cultures focus on performance, achievement, heroism and progress. They are more materialistic. People's behaviour is more

31. We believe that this fact will then be reflected in the approach to mediation and in the selection of mediation style.

aggressive and direct. Conflicts are more often resolved by fighting. The upbringing of girls and boys differs; girls are supposed to be gentle and sensitive, while boys are supposed to be pugnacious and ambitious. Feminine cultures, on the other hand, focus on interpersonal relationships, quality of life, taking care of oneself, other people and the environment. Conflicts are more often resolved through compromise and negotiation. Girls and boys are raised similarly; they may cry but they are not supposed to fight.

Partial conclusion: Cultural bases of mediation are more likely to be found in feminine cultures focused on the quality of relationships and tendencies towards negotiation and consensus.

[E] Long-Term Orientation

The dimension of LTO signifies a society's coming to terms with its own past, learning from history and mistakes, and responding to current challenges and development. Cultures with low scores are short-term oriented, honour tradition and view innovation with respect. They prefer immediate results and delivering on commitments. They are ideologically oriented. Cultures with high scores are long-term oriented and they accept social and other changes as a challenge. They aim for future results, long-term investments. They are better prepared to adapt to new circumstances. They learn from others, are thrifty, persistent and competitive.

Partial conclusion: With regard to the search for new ways of operating in the future and innovative approaches to conflict resolution, sources of mediation are more likely to be found in long-term-oriented cultures.

Hofstede originally defined only five dimensions, but in 2010, in collaboration with Minkov, a sixth dimension was added to the theory: *indulgence*. Indulgence is related to the relatively free satisfaction of needs and desires, where individuals 'enjoy life'. They are more satisfied, feel freer, and focus on positive experiences and emotions. In contrast, restraint is related to the suppression of individual desires through very strict social norms. The features that characterise restrained cultures are the existence of relatively fewer happy people, perception of powerlessness, indifference to free speech, lower importance of leisure time, and remembering rather negative emotions.[32]

Partial conclusion: We believe that mediation will be applied more in an indulgence culture, oriented towards satisfaction and fulfilment of personal needs.

Based on the above, it can be summarised that the sources for the introduction and development of mediation are more likely to be found in cultures that prefer a small PDI, do not avoid uncertainty, and are more collectivist and feminine, long-term oriented and more indulgence oriented. Since it would be probably hard to find a culture that fulfils all these attributes, we can conclude by expressing hope that in every culture we are likely to find characteristics that can be considered as potential sources

32. Geert Hofstede, *Dimensionalizing Cultures: The Hofstede Model in Context*, 2 Online Readings in Psychology and Culture 1–26 (2011).

of mediation and, under favourable social conditions, can be further developed. Specifically, in line with Ross, it can be said that mediation will be cultivated in cultures with a constructive approach to conflict resolution that share common characteristics such as low levels of inclination towards aggression and violence, a strong alignment of individual and community interests, preference for self-determination, desire for control over dispute resolution, an interest in restoring peace and cooperation, and the ability to withdraw if an acceptable solution cannot be reached.[33]

§3.03 CULTURAL INTEGRATION OF EUROPE AS A STARTING POINT FOR EU MEDIATION EFFORTS

As the book deals with mediation in the reflection of law and society in the European context, the analysis of cultural sources will not avoid the issues of European culture. However, our research interest goes even further as we are interested in the reflection on mediation specifically in the EU setting. This implies the need to focus here on issues of cultural integration in Europe as a cultural starting point for EU mediation efforts. The topic of European integration seems to be a very attractive one for contemporary researchers. They address it from many angles – sociocultural, migration, political, economic and others.[34]

'Integration' is a polysemic concept that has no generally agreed definition. When considered in its sociocultural dimension, the concept of integration challenges a society to realise which features it considers existential in such a way that their absence would undermine its very essence. This requires a process of introspection and connection to the concept of 'identity'.[35]

Identity itself is a multifaceted concept composed of individual and collective layers: biological, social, geographical, cultural, political, religious and others. While some of these aspects can easily coexist, others can be problematic and create internal or external tensions. For example, while being a heterosexual man is unproblematic from this perspective, being a homosexual man who identifies as a woman can be problematic. The element of complexity relates to the perception of identity. There is a conflict between how individuals perceive themselves and how society perceives those individuals. In other words, a particular aspect of a person's identity may be selected as their dominant feature regardless of their will or self-identification.[36]

In the context of international integration, researchers and policymakers often simplify this complexity by explicitly or implicitly recognising individuals as primarily

---

33. Marc H. Ross, *The Management of Conflict* (Yale University Press 1993).
34. *See* Cris Shore, *Building Europe: The Cultural Politics of European Integration* (Routledge 2000); Steven Dijkstra et al., *Multiculturalism and Social Integration in Europe*, 22 International Political Science Review 55–84 (2001); Zuzana Lehmannová, *Integrace Evropy z hlediska kultury*, 3 Mezinárodní vztahy 24–40 (2001); Tommaso Virgili, *Whose 'Identity'? Multiculturalism vs. Integration in Europe*, 19 European View 45–53 (2020).
35. Bhikhu Parekh, *A New Politics of Identity: Political Principles for an Interdependent World* 4 (Red Globe Press 2008).
36. Elham Manea, *Women and Shari'a Law: The Impact of Legal Pluralism in the UK* 15 (I B Tauris Academic 2016).

members of a group.[37] This has given rise to what we refer to as 'identity politics'. It is strongly associated with political multiculturalism. Political multiculturalism does not build on the values of pluralism but institutionalises diversity by placing individuals into ethnic and cultural groups. Their individual needs and rights to shape public policy are then defined on the basis of these groups.[38] Virgili is critical of identity politics, and he is particularly concerned in practice with the creation of semi-autonomous communities living according to their cultural traditions and without significant intergroup exchanges.[39] Virgili's ideas are supported by Triandafyllidou's adherence to the 'simple reality' of a conglomeration of human beings sharing certain characteristics, traditions, beliefs and goals. And at the same time differing, even significantly, from others.[40]

[A] The Value Paradigm of European Cultural Integration

What does this mean for the European process of cultural integration, which can be seen as the source of the EU's efforts to introduce elements of peaceful conflict resolution into the legal systems of the Member States? The starting point, and at the same time a safeguard against simple descriptions, becomes once again a value paradigm. In the European context (but not only there), it can be said that in connection with integration processes in the political, economic, social or legal spheres, the question of the possibilities and limits of the integration process in the cultural sphere arises. However, the problem of the cultural dimension of processes of European integration is, as Lehmannová notes, '… a very complex one, the solution to which can only be formulated intuitively'.[41] Considering the intricacy and complexity of cultural reality, the topic needs to be examined with a broad sociological and anthropological approach. In this sense, we arrive at the concept of 'sociocultural system', which we already discussed in the first chapter. From a systemic point of view, the basic question can be formulated as follows: is it possible to define European culture as a historical type of sociocultural system of a 'transnational' type or is Europe moving towards such a system? Lehmannová has addressed this question in her study. She started from the value paradigm, whose function is primarily to integrate sociocultural systems, to define the specifics of a given culture and to navigate communities in reality. In doing so, it is itself the basis of this navigation. In other components of culture (e.g., in legal and ethical norms or in the structure of institutions), it is already manifested indirectly. The value paradigm allowed Lehmannová to get to the level of the internal integration, coherence and orderliness of the whole and to answer other questions that arose from the principle of this paradigm. For example, are there

37. Vít Novotný, *Politics of Identity in Focus: What Next after Multiculturalism* (Wilfried Martens Centre for European Studies 2015).
38. Bhikhu Parekh, *supra* n. 35, at 31.
39. Tommaso Virgili, *supra* n. 34, at 47.
40. Anna Triandafyllidou, *The Multicultural Idea and Western Muslims* 214–229 (Roberto Tottoli ed., Routledge 2015).
41. Zuzana Lehmannová, *supra* n. 34, at 24.

spiritual foundations for European cultural unity? Is there a European cultural paradigm? And what are the basic European value principles?

The majority of researchers answer the above questions regarding the existence of the European value paradigm affirmatively. European thinkers have been trying to define a basic European value orientation (European idea) since the nineteenth century. Certain common spiritual features of Europe exist, and thus the existence of a European value paradigm can be assumed. However, as Lehmannová argues, in order to verify such an assumption, an appropriate method of identifying the underlying value structure must be chosen. This is possible in several ways. Alongside classical cultural-anthropological empirical research, the most effective is the analysis of the spiritual component of culture because the value paradigm is most strongly expressed in this component. In order to identify the European value paradigm, it is necessary to identify the main factors that have co-created it. These are, first, the way of life of a particular human community in its geographical and climatic conditions, the ethnic composition of the population, the specific historical processes and events that have influenced the development of culture, and the spiritual systems that spiritually 'process' these initial factors. We do not have sufficient space here to explore the characteristics of the values of European culture, which have certainly also influenced the European practice of mediation. Therefore, out of a large number of topics, we will limit ourselves to the new concept of man and his place in a changing world because this topic is very closely related to mediation as a method of solving problems of particular people. The concept of man will thus also be an appropriate link to the chapter on the social sources for introducing mediation.

While the classical period is mainly concerned with the developmental patterns of the human race and the individual is understood as a modus of gender, the modern period emphasises the human being in his uniqueness and unrepeatability. With this shift, the interpretation of the topic of freedom in European thought changes. In the modern period, freedom is understood as the defence of the individual and the individual's existence against enslavement in an expanding civilisation. The topic of freedom is a topic of human responsibility towards oneself and one's environment.[42] This resonates very closely with resolving interpersonal conflicts with one's own resources, taking responsibility for this and freely choosing to manage one's adverse personal situation in this way. As Bruno Leoni, an Italian political philosopher and lawyer, states in his book *Freedom and the Law*,[43] the content of freedom remains spiritual development, but with an even stronger emphasis on individual responsibility and the law.[44] At the same time, this new image of the world means that humanity is becoming aware of itself as a whole and as part of an even greater whole. All modern

42. Harrie Salman, *Evropa v novém světle* 50 (Eós 1995).
43. Bruno Leoni, *Freedom and the Law* (D. Van Nostrand Company 1961).
44. At the same time, Leoni says that the biggest obstacle to the rule of law in our times is the problem of excessive legislation. In modern democratic societies, legislatures are increasingly usurping functions that were and should be performed by individuals or groups rather than by the government. This is where we see the starting point for the introduction of amicable procedures for dispute resolution. These seek to consider the interests of both parties and to reach a mutually acceptable outcome that the parties can identify with and implement. In this

European schools of thought stress the development of free individuality as a prerequisite for human responsibility. These principles are associated with the importance of the personal responsibility of each individual person for the direction towards the good and freedom.[45] And it is the emphasis on personal responsibility, the development of free individuality and free decision-making and the direction towards the good that are the cultural-value sources of mediation. We will come to the interdependence of the global and the individual several more times in this book in different contexts.

[B] The European Cultural System: Transformations of a Common Identity

When asked whether there are preconditions for the creation of a unified European cultural system and whether European cultural integration (as a value basis for integration in all areas of human life) is under way, Lehmannová, for example, answers affirmatively. In her view, Europe has a unified civilisational sphere. The rapid development of science and technology, the development of new production processes, overseas discoveries and the expansion of Europe into the whole world have all enabled Europe to create a dynamic civilisational system and the basis for globalisation, which has been fully under way since the twentieth century.[46] From a cultural point of view, this is a transition from a period in which individual cultural formations were relatively closed entities to a period of global multicultural civilisation. This means that the sociocultural systems of the countries of Europe are integrated into some parts of their structure, while other parts are not integrated or, on the contrary, have the opposite tendency of disintegration (e.g., in the field of spiritual culture).[47]

Europe today is carrying out a unique experiment in the history of mankind. For the first time in history, a transnational sociocultural system is being created on the basis of a free and deliberate decision by the entities that make up the system. The subjects of this integration process are mature, stable and historically and culturally fixed national systems that are working together to create Europe. This purposeful decision is the logical consequence of the European worldview, the European worldview and the European value paradigm. In it, Europe realises its fundamental idea and completes its historical role. Europe not only has created the preconditions for globalisation and a new relationship between cultures in the world and formulated new values for the globalisation phase but is also performing a historic example of a purposeful procedure in creating a modern community made up of specific and culturally distinct entities: entities that work together to solve common tasks and problems on the basis of consensus and commonly accepted principles.

---

way, we are gradually returning to the original, natural and more amicable ways of resolving disputes, where the focus of responsibility for resolving disputes is shifted from society to the individual.

45. For more detail *see*, e.g., Christopher H. Dawson, *Zrození Evropy* (Vyšehrad 1994).
46. Zuzana Lehmannová, *Odkaz Evropy globalizaci*, 5 Acta oeconomica Pragensia 166–184 (2000).
47. *Ibid.*, 55.

However, contemporary (not only European) society is becoming less and less homogeneous in terms of cultural typology. On the one hand, there are European integration processes, and, on the other hand, due to postmodernity, there is a growing global differentiation based on new conceptions of ways of life, lifestyles and life practices. The postmodern era is a state of feeling and spirit that rests primarily on plurality, heterogeneity and discontinuity as a basic orientation directive while at the same time denoting a diverse cultural set.[48] The essential element of postmodernity is the plurality of opinions and their equalisation.

Is not the creation of a transnational European sociocultural system in the current pluralistic postmodern era swimming against the tide? Is this not creating a utopia of European values in an age of multiplicity of cultures of European countries? The answer is found in Welsch's 'radical pluralism'.[49] What does he mean by this? In his view, the present postmodern age is characterised by the fact that we are confronted with an increasing number of different life forms, conceptions of knowledge and ways of navigating ourselves in the world. At the same time, we realise that each individual form is as valuable as the others and we recognise and appreciate this multiplicity of life more and more with further experience. The problem to which this pluralisation leads is thus obvious. With each new possibility, orientation of the members of a given culture becomes more difficult. What values are we to live by when in a postmodern world each of the choices is equally justified? Radical plurality goes beyond and intensifies its own plurality. Radical pluralism breeds a world in which there is consensus that we disagree with each other. It is essential that we operate on the basis of acceptance of each other's differences. This is both a requirement and a goal that is also characteristic of mediation. Mediation is a distinctly pluralist method in its acceptance of differences. Its aim is not to find a common truth but to find common solutions in perceiving and understanding differences. The same can be said in the context of the European cultural values with which mediation is associated in the EU.[50]

Postmodern pluralism is based on ethics. It advocates the right to different orientations in life, the right to live different forms of life. It believes that acceptance of the difference is only possible when we look inside it. Tolerance is not enough. The consciousness of the subject should abandon its limited perspective and be able to see things through the eyes of the other. Postmodern plurality means that the logic of one form of life must not be made a criterion for another. Through the lens of postmodernism, the idea of European integration is possible with the simultaneous plurality of its individual cultures, values, the purposeful processes of creating a European community and the awareness of the limits to which individual decisions reach.

48. Thomas Koenig, *Existentialism and Human Existence: An Account of Five Major Philosophers* (Krieger 1992).
49. Wolfgang Welsch, *Postmoderne – Pluralität als ethischer und politischer Wert* 22–24 (Wirtschafts-Verl. Bachem 1988).
50. Above we related mediation to one of them, namely the new concept of man.

§3.04 VALUE SOURCES OF MEDIATION WITH EMPHASIS ON CULTURAL VALUES

Questions associated with 'good life' have been among the fundamental philosophical themes from the very beginning. However, older philosophy usually addressed them as a search for the good or virtues, as a search for specific values that lead to the 'good life'. It explored their nature and formation. The notion of 'value', however, like the notion of 'culture', seems highly problematic. It invites the idea that these are things that are just to be found and followed. If we are to define values more precisely, we would have to turn to evaluation and define them in a circle: values are what guide our evaluation. By imagining value, we additionally try to answer the question of why we prefer something over something else. Therefore, the more demanding philosophical enquiry today starts from acts of evaluation rather than from pregiven values. Value is a concept that transcends the boundaries of several disciplines. Values have long been the focus not only of philosophy, psychology and sociology but also of education, political science, economics, mathematics, anthropology and theology. To fully understand their significance in mediation, it would be necessary to address them from the perspective of all these relational disciplines. However, there is no space for that here. Therefore, to maintain thematic consistency, in this chapter we will focus on cultural values as important attributes of society that we believe are relevant to mediation and vice versa.

The emphasis on value within a group, culture, society or institution is crucial for sociological approaches. According to sociologists, values are the basic building blocks of social structure.[51] They form the framework, orientation and regulations of individual behaviour, which is reflected in the regulations of the group or society. Values express what is desirable, appropriate or good for an individual or group and what guides their direction. Therefore, we might consider values as ideals, influencing rules and norms. For example, Schaefer defines values as the collective conception of what is considered good, desirable and appropriate, or bad, undesirable and inappropriate in a given culture.[52] The sociological conception of values is closely intertwined with the psychological conception, particularly the social-psychological conception, which will be addressed in the next chapter.

From the perspective of sociological research on values, the relationship between values and culture forms a separate part. In this context, Rickert speaks of two types of objects: cultural (i.e., value-dependent) and natural (value-independent).[53] He believes that it is impossible to observe cultural reality without considering its value-dependence because this would be a naturalistic view. Durkheim has a similar conception of cultural values. In his view, values are one of the basic elements necessary for the existence of society. Culture is made up of the values that the

51. *See*, e.g., Ronald Inglehart & Christian Welzel, *How Development Leads to Democracy: What We Know About Modernization Today?*, 88 Foreign Affairs 33–48 (2009).
52. Richard T. Schaefer, *Sociology: A Brief Introduction* (McGraw-Hill Higher Education 13th ed. 2019).
53. Heinrich Rickert, *Kulturwissenschaft und Naturwissenschaft* (J.C.B. Mohr 1915).

members of a society hold.[54] The sociological-cultural line is to some extent inherent in Freud as well – he is also concerned with cultural anthropology and the formation of cultural values on the basis of individual values. In *Totem and Taboo*, Freud elucidates the psychology of nations through psychoanalysis and, among other things, compares individual norms with group rules. These individual norms are formed on the basis of values and if they are incompatible with the demands of the group (society), the individual is frustrated, according to Freud.[55] As a result of (one's) evaluation, a value is always a value to someone. It is therefore subjective in nature. However, the evaluations of different people often resemble or even coincide, especially if these people belong to the same society, to the same culture or have shared experience. The upbringing and culture in which a person has grown up and lives therefore have a considerable influence on their evaluation. What follows is the fact that the values that are recognised by the individual members of a society somehow become norms. Society is built on the values that its members hold.

The values of the culture (society) are therefore one of the factors that will influence the choice of the preferred way of conflict resolution. Mediation is tied to the influence of social influences and, as we have stated above, is associated with the emergence of a postmodern society that is moving towards alternatives. These are based on the search for individual responsibility and active involvement in conflict resolution. The decision to resolve conflict amicably is not a matter of law or a primarily legal decision. The choice between cooperative and competitive approaches is a demonstration of cultural maturity and individual maturity.[56]

If we talk about mediation as a philosophy, an approach to conflict resolution based on cooperation, reciprocity and reconciliation, then it can be considered a kind of moral ideal, a value. Another argument for explaining the processes and relationships in mediation through values is due to their interrelationship. Social behaviour is closely related to (moral) values and the (moral) norms derived from them. Mediation is also guided by certain norms. From this it can be deduced that it has values. Moreover, mediation itself is an instrument for mediating values. It should be added that values in mediation are the sum of the values of mediation as an approach and method, the values of the participants in mediation and the values of the outcomes of mediation (the values of all observable outcomes). Here, then, a number of specific questions arise. For example, which values may influence participants' choice of a constructive approach to conflict resolution? How are they reflected in the choice of mediation and its evaluation? What values influence the motivation to change from competition to cooperation? What values influence expectations of mediation; that is, what outcome do participants consider desirable so that they can be satisfied with it? And what are the values that guide the person of the mediator, how are they reflected

54. Émile Durkheim, *Les Règles de la Méthode Sociologique* (Librairie Félix Alcan 1919).
55. Sigmund Freud, *Totem and Taboo: Resemblances Between the Psychic Lives of Savages and Neurotics* (Penguin Books 1938).
56. Lenka Holá, *Hodnoty v mediaci* 6–25 (Slávka Karkošková & Renata Dolanská eds., Prešovská univerzita v Prešove 2013).

in their choice of mediation concept, approach to mediation and choice of specific mediation techniques?

For example, according to Baine and Sawatzky, Eastern mediators may find it difficult to use harmonisation techniques, especially in face-to-face negotiations.[57] In response, Gire and Carment state that the desire of Eastern cultures for upliftment and harmony is not very conducive to mediation.[58] This is quite a surprising position. The authors add that these cultures use coercive tactics quite extensively because their society gives them a strong position and thus the possibility of such an approach. According to Abu-Nimer, mediators in Western civilisations are more assertive than mediators in Eastern civilisations, but their society does not empower them to create pressure on clients or to use pressure from another institution.[59] Therefore, the cultural background of conflicts will significantly influence the choice and the actual course of mediation. This is of course true in general of any other method of conflict resolution, not just mediation. It is also interesting to think in the opposite direction, that is, what is the importance of values in mediation for culture and society? And how do they influence individuals through society? Is the introduction of mediation as a common method of conflict resolution in a given society and its support by the state an expression of the values that a given society recognises or, more accurately, prefers?

§3.05 PARTIAL CONCLUSION

We can conclude that value as a philosophical category applies in cultural, social, psychological and ethical domains. It manifests itself on a social and individual level. It is equally multilayered in mediation. We are concerned with the values of mediation for its participants, the mediator and society; we pursue the values of mediation, working together towards a mutual mediation of values. We see values as philosophical assumptions that influence the purpose of mediation, its conception, course and outcome. These assumptions have a fundamental influence on the experience and thinking of the individual, on the choice of the way of conflict resolution, on the evaluation of the other party's behaviour and on their interests and needs. In the context of mediation, it can be said that the effect of mediation can be achieved if the values of cooperation, justice, freedom and reconciliation are applied. It is manifested in the way individuals balance their own needs with the needs of the whole. If mediation is to create the reciprocity that conditions cooperative relations, there must be shared values to which individual societies subscribe, including through their legal norms. The topic is gaining in relevance with the search for the place and identity of mediation in Europe and its individual countries, also in the context of European processes of cultural integration.

57. David Baine & Donald Sawatzky, *Mediation Methods as an Adjunct to Counseling Couples*, 4 International Journal for the Advancement of Counseling 273–284 (1991).
58. James Gire & Dessauer W. Carment, *Dealing with Disputes: The Influence of Individualism-Collectivism*, 133 Journal of Social Psychology 81–95 (1993).
59. Mohammed Abu-Nimer, *Conflict Resolution Approaches: Western and Middle Eastern Lessons and Possibilities*, 55 American Journal of Economics and Sociology 35–52 (1996).

CHAPTER 4

Social Sources for Introduction of Mediation: Empowerment as Acceptance of Responsibility

Lenka Holá

From the perspective of social disciplines, what is significant for the introduction of amicable procedures into our legal system is that social functioning relates to human efforts to resolve situations that can be perceived as social tasks or problems of life. This allows us to perceive both the question of individual or group capacity to solve them and the question of the social context in which the individual or group seek to solve the problems. In social sciences, this is a multilevel perspective through which these sciences focus on a 'person in a situation'. At the same time, the starting point of our analysis of social sources is a perceptive and empathetic reflection on a person's life situation, which is usually so specific that it is difficult to fit it into paradigms, a single theoretical approach or a single method. In order to provide effective and appropriate assistance, attention must be paid to each person's individual circumstances. Reflecting on a person's life situation is the first and necessary step towards selecting intervention goals and methods that can help change that situation, strengthen that person's ability to cope with the demands of their environment and contribute to restoring or maintaining that person's social functioning.[1]

In analysing the background of the development of mediation, we thus move from a broad cultural and social context to a narrower social-psychological level. As has been pointed out several times, the interdependence of the global and the individual is unavoidable in the topic of amicable procedures of dispute resolution. It

1. *See*, e.g., Charles Horejsi & Bradford Sheafor, *Techniques and Guidelines for Social Work Practice* (Allyn and Bacon 2000); John Longres, *Handbook of Accreditation Standards and Procedures* (Itasca 1995); Robert L. Barker, *The Social Work Dictionary* (National Association of Social Workers 1995); Beata Balogová, *Model posúdenia životnej situácie rodiny* 157–195 (Pavel Navrátil, Radka Janebová eds., Gaudeamus 2010).

is with this ideological background in mind that we have approached the writing of this chapter. Although our primary focus will be on the social and individual levels, we will also refer to the broader social level in the spirit of modern social cognitive theories.

§4.01 AMICABLE PROCEDURES AS A SUPPORT FOR SOCIAL FUNCTIONING

With reference to the discussion of the value paradigm of the European cultural civilisation in Chapter 3 of this book, we can now aptly follow up on the new concept of a human being and their place in a changing world as one of the main factors that co-created the European value paradigm. As noted, the contemporary period emphasises the human individual in his or her uniqueness. All modern European schools of thought stress the development of human beings' free individuality as a prerequisite for human responsibility. This emphasises the importance of each individual's personal responsibility for coping with their situation. This allows us to anchor amicable procedures as promoting social functioning and also to find possible social sources for them in this concept.

[A] Person in a Situation

The multilevel perspective of a 'person in a situation' tends to be a comprehensive theory, not only a partial one. This tendency is underpinned by an ongoing extensive research activity. It is all the more valuable because it is both relevant to contemporary mature needs and relatively unique. We will not delve further into the analysis of contemporary theories here but focus on the mediation situation itself, in which the actor is the human being. What can be considered a mediation situation in accordance with the social-psychological concept is the individual's understanding and interpretation of the social context of mediation, that is, how that individual understands the situation in which they find themselves. The definition of the situation is an important concept in the interpretive school in social sciences. This is based on the idea that social reality is how its actors understand it.[2] It is defined by these actors. Paraphrasing the theorem above, we can say that if a mediation situation is defined as real by the mediation participants, then it is also real in its consequences.[3]

The modern social cognitive theory is based on a triadic, mutually interacting determinism in the interpretation of human behaviour. It contrasts it with a one-sided interpretation of behaviour based only on environmental influences or only on internal dispositions. The triad takes into account three groups of factors: behaviour, internal personal dispositions and the external environment (Figure 4.1). These factors interact with and influence each other.

2. Paul Watzlawick, *Wie wirklich ist die Wirklichkeit? Wahn – Täuschung – Verstehen* 53 (Piper 1976).
3. Lenka Holá, *Mediace v teorii a praxi* 44 (Grada Publishing 2011).

Figure 4.1 Diagram of Triadic Reciprocal Determinism (Adapted Loosely from Bandura, 1986)

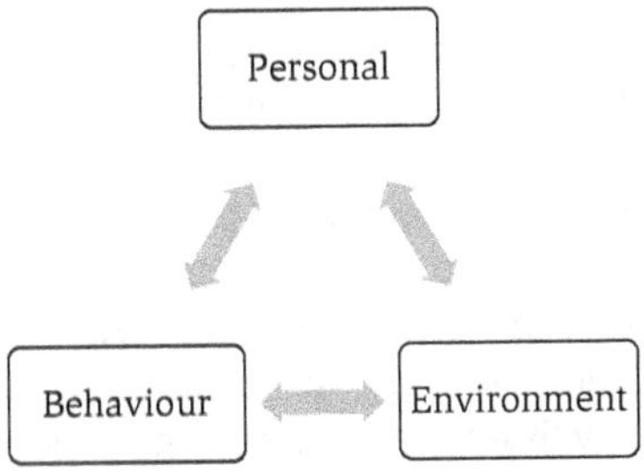

Canadian psychologist Albert Bandura served as the author and a prominent exponent of social cognitive theory (originally termed 'social learning theory'). Bandura assumes that regulation of human behaviour takes place in a social context with the dynamic interaction of human behaviour and the environment. A unique element of the theory is its emphasis on social influence and its impact on external and internal social improvement. In doing so, new social experience is also taken into account. The goal of social cognitive theory is to explain how people manage their behaviour through control and improvement in order to achieve behaviour that will produce expected gains.[4] This is where we can see the social sources of mediation because the parties to the dispute will try to control their aggressive behaviour and choose mediation as a resolution tool if they expect that this will produce effects, that is, an improvement in their situation. According to Bandura's theory, not only can direct personal experience of mediation bring about a behavioural change but also observation of the behaviour of other mediation participants. For example, a friend's positive experience with mediation can lead a person to decide to change the way they approach their own conflict situation and try to resolve it in an amicable way. Bandura argues that people can also gain new social experience and change their behaviour by observing others.

In the interplay between the three groups of factors, the human being as a whole is always implicitly and explicitly involved, both as a precondition and as a result of these processes. Consideration of a person is an important manifestation of the tendency towards a complex understanding of their conflict situation. In relation to the general nature of human beings, Bandura defines the main human capacities. These are either cultivated or remain undeveloped in individual development, and people differ from one another in the particular forms of these capacities.[5] Thus we come very close to the concept of 'self-efficacy',[6] which stems from the broad background of

4. *See* Albert Bandura, *Social Learning Theory* (Prentice Hall 1977); Albert Bandura, *Social Foundations of Thought and Action: A Social Cognitive Theory* (Prentice Hall 1986).
5. Albert Bandura, *Human Agency in Social Cognitive Theory*, 44 American psychologist 1175–1184 (1989).
6. Self-efficacy is defined as self-confidence in one's own abilities, self-validation, belief in one's own ability to plan and act in the manner necessary to achieve a goal and manage a situation. The level of self-efficacy is directly related to the level of human self-regulation. It is perceived as

human action in general. Self-efficacy is realised, for example, by on the one hand coping behaviour and, on the other hand, resignation when failing to manage conflict in a desirable way. The principles of self-efficacy can also be applied to collective efficacy. Then, in order to bring about reconciliation, it is necessary to have the means to bring partial (personal) interests into relation with shared purposes, that is, common interests and values. The unifying purposes must be explicit and achievable through joint efforts.[7]

In relation to the principles of mediation, in particular voluntariness, freedom of choice and the related right to self-determination of the parties, the social cognitive model includes an interesting concept of freedom. Freedom is not defined negatively as the absence of influences and external constraints, but positively. Without entering into philosophical issues, psychologically speaking, freedom is associated with self-regulation and socially speaking, it is viewed as the presence of a set of choices and the right to exercise them.[8] The personal influence on the mediation participants' own behaviour implies personal responsibility for them and at least a partial possibility to influence their life situation. By accepting personal responsibility, we come very close to the notion of empowerment, which will be discussed later in this chapter.

To summarise the above, the model of triadic determinism of a person in a situation corresponds to the multilevel perspective of a person in a conflict situation, and some social-psychological sources and interpretive tools for mediation can be found in it.

[B] Life Situation and Support for Social Functioning

Very closely related to the concept of social functioning is the concept of life situation. A life situation can thus be interpreted as a set of life circumstances at a particular point in time, which evolves over time and can be influenced by social events, transformation or the course of an individual's life.[9] Life situations are assigned connotations by

confidence and belief in human thinking, decision-making or control over behaviour. The sense of self-efficacy plays a very important role in conflicts because it is a reflection of how one approaches and resolves them. In general, people with positive levels of self-regulation have a confident, goal-oriented nature, are more successful in life, and are able to handle conflicts prudently. The main pillars of their characteristics are perseverance, high aspiration, motivation, creativity, skill and resilience to failure. It is an effective attitude that promotes not only an individual's intrinsic interest in constructive conflict resolution but also high commitment to its implementation. Conversely, a low level of self-efficacy leads to psychological vulnerability and succumbing to psychological disorders. If there is a lack of self-belief, which is especially common at the beginning of mediation, that person suffers from self-blame, doubt and hopelessness. The basic symptoms are unpreparedness, anxiety, tension and fear of failure or ineffectiveness of the mediation. The person lacks motivation and commitment to change. This creates a vicious circle that can be broken with the help and support of the mediator. Albert Bandura, *Self-Efficacy: The Exercise of Control* (Freeman 1997).

7. Frank Pajeras, *Self-Efficacy Beliefs in Academic Settings*, 66 Review of Educational Research 543–578 (1996).
8. Jaromír Janoušek, *Sociálně kognitivní teorie Alberta Bandury*, 36 Československá psychologie 385–398 (1992).
9. Oldřich Matoušek et al., *Encyklopedie sociální práce* 228 (Portál 2013).

individuals themselves according to their subjective and emotive meaning. Simply put, whether a person perceives their conflict situation as positive or negative depends on their perception and evaluation of the situation.

The concept of life situation was brought to the helping professions by Harriett Bartlett, an American sociologist and professor of social work.[10] The basis of the concept is that the life of an individual does not take place in isolation from the environment, but in interaction with it. The author developed the idea further and addressed those events between the individual and the environment that have a negative impact on the individual's functioning in social (life) situations. She discusses life tasks and coping with them, which together with other factors forms the concept of an individual's coping with life situations (Figure 4.2).[11]

Figure 4.2 The Concept of Life Situation: Adapted Loosely from Bartlett, 1970

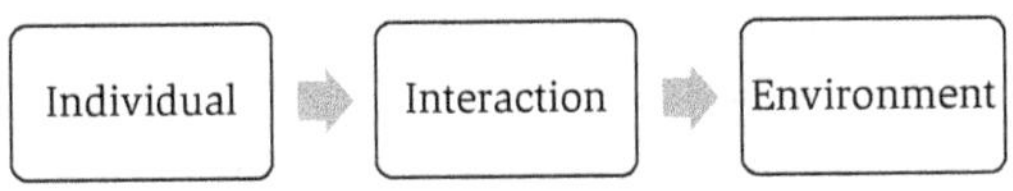

In Bartlett's view, there are four factors that influence a life situation: (1) the personal characteristics of the person, (2) the expectations of the social environment, (3) support in the social environment and (4) interaction between the expectations of the social environment and the person's ability to cope with them. The fourth factor is a combination of the previous three. In this way, we can state even more briefly that a living situation is the result of the interaction between a person and their environment. Even Bartlett considers the environment in which a person lives to be one of the important factors in coping with challenging life situations, which also include conflict situations.[12] However, we are critical of the linear causal conditioning of the factors (an individual → an interaction → the environment) as opposed to the multilevel perspective of Bandura's model of mutually contingent and influencing triadic determination, which affects the mutual contingencies more comprehensively and in their dynamic interplay.

Bartlett sees problems of life as tensions in the social environment.[13] Therefore, this concept not only includes interaction of the individual and the environment but also is about the interaction of the individual's skills to manage the expectations that the environment has for them in different life situations.[14] In doing so, an imbalance may occur which the individual is unable to resolve on their own. This imbalance can then be addressed through social intervention to strengthen the individual's social

10. Harriett M. Bartlett, *The Common Base of Social Work Practice* (National Association of Social Workers 1970).
11. *Ibid.*, 96.
12. Michael Ungar et al., *Studying Resilience across cultures*, 38 The British Journal of Social Work 218–235 (2008).
13. Bartlett 1970, *supra* n. 10, at 100.
14. Steven M. Southwick & Dennis S. Charney, *Resilience: The Science of Mastering Life's Greatest Challenges* 13 (Cambridge University Press 2012).

functioning.[15] If we apply this to mediation, it should focus on the impact of the disturbed balance in interpersonal interactions. The term 'life situation' thus refers to the multiplicity and non-repeatability of factors that impede or, on the contrary, facilitate the social functioning of an individual or a group of people. A life situation is a concept that represents a set of circumstances and factors that need to be understood in a person's conflict situation so that appropriate help and support can be chosen to manage the situation. What is significant for mediation as a method of interpersonal conflict resolution is that social functioning relates to human efforts to resolve situations that can be perceived as social tasks or problems of life. This allows us to focus on the issue of the individual's ability to resolve the conflict as well as the issue of the social context in which the individual or group seek to resolve the conflict. This brings us back to the multilevel perspective, through which we again focus on a 'person in a situation'. At the same time, our starting point is a perceptive and empathetic reflection on a person's life situation, which is the first and necessary step towards selecting intervention goals and methods that can help change it, strengthen that person's ability to cope with the demands of their environment and contribute to restoring or maintaining that person's social functioning in the interest of the functioning of the society as a whole.

In this sense, mediation can be understood as promoting the social functioning of a person in their life situation marked by conflict.

§4.02 MEDIATION AS MUTUAL PARTICIPATION AND EMPOWERMENT

Social sciences do not have a clearly accepted theoretical model of social functioning. Yet, they have a number of concepts that can be applied to help in their various fields. One of these is the concept of empowerment. It is usually cited in conjunction with the participatory concept, with each other as both a means and the goal. In the Anglo-Saxon environment, both concepts have been used since about the 1990s. This has cultural, social and historical roots. The growing interest in the subject is linked to the struggle for human rights, the development of liberation pedagogy, non-formal adult education, the work of children's and parents' rights organisations, the development of self-help and mutual help, volunteering, the movement to protect users of health and social services, and the feminist movement.[16] McNeish even speaks of a development of participatory discourse in the social sciences.[17] In the Central European region, the concept of empowerment began to be applied some fifteen years later, especially in the context of community living. Here, definitions of empowerment are primarily related to

15. Bradford W. Sheafor, *Measuring Effectiveness in Direct Social Work Practice*, 1 Revista de Asistenţa Sociala / Social Work Review 25-33 (2011).
16. Robert Adams, *Empowerment, Participation and Social Work* (Palgrave 4th ed. 2008).
17. Diana McNeish et al., *What Works for Children?: Effective Services for Children and Families* (Open University Press 2002).

power. They mention political influence, control over all aspects of life and the achievement of social justice.[18]

Because of its multiple meanings, the term 'empowerment' is difficult to define.[19] Adams considers it as an idea that takes on different contents in different contexts.[20] Most definitions of empowerment work with the root of this word, namely, 'power'. Without going into a deeper analysis of the definitions of the term, it can be said that two attributes are evident in these definitions: the concept of powerlessness and the desire to overcome it. However, according to Smith, it is power that is the problematic aspect that complicates the understanding and subsequent implementation of empowering practice.[21] Adams responds to this by suggesting that this scepticism can be undermined by the use of the constructivist perspective we have outlined above, which allows for changing the ways in which people's life situations are constructed.[22] Adams' definition of empowerment seems relevant in the context of mediation as promoting social functioning and managing human conflict: '... empowered may be defined as the process by which individuals, groups and/or communities become able to take control of their circumstances and achieve their own goals, thereby being able to work towards maximizing the quality of their lives'.[23] To be empowered, then, is to acquire certain qualities.[24] And even closer to Bandura's social cognitive model of behaviour, according to Mondros and Wilson, empowerment is a process whose outcome may then encourage participation in another empowering process.[25] Empowering activities can be defined as those that allow access to the components of power, which may include knowledge, skills, decision-making, networks or resources.

If, in agreement with Labath, we start from the view that mediation is a method of participatory conflict resolution,[26] then we can assume that:

(1) if conflict is a specific communicative (interactional) situation, then mediation cannot do without a certain degree of interaction (participation);
(2) if mediation is a participatory method of conflict resolution, then participation is its guiding principle.

18. *See*, e.g., Ingrid Burkett, *Traversing the Swampy Terrain of Postmodern Communities: Towards Theoretical Revisionings of Community Development*, 4 European Journal of Social Work 233–246 (2001); Gerard Hautekeur, *Community Development in Europe*, 40 Community Development Journal 385–398 (2005); Alice Gojová, *Teorie a modely komunitní práce* (Zdravotně sociální fakulta Ostravské univerzity 2006).
19. Lena Dominelli, *Empowerment: Help of Hindrance in Professional Relationship* (Paul Stepney & Deirdre Ford eds., Russel House Publishing 2000).
20. Robert Adams, *supra* n. 16, at 6–9 and at 50–58.
21. Roger Smith, *Social Work and Power* (Palgrave Macmillan 2008).
22. Robert Adams, *supra* n. 16, at 60.
23. Robert Adams, *Social Work and Empowerment* 8 (Palgrave 3rd ed. 2003).
24. Nick Walters et al., *Empowerment Indicators: Combating Social Exclusion in Europe* (Policy Press 2001).
25. Scott M. Wilson & Jacqueline B. Mondros, *Organizing for Power and Empowerment* 279 (Columbia University Press 1994).
26. Vlado Labath, *Kontext uplatňovania mediácie* 79–80 (Lenka Holá, Michal Malacka et al. eds., Leges 2014).

In the theoretical analysis of both assumptions, we draw on Vybíral and anchor them in the communication theory with a systemic interpretation.[27] In doing so, the focus is on participation and empowerment. In the context of mediation, we do not conceive them as a theoretical concept but as an underlying principle of mediation that is manifested in all its basic aspects (concepts, principles, goals, relationships, phases, etc.). Our reference approach is facilitative mediation. Facilitative mediation does not explicitly work with empowerment, but by focusing on participation we reasonably assume that it is a consequence of it. Participation and empowerment of clients and of the mediator are then mutually contingent.

The application of a participatory philosophy is a fundamental change in one's status. The person ceases to be an object of social policy and becomes a full, responsible and respected subject.[28] In this context, we may draw attention to risks associated with disclaiming responsibility on the part of society (social institutions) and transferring inadequate responsibility to citizens, which could lead to their secondary powerlessness. As in mediation, it is a question of constantly balancing the degree of responsibility that is placed on a person in dealing with their difficult life situation. As noted above, the concept of empowerment is multifaceted, and there is no consensus on its understanding and application. On the contrary, there is agreement on its conception at two levels, namely, individual and societal (structural). The individual level includes changes at the level of individuals, while the structural level focuses systemically on social inequalities and structural resources. Many authors believe that the two levels are mutually contingent and that personal empowerment is the first step towards social empowerment.[29] At the individual level, this leads us to the concept of empowerment as recognising individuals' values, identifying and strengthening their resources for change, fostering individual responsibility and developing free, informed decision-making in their life situation, all with respect to the context and other individuals with whom they are in contact. Therefore, the basic principle of empowerment is participation.

Participation is often seen as both a means of empowerment and the goal of the empowerment process. The different levels of participation were already discussed by Arnstein in 1969. He sees empowering potential only in participation at the level of partnership, delegated power and citizen control. The main criterion for such a conclusion is whether a given form of participation gives its participants the possibility of controlling and thus influencing the situation.[30] Such a conception of participation is also essential for mediation. We see the empowerment approach as the strengthening of individuals, groups and communities in their ability to manage or constructively create their life situation through their own activities. Mediation can then be seen as a method of amicably resolving people's conflicts, and the essence of this method lies in

27. Zbyněk Vybíral, *Psychologie komunikace* 201–202 (Portál 2009).
28. Vojtěch Krebs et al., *Sociální politika* (Wolters Kluwer 2010).
29. *See*, e.g., Judith A.B. Lee, *The Empowerment Approach to Social Work Practice* (Francis Turner ed., The Free Press 1996); Elizabeth M. Rocha, *A Ladder of Empowerment*, 17 Journal of Planning Education and Research 31–44 (1997); Lena Dominelli, *supra* n. 19, at 125–138.
30. Sherry R. Arnstein, *A Ladder of Citizen Participation*, Duncan online (April 29, 2021), https://lithgow-schmidt.dk/sherry-arnstein/ladder-of-citizen-participation.html.

identifying people's own resources for managing and resolving the conflict situation. It is a method that is not primarily focused on the problems of persons but a method that is focused on the persons themselves. As Holá writes, 'Through mediation and with the help of the mediator, their untapped resources are activated to resolve their conflict situation.'[31] In the context of social sciences, mediation is aimed at improving the social functioning of persons through their mutual participation and empowerment.

§4.03 VALUE SOURCES FOR MEDIATION WITH EMPHASIS ON SOCIAL-PSYCHOLOGICAL VALUES

If we speak of amicable procedures as a philosophy, an approach to conflict resolution based on cooperation, reciprocity and reconciliation, then they can be considered a kind of a moral ideal, a value. Social behaviour is closely related to values and the social norms derived from them. Institutions of amicable dispute resolution are also governed by certain norms. This implies that they have values. Value as a multidisciplinary category allows us to join discussions on the cultural, social and legal sources for amicable procedures with particular regard to mediation. By imagining value, we additionally try to answer the question of why we prefer something over something else. The cultural and social aspects of values in relation to mediation were discussed in Chapter 3. We now turn to the social-psychological aspects. What remains in the focus of our attention due to the 'social' view is a person in a conflict situation. We will approach the topic analytically by examining the functions of values in mediation.

Values are one of the longest-studied concepts in terms of social science and psychology, and they have received much attention. Indeed, it is values that shape a person's basic attitudes towards virtually all areas of their life. They are key aspects of self-concept, directly linked to people's personal and social identity. They influence all human activities, thoughts and feelings and are an important component of human motivation.[32] Hermann Lotze, a German philosopher, doctor and one of the founders of scientific psychology, was the first to point out the psychological importance of the concept of value at the turn of the nineteenth and twentieth centuries. In his view, values as important factors influencing human experience and action (already in his time) deserved more attention.[33] A comprehensive concept of scientific investigation of values can be found for the first time in Durkheim, who considered life values as a factor that directly influences the behaviour not only of a human being as an individual but also of the whole society.[34] The link between individual and social levels of values is evident in his work. Values are central components of personality and 'relate to what is good and valuable'.[35] Schwartz points out the dynamic relationships between

31. Lenka Holá, *Mediace. Způsob řešení mezilidských konfliktů* 7 (Grada Publishing 2003).
32. Andrew Miles, *The (Re)genesis of Values Examining the Importance of Values for Action*, 80 American Sociological Review 680–704 (2015).
33. Rudolf Hermann Lotze, *Logic* (Clarendon Press 1887).
34. Émile Durkheim, *Suicide* (Free Press 1964).
35. Shalom H. Schwartz, *The Refined Theory of Basic Values* 2–30 (Sonia Roccas & Lilach Sagiv eds., Springer 2017).

values. More than hierarchical ordering, he was interested in how they interact with, complement or conflict with each other. In his theory, he focused on the values that people from different cultures have in common. He thus identified ten core values that help people cope with the existential demands.[36] These are self-direction, stimulation, hedonism, achievement, power, safety, conformity, tradition, benevolence and universalism.[37] It is possible that the ability to understand the needs, interests and values of the mediation partner has its starting point here, and that some of the values communicated in mediation are understood similarly by the participants. If a person is to cope with their conflict situation and manage it successfully, the effectiveness of the process used could be evaluated by these values and the degree to which they are fulfilled. At this point, let us take this as possible inspiration for future research.

Attempting some generalisation, it can be said that views have shifted, in line with the development of psychology, from attitudes that only accounted for instinctive conditioning of values, through attitudes that consider social conditioning, to attitudes that emphasise human autonomy and free choice. Of course, there is a diversity of views also today, but the current trend in looking at the dynamics of values considers the development of values as something that is largely within the power of a person. It is therefore necessary to examine the importance of individual values for mediation and its participants, the differences in activity in shaping or changing them, and the extent to which individual factors influence the positive changes in values that can be achieved through mediation.

§4.04 FUNCTIONS OF VALUES IN MEDIATION

So far, we have presented considerations concerning values in a broader social-psychological context. We now turn to the individual meaning of this construct. We will look in turn at various functions of values and examine what role they may play in mediation. In doing so, we are aware of limitations that this approach can bring, namely, limitation by any categorisation in terms of simplification and superficiality. Nevertheless, we would like to offer at least basic guidelines for further development of the theory and research of mediation.

[A] Motivational Function

Max Weber, a prominent German sociologist and economist, contributed to the understanding of values especially by his conception of their motivational function. As he put it, 'An object is as valuable as it is needed.'[38] Values and value orientation are related to needs and interests. They determine which needs are to be satisfied sooner and which later. If they are threatened by a conflict, they stimulate the parties to the

36. Shalom H. Schwartz, *An Overview of the Schwartz Theory of Basic Values*, 2 Online Readings in Psychology and Culture 1–20 (2012).
37. *Ibid.*, 9–10.
38. Ján Grác, *Pohľady do psychológie hodnotovej orientácie mládeže* 30 (Slovenské pedagogické nakladatelství 1979).

conflict to behave in certain ways. The behaviour will be chosen according to how the parties expect it to bring them satisfaction. Therefore, values are an important dynamising component in conflict resolution. They form a fundamental component of attitudes and shape the positions that parties to a conflict take on the subject matter of the dispute and the manner of its resolution. If mediation is more focused on conflict resolution and reaching a specific agreement, the parties may have more performance goals. If it is more focused on the quality of relationships, they may have more relational goals. It can be said that the concept of mediation can inspire individuals to certain values or lead them towards or away from those values.

[B] Emotional Function

Weber also considers emotions an important principle that determines the motivational function of values.[39] Therefore, in his view, values also have an emotional function. A large part of theories of emotions assigns a central position to goals, that is, the values that an individual pursues. Mediation is influenced by the emotional experience of the participants and also feeds back into their emotional experience. For this reason, it is important to be able to recognise if and when expression of emotions is related to the coming to a new understanding of conflict and a new approach to its resolution.[40] Values are in a feedback relationship with emotions and motivation. Recognition of certain values is important, for example, for satisfaction and feelings of happiness.[41] If we depart from the postulate that values influence attitudes, emotions and behaviour,[42] then mediation (as a value) also influences the attitudes, motivation, behaviour and emotional experience of its participants.

[C] Moral Function

Values are, of course, closely related to morality. Values influence behaviour in terms of content (goals, means) and motivation. Values are a factor influencing moral reasoning and resolution of moral situations. Therefore, participation as a value in mediation influences moral reasoning and resolution of ethical dilemmas that arise in the course of mediation. This, of course, applies to all mediation participants, including the mediator. We can also interpret this to mean that interests are always limited in scope. They influence the actions of mediation participants within a limited time frame. Generalised values in the form of ideas or images of the world are always relevant to a

39. Guy Oakes, *Max Weber on Value Rationality and Value Spheres*, 3 Journal of Classical Sociology 27–45 (2013).
40. Cheryl Picard & Janet Siltanen, *Exploring the Significance of Emotion for Mediation Practice*, 31 Conflict Resolution Quarterly 31–55 (2013).
41. Jessica Katz Jameson et al., *Exploring the Role of Emotion in Conflict Transformation*, 27 Conflict Resolution Quarterly 167–192 (2009).
42. Max Weber, *Metodologie, sociologie a politika* (Oikoymenh 2009).

larger number of situations.[43] Therefore, mediation expressed in terms of ethical values of cooperation, reciprocity, respect for dignity, decency, fairness and others can be considered a relevant approach to resolving a larger number of conflict situations.

[D] Cognitive Function

This brings us back to Weber, who emphasises the cognitive function of values through his description of interpretive schemes. Values are a kind of filter that determines what one notices, how one perceives it and what one remembers.[44] A participant in mediation thus has the opportunity to assess the meaning, the importance and the benefits of mediation as well as their needs and expectations, and to decide accordingly, that is, to process their motive cognitively. We investigate the effect of mediation on cognitive processes (perception, thinking, understanding, adaptation, etc.) and vice versa. The interconnectedness of value development with cognitive development is typical of Piaget's theories. Piaget names the different stages of thinking according to their maturity and derives how morally capable an individual is of behaving at a given stage. According to Piaget and his followers, there is a linear causality – morality is dependent on intellect but not vice versa.[45] The relevance of this finding for mediation may, for example, mean posing the question of to what extent one can expect positive changes in mediation participants' values with respect to their cognitive maturity and understanding in mediation.

[E] Social Function

The social function of values is of particular importance for mediation. As part of socialisation, people have to come to terms with the values of others. Some values are consciously and unconsciously internalised, some are rejected. The mediators of values in mediation are individuals (the mediator or the parties to a dispute between each other) and institutions (i.e., probation and mediation services, which lead offenders to accept responsibility for their actions). Values are, of course, influenced by the social environment (the broader social and mediation environment), and participants in mediation feed back into the social environment. Sharing the importance of values facilitates communication in mediation. Roccas and Schwartz investigated the importance people attach to particular values depending on their identification with the group. They concluded that specific values influence how an individual identifies with a group.[46] That is, the values that mediation presents, the principles it works on, and the values it conveys to the participants all influence how clients adapt to conflict

43. Jürgen Habermas, *The Theory of Communicative Action, Volume I – Reason and the Rationalization of Society* 172 (Beacon Press 1984).
44. Calvin Hall & Gardner Lindzey, *Theories of Personality* 260 (John Wiley 1957).
45. Jean Piaget, *La psychologie de l'intelligence* (Armand Colin 1961).
46. Sonia Roccas, *Identification and Status Revisited: The Moderating Role of Self-Enhancement and Self-Transcendence Values*, 29 Personality and Social Psychology Bulletin 726–736 (2003).

resolution through mediation, how they accept it as suitable for them, and with what effort they will cooperate.

We will conclude our discussion of the function of values in mediation with a few additional ideas that are more difficult to categorise under the above functions. We therefore present them separately and leave it to the reader's kind judgment in what context to place them. For example, Inglehart believes that the values of individual members of communities change as those communities change.[47] Therefore, a change from competition to cooperation, the pursuit of mutual understanding, and the search for a mutually acceptable solution are changes occurring in mediation that can affect the values of mediation participants. If we depart from Sagiv and Schwartz and take, for example, facilitative mediation, which works with the structure of the process, the roles of the participants are clearly defined and the goal of mediation is continuously verified, then the 'mediation groups' behave (very broadly) similarly at a certain stage of the negotiations.[48] Therefore, values may also change similarly. One group of researchers would look at the social climate of mediation and how it evolves depending on case resolution. They would investigate how the different phases of mediation affect the change in the participants' values. Other researchers would examine specific social events that participants experienced in mediation that affected them in some way. These, in their view, cause their values to change.

It is interesting to think about how values are understood between mediation participants and whether it is possible to understand the value system of the other. Berlin's concept of 'value relativism and pluralism' can be used. It is a fundamental doctrine in his theory of values. He rejects a relativistic conception of values in the sense that 'if I like a cup of milk before bed and you like a glass of wine, you can never understand how I can like milk in the evening, and I equally cannot understand you'. He translates the example into ethics and says that this type of relativism pushed to the extreme could look like this: I like hurting other people, you do not; our customs, our traditions are just different, and there is nothing we can do about it. There is no room for communication and consensus in such an approach to values, he says.[49] In Berlin's view, communication, understanding of moral attitudes between people and consensus is made possible by value pluralism. The fundamental principle of value pluralism is the view that a value is binding on a person by privileging their own goals on their own terms, not on terms that define someone else's goals. However, that person is capable of understanding the values that define the goals of others. Value pluralism in mediation means that one party has the capacity to understand the values of the other party and also seeks to do so.

47. Ronald Inglehart, *Changing Values, Economic Development and Political Change*, 47 International Social Science Journal 379–403 (1995).
48. Lilach Sagiv & Shalom H. Schwartz, *Value Priorities and Subjective Well-Being: Direct Relations and Congruity Effects*, 30 European Journal of Social Psychology 177–198 (2000).
49. Isaiah Berlin, *A Value Pluralist and Humanist View of Human Nature and the Meaning of Life* (Rodopi 2006).

§4.05 PARTIAL CONCLUSION

Social functioning in mediation refers to people's efforts to resolve the conflict situation in which they find themselves. This enables them to perceive both their own problem and the issues of the social context in which they seek resolution. This brings us back to the multilevel perspective, through which we focus on a 'person in a (conflict) situation'. With the support of a perceptive reflection on this situation, it is then possible to choose intervention goals and methods that can contribute to its change, strengthen the individual's ability to cope with the demands of the environment, and contribute to the restoration or maintenance of their social functioning.

Mediation can then be seen as a method of amicably resolving conflicts, the essence of which lies in identifying people's own resources for managing and resolving the conflict situation. The empowerment approach applied in mediation is the strengthening of individuals, groups and communities in their ability to manage or constructively create their life situation through their own activities. In the context of social sciences, mediation is aimed at improving the social functioning of individuals through their mutual participation and empowerment.

Social behaviour is closely related to values and the social norms derived from them. The social-psychological aspects of values and their function in mediation are related to the analysis of values from a cultural and social perspective. We consider the values of cooperation and justice as central values in the context of amicable practices. All this now allows us to move smoothly on to the next topic, namely, the legal sources for mediation.

CHAPTER 5
Legal Sources of Mediation: Justice, Decency and Satisfaction

Lenka Holá

The beginning of the twenty-first century in Europe can be described without exaggeration not only as a period of revolutionary socio-economic change but also, from a legal perspective, as a period of searching for new forms of justice to replace or at least complement some traditional, somewhat inflexible practices. The belief that the courts are the main forum for resolving disputes has increasingly been undermined. Alternative forms continue to expand and become institutionalised, which leads to their characterisation as 'appropriate', 'amicable' (ADR) or 'proportionate' (PDR) dispute resolution.[1]

Mediation in the judiciary has its origins in the Anglo-Saxon legal culture, where the judicial process is essentially uniform for both criminal and civil cases and its purpose is to reach agreement between the parties. Mediation contributes to making proceedings more flexible while maintaining high standards of accuracy and fairness of decisions, and at the same time, it helps understand the causes of violations of legal norms. As a result, it creates conditions not only for resolving conflicts that have already arisen but also for preventing future conflicts. Therefore, the state can leave its established position and delegate efforts for 'rehabilitation' to the parties to the conflict and the professional mediator. The mediation process greatly humanises the justice system. It can enhance the justice system's sense of fairness, create conditions for individual assessment of each case, and it represents a promising approach in terms of preventing further conflicts.[2]

1. Lorna McGregor, *Alternative Dispute Resolution and Human Rights: Developing a Rights-Based Approach through the ECHR*, 26 The European Journal of International Law 607–634 (2015).
2. Lenka Holá, *Mediace v teorii a praxi* 155 (Grada Publishing 2011).

§5.01 LEGAL-THEORETICAL SOURCES OF MEDIATION

When anchoring amicable dispute resolution procedures in legal theory, we will depart from the ideas of legal philosophy and theory of law. For a deeper understanding of legal practice, we consider it important to uncover the theoretical conceptions of law that are likely to have influenced the emergence and development of amicable procedures, the interrelationships between law and these procedures, and the common goals towards which law and amicable (cooperative, alternative, out-of-court) methods are directed. Theoretical interpenetration of philosophy as the cradle and constant inspiration of theoretical knowledge, law and other disciplines is evident in this respect.[3] Specific conceptions and approaches to out-of-court methods are then, from a legal perspective, part of the legal culture, legal system and legal order of a particular state as we discussed in detail in the first part of this book.

The philosophical principles of law and justice are found in the philosophy of law. From the time of Plato to the emergence of modern legal theories, these principles were part of ethics.[4] The oldest and most influential school of thought is that of natural-law philosophy concerning an ideal law independent of men, the state and religion. Law is a product of human nature, divine will. According to this philosophy, legal norms arise from nature or from some supernatural authority. Some of the earliest representatives of the natural-law philosophy were the Sophists. In Greek thought, there was a contrast between *physis*, the process of growth in the physical sense, and nomos, the formulation of rules concerning this growth by man.[5] The early Greek philosophers thought primarily about the physical world, but the Sophists turned their attention to the state and its relationship to individuals. The Sophists sought to shift considerations about the natural order into the realm of human life. They argued that all human orders must be measured against the natural order, and should the human order not be in harmony with that natural order, then it is just a foolish human creation bereft of legitimacy. Sophistry thus laid the foundations for the idea of legal dualism. It has remained for more than a thousand years both the axis and the driving force of all European legal and political thought. The Sophists recognised justice as an objective phenomenon, a relatively permanent phenomenon. Every human being has an eternal desire for self-assertion, which leads to mutual conflicts. Therefore, according to the Sophists, it would be more advantageous for all to agree not to commit violence and therefore not to suffer from it. Justice and laws are regarded by Sophists as conventions, agreements between people.[6] In this, we can see the initial theoretical sources of amicable procedures built on agreement where, for example, mediation is a norm-generating agreement. It creates for the parties to the dispute rules and obligations which they agree to follow.

3. Lenka Holá & Miluše Hrnčiříková, *Mimosoudní metody řešení sporů* 11 (Leges 2017).
4. Viktor Knapp, *Teorie práva* 16 (C.H. Beck 1995).
5. John L. Myres, *The Political Ideas of the Greeks* 270 (The Abingdon Press 1927).
6. Andreas Graeser, *Řecká filosofie klasického období: sofisté, Sókratés a sokratikové, Platón a Aristotelés* (Oikoymenh 2000).

The natural-law theory influenced the conception of law until the late eighteenth century. However, by the turn of the eighteenth and nineteenth centuries, doubts about man's relationship to others (and to the state) were emerging. The idea that we cannot be governed by natural rules alone but primarily by laws – rules set and enforced by the state – was gaining ground. If we speak of natural law as a natural creation, then positive law is an artificial creation, a creation of human beings. Positive law must be established in order to be valid and effective. It is tied to the expression of the will of the rule-maker, to a certain procedure in the adoption of legal norms and to the institutions involved in that procedure. This law is changeable through the expression of the will of people. Legal positivism ceases to function as a philosophy of law and narrows its theoretical interest to the form of law.[7] It is in the form of law that the differences have gradually deepened to such an extent that legal positivism has prevailed as the new theoretical direction of legal doctrine.

Based on the above and in relation to the legal-theoretical anchoring of amicable procedures for dispute resolution, we will express the opinion that natural-law philosophy is the source of the idea that these procedures are an effort of people to arrange mutual functioning for the benefit of both of them and of the whole, to achieve mutual reconciliation and justice. Positive-law philosophy then forms the theoretical source for the application of these practices in terms of the process and content of negotiating the rules of such mutual functioning[8] and for the existence of the various institutions of out-of-court methods that are 'normative'; that is, they produce rules as a result of negotiations. If the disputed area is regulated by law (if it concerns violation of legal norms), even amicable procedures cannot escape the law since they aim at the creation of a contract (agreement), which serves to apply law.

However, the central concept of conciliation is the human being. This brings us to the revival of natural law, where the essential element of this discourse is the priority of the free and autonomous individual over the claims and interests of society. However, the autonomy, integrity and sovereignty of an individual are not absolute. The issue of the autonomous status of the human personality has gained importance with the concept of human rights. Human rights stem from a consensus on basic human interests and needs. It would seem that moving towards agreement and mutual consensus is a central element of human personality, which has decisive consequences for law as well. From here, it is only a small theoretical step to the extremely important principle of equality, reciprocity and cooperation. We speak of a consensual theory of law (also called social contract theory). The consensual theory assumes that at the heart of the social order is an unwritten convention whereby people consciously commit themselves to abide by rules that enable them to coexist with each other.[9] From the perspective of social disciplines, an accepted mediation agreement is a social contract, and from the perspective of law, it is a normative regulation, an expression of subjective law. It determines the possibility of the behaviour of the mediation participants (guaranteed by objective law), the degree of possible behaviour resulting

7. Miloš Večeřa, *Sociální stát: Východiska a přístupy* 8 (Sociologické nakladatelství 1996).
8. *See* Ondrej Hamulák ed., *Principy a zásady v právu – teorie a praxe* (Leges 2010).
9. Jan Keller, *Úvod do sociologie* 101 (Sociologické nakladatelství 5th ed. 2010).

from their specific (legal) relationship. It is defined as a set of authorisations, obligations and responsibilities of each of the mediation participants. As Veverka et al. write, 'Law does not regulate human relationships merely by setting out an order for them. If law is to be correct, it must meet two expectations – relying on the nature of things and professing a legal idea.'[10]

§5.02 JUSTICE AS A VALUE IN LAW AND MEDIATION

The idea of law in any legal thought always points to the essence of law, to the area of values in law and to its ethical foundations. Contemporary legal philosophy illuminates the deeper meaning of law and its anchoring in a system of vital social factors in interpersonal relations. Some authors even speak of ideals of law.[11] In their view, these ideals are justice, expediency and legal certainty. In other authors' views, these are justice, human freedom and legal certainty.[12] From the point of view of axiological legal philosophy, justice is the central idea of law and is perceived here as the highest legal value.[13]

We now turn our reflections on the legal-theoretical sources of amicable dispute resolution procedures to the ultimate goals of law. In a simplified form, this is what is to be, what is forward-looking and what pursues the fulfilment of certain purposes. Directing the law towards certain goals and values is a generalisation that allows us to overcome the substantive dispersion of legal regulation in a multitude of legal norms.

[A] Justice as a Central Value of Law

Justice is consistently cited as the ultimate goal of law and the highest level of the hierarchy of values transformed into law.[14] It is the central category of law and its fundamental value: 'Law seeks to be realized in the name of justice, and justice seeks to be embodied in law.'[15] Law is a reality belonging to the realm of culture and thus standing between the natural and the ideal. It relates to values and is to be measured by the idea of justice. Positive law must therefore be upheld even though it may appear to us to be substantively unjust and inexpedient. The principle of legal certainty takes precedence, but this is only up to the point where this positive law comes into extreme conflict with justice. Natural law takes precedence then. What matters is the degree of intolerability. The dividing line of the degree of intolerability is not entirely clear, but

10. Vladimír Veverka et al., *Základy teorie práva a právní filozofie* 267 (Codex 1996).
11. Veverka, Boguszak & Čapek, *supra* n. 10, at 267 and following.
12. Petr Osina, *Teorie práva* 87 (Leges 2013).
13. Jan Pinz, *Hodnoty, hodnocení a hodnotová orientace v obecném a právním smyslu* 127–146 (Petr Osina ed., Tribun EU 2016).
14. Aleš Gerloch, *Teorie práva* 22 (Aleš Čeněk 2017).
15. Jacques Derrida, *Force of Law: The 'Mystical Foundation of Authority'* 22 (Drucilla Cornell et al. eds., Routledge 1992).

an important criterion for assessment is whether positive laws were made with the intention of being fair.[16]

Justice has been one of the great themes of philosophical and legal thought since Aristotle. Even Aristotle's now universally accepted doctrines of distributive justice (a fair distribution of property, duties, responsibilities, rights and functions in a community) and commutative justice (a fair reciprocal measure of reciprocal behaviour) are the consummation of the concept of justice in interpersonal relations and also in law.[17] Justice is one of the basic criteria for evaluating the ordering of social relations.[18] Fair behaviour and thinking of an individual belongs to the field of ethics, while the objective concept of justice belongs to legal theory.[19] Justice is a value that has an exceptional position in law and must be present in it at all times. Justice in law is therefore not only related to normativity but also expressed in the overall solution and approach. Then, too, the parties to the dispute resolution are themselves the measure of the fairness of the procedure and the outcome.[20] It is distinctly a question of value. In terms of legal theory and practice, it is a fundamental principle but one that is difficult to define. The question naturally then arises of how a principle that is not defined can be applied and controlled. While this would be an interesting enquiry, it is not the subject of our chapter. We will therefore move on in our considerations.

Reflection on legal principles is essential to the analysis of justice. Legal principles are certain minimum standards of justice, basic value judgments.[21] However, attempts to formulate legal principles and create a catalogue of them can only achieve partial success. Legal principles, due to their fundamental characteristic – vagueness – either resist explicit formulation or, even after explicit formulation, still contain a lot of ambiguity.[22] At the same time, we encounter another limitation, namely, the terminological inconsistency of the concept. Most authors agree, however, that legal principles have a high degree of generality and are always valid. As a rule, they are not expressed anywhere and information about them must be obtained by reflection.[23] Legal principles arise from the system of law as such. In our view, they are very close to values as the essence of law and the meaning and purpose of law.

[B] Mediation Through the Lens of Justice

We will accept this understanding of the basic legal principles and focus on the anchoring of amicable procedures through them. In doing so, we will also note the

16. Gustav Radbruch, *O napětí mezi účely práva* 62 (Wolters Kluwer 2012).
17. Aristotle, *Etika Níkomachova* (Rezek 2009).
18. Miloš Večeřa, *Spravedlnost v právu* 17 (Masarykova univerzita 1997).
19. Lubomír Kubů, Pavel Hungr & Petr Osina, *Teorie práva* 268 (Linde 2007).
20. Chaïm Perelman, *The Idea of Justice and the Problem of Argument* (Routledge and Kegan Paul 1963).
21. Filip Melzer, *Metodologie nalézání práva* 46 (C.H. Beck 2011).
22. Osina, *supra* n. 12, at 85.
23. *See*, e.g., Zdeněk Kühn & Jiří Boguszak, *Právní principy* 91–103 (Vydavatelství 999 1999); Aleš Gerloch, *Teoretické problémy práva na prahu 21. století: pocta k 75. narozeninám prof. JUDr. Jiřího Boguszaka, DrSc* 65 and following (Karolinum 2002); Jan Wintr, *Říše principů: obecné a odvětvové principy současného českého práva* (Karolinum 2006).

underlying principles of amicable procedures. These include informality, direct participation and communication between the parties, voluntariness, confidentiality, impartiality and the professionalism of the mediator.[24] In view of the topic of this book, we will narrow the subject matter to mediation. As we noted above, among the basic legal principles, justice, legal certainty and human freedom are cited. Experts differ greatly in the formulation of other principles. Therefore, in our further examination, we will focus only on justice, which we consider to be relevant also for mediation. In mediation, however, we are not directed towards the legal concept of justice (in the sense of rights and obligations) but towards justice as a social and value-based idea.

Mediation in the sense of value anchoring relates to a number of disciplines and fields, in particular philosophy, psychology, sociology, social work, counselling, law, management theories and mathematics. It is therefore difficult to find universal principles underlying mediation. Equally, justice is a concept that transcends the boundaries of several disciplines. Justice has long been the focus not only of philosophy, psychology and sociology but also of education, political science, economics, anthropology and theology. Therefore, no single view of justice has become universally accepted. There may be several reasons for this. This is very aptly expressed by the thought of John Rawls, an American political philosopher and author of *The Theory of Justice* (1971), which made him world-famous: 'Justice is the first virtue of social institutions, as truth is of systems of thought'.[25] The understanding of justice is strongly influenced by social experience. It is an attribute of reality that is generalised and turned objective.[26] Each person's conception of justice is different. People usually have different views on what is fair.[27] An individual's conception of justice is also influenced by their personality, moral level or emotional maturity.[28] In this sense, we speak of psychological aspects of justice.

Since we conceive of mediation as a method of communication (interaction), it is relevant to operationalise the concept of 'justice' also in psychology. However, a psychological analysis of the concept of 'justice' is at least as difficult as a legal characterisation because the understanding of justice is strongly influenced by many factors. These include an individual's personality characteristics, the level of their moral, intellectual, and emotional development, social experience and others. Psychology has not paid sufficient attention to the concept of justice in its literature, and justice has become a subject of research only in relatively recent times. It can be understood as behaviour that is not perceived by an individual as unfair. While this negative definition of justice on the basis of defining injustice is something of a betrayal of the positive connotation of mediation, in the psychological and especially psychopathological literature, one often encounters definitions of the positive and of the normal on the basis of the abnormal, the dysfunctional, the negative. Fairness is particularly

24. For more details on the topic, *see* Holá & Hrnčiříková, *supra* n. 3, at 22–23.
25. John Rawls, *A Theory of Justice* 17 (Oxford University Press 1999).
26. Večeřa, *supra* n. 18, at 13.
27. Stanislav Myšička, *John Rawls a teorie mezinárodní spravedlnosti* 26 (Centrum pro studium demokracie a kultury 2014).
28. Vladimír Veverka, *K otázce poznatelnosti spravedlnosti v právu*, 134 Právník 538–539 (1995).

emphasised in social psychology because it is most often interpreted as the result of a distribution of resources that a person perceives as unfair in comparison with another person. The current understanding of social injustice in social psychology focuses on the individual as the object of another person's action. Of crucial importance is the evaluation and opinion of the person who believes to have become the object of another person's unfair behaviour.[29]

The theory of justice was developed in the 1960s by the American psychologist John S. Adams.[30] He sees the causes of feelings of (in)justice in social relations. Inequality in relationships will cause people in those relationships to become dissatisfied to a degree proportional to the amount of inequality.[31] According to Adams' theory, parties to a dispute will value fair treatment, which will motivate them to maintain or restore good relations. Important in this area is the research carried out by Mikula who, using content analysis of the term 'injustice', generated a taxonomy of its lay typisations. He defined eight groups of unfair events:

(1) leaving someone helpless;
(2) lack of loyalty;
(3) acting selfishly;
(4) exercise of parental authority;
(5) cheating, theft;
(6) hostile or aggressive treatment;
(7) arbitrariness of officials;
(8) distribution of goods and benefits.[32]

The fundamental importance of this classification is that it presents specific situations experienced and evaluated as injustice. The classification can be seen as a list of basic types of social injustice in interpersonal relationships. Interestingly, however, only a minority of the categories relate to traditionally researched issues of distributive and procedural justice, while the majority relate specifically to interpersonal relationships. It can therefore be concluded that the quality of interpersonal interactions plays a dominant role in the perception of justice.[33] Mikula's research was followed up by Lovaš. He investigated the influence of gender and age on the

29. Laura K. Guerrero et al., *Close Encounters: Communication in Relationships* 263 (SAGE Publications Inc. 4th ed. 2014).
30. John S. Adams, *Toward an Understanding of Inequity*, 67 Journal of Abnormal and Social Psychology 422–436 (1963).
31. John S. Adams, *Inequality in social Exchange*, 62 Advanced Experimental Psychology 335–343 (1965).
32. Gerold Mikula et al., *What People Regard as Unjust: Types and Structures of Everyday Experiences of Injustice*, 20 European Journal of Social Psychology 133–149 (1990).
33. As early as in 1976, Miller was convinced of the importance of interactions in the perception of (in)justice. He argued in his book *Social Justice* that the importance one gives to justice is strongly influenced by the nature of the relationships that person has with other people. The social structure of a given society creates a certain type of interpersonal relationships, which in turn give rise to certain types of judgment and evaluation of others. David Miller, *Social Justice* 255 (Clarendon Press 1976).

occurrence and experience of social injustice and found higher levels of sensitivity to situations evoking injustice in women and in younger persons, regardless of gender.[34] What does this mean for mediation? It can be said that if the mediator conducts mediation in such a way as to prevent the situations of injustice mentioned above, there is a good chance that the mediation participants will perceive the conflict resolution process as fair and that this will contribute to their sense of satisfaction. What we consider to be the primary goal of mediation is that the parties to the dispute are satisfied with mediation and perceive the process and outcomes as fair. How a person feels and what state of mind they are in is an unquestionable and immediate reality about which they can provide more or less accurate information. If mediation participants describe their state of mind as positive, they use the words 'good', 'happiness', 'calm', 'great', 'well-being', and so on, in common speech. In psychological research, the terms 'subjective well-being', 'contentment' and 'happiness' are used to describe a positive state of mind. Interestingly, colloquial terms do not differ significantly from psychological terms.

If we want to look at research on perceived fairness in mediation, we can cite Tyler: '... in civil cases, defendants rate mediation to be fairer than a formal trial, and it is typically rated as more satisfactory'.[35] Although the lay public are often unfamiliar with the exact procedures of institutionalised conflict resolution, according to Hollander-Blumoff and Tyler, they have a very clear idea of whether or not these procedures are fair.[36] A suitable criterion in the context of this paper is whether the participants' perceived fairness plays a role in mediation. The answer was provided by Pruitt et al., who demonstrated in their research the importance of perceptions of mediation as fair in relation to adherence to a negotiated agreement.[37] That this was not an isolated result, but one of the potential advantages of mediation over litigation was also confirmed by Emery et al. in their longitudinal study. Over a twelve-year period, they followed randomly divided parenting couples who resolved child-custody disputes either through mediation or standard court proceedings. In successive measurements after six weeks, a year and a half, and twelve years apart, they found, *inter alia*, that the satisfaction of parties was always higher in mediation than in standard court proceedings.[38] The relationship between procedural fairness and party satisfaction was also demonstrated previously by Kitzmann and Emery. Although the outcome of the dispute resolution in mediation and court proceedings was essentially the same (e.g., the child remained in the sole custody of the mother after the separation), the criteria

34. Ladislav Lovaš, *Nespravodlivost' v interpersonálnych vzt'ahoch*, 39 Československá psychologie 203–212 (1995).
35. Tom R. Tyler, *Social Justice: Outcome and Procedure*, 35 International Journal of Psychology 121 (2000).
36. Rebecca Hollander-Blumoff & Tom R. Tyler, *Procedural Justice and the Rule of Law: Fostering Legitimacy in Alternative Dispute Resolution*, 2 Journal of Dispute Resolution 1–20 (2011).
37. For more details *see* Dean G. Pruitt et al., *Long-Term Success in Mediation*, 17 Law and Human Behavior 313–330 (1993).
38. *See*, e.g., Robert Emery et al., *Child Custody Mediation and Litigation: Custody, Contact, and Coparenting 12 Years After Initial Dispute Resolution*, 69 Journal of Consulting and Clinical Psychology 323–332 (2001); Robert Emery et al., *Divorce Mediation: Research and Reflections*, 43 Family Court Review 22–37 (2005).

influencing the perception of satisfaction were the presence and quality of elements of procedural justice as monitored through the possibility of control over the outcome, the feeling of understanding, interest on the part of the dispute resolution's intermediary (mediator, judge) and their respect for the parties.[39] Therefore, distributive justice was not a key factor influencing parents' perceptions of fairness and satisfaction. Although mothers reported essentially the same level of satisfaction in both mediation and court proceedings, men perceived mediation as fairer, felt more control over the process, and were also more satisfied with the outcome than men who reached a similar outcome in court proceedings. In light of the above, it can be concluded that perceived fairness plays an extraordinary role in mediation, which is confirmed even several years later.

To further examine the topic of justice in mediation, let us return to the ideas of Aristotle, whose work laid the foundation for the understanding of this concept. He interprets justice as the most perfect virtue.[40] Aristotle thus breathed life into what is referred to as legal justice. The notion of justice primarily as a virtue was further developed by John Rawls. He elaborates on Aristotle's ideas in two areas. The first he refers to as the virtue of institutions.[41] Applied to mediation, it is the 'virtue' of the institution of mediation. One of the fundamental issues in the coexistence of out-of-court means of dispute resolution and judicial proceedings is the degree of obligation of these means and their institutional integration into the judicial process. In order for mediation to function socially and legally, two fundamental questions must be answered. Namely, what standard of justice is expected from mediation and what instruments of coercion can be imposed on the parties?[42] The basis for assessing under what circumstances parties can be 'subjected' to mediation is to resolve the dilemma between the social value of a judicial decision and the outcome of an out-of-court method of dispute resolution. According to Cohen, a judicial decision is based more on social responsibility than on individual decision-making. It is an expression of social welfare and reflects and promotes the public interest more than private values.[43] The basic argument for incorporating mediation into justice systems is that law and justice are not synonymous.[44] Mediation offers more in terms of consent, agreement, active participation, quality solutions, efficiency, accountability and justice.[45]

The second area Rawls addressed is the virtue of individual action. He sees justice as a virtue of human conduct. Mediation as a communication method has a dynamic (procedural) component in addition to the relational and substantive ones. The influence of mediation on the participants' values stems from the fact that mediation

39. Katherine M. Kitzmann & Robert E. Emery, *Procedural Justice and Parents' Satisfaction in a Field Study of Child Custody Dispute Resolution*, 17 Law and Human Behavior 553–567 (1993).
40. Aristotle, *supra* n. 17, at 116.
41. Rawls, *supra* n. 25, at 46.
42. Miluše Hrnčiříková & Lucia Valentová, *Judiciální trendy v mimosoudním řešení přeshraničních sporů* 97 (Leges 2016).
43. Amy J. Cohen, *Revisiting Against Settlement: Some Reflections on Dispute Resolution and Public Values*, 78 Fordham Law Review 1143–1170 (2009).
44. Andrew W. McThenia & Thomas L. Shaffer, *For Reconciliation*, 94 Yale Law Journal 1660–1669 (1984).
45. Carrie Menkel-Meadow, *Whose Dispute Is It Anyway?: A Philosophical and Democratic Defense of Settlement (In Some Cases)*, 83 Georgetown Law Journal 2669 (1995).

takes place on the basis of the values recognised by the participants. Mediation is an influence towards values through values. It allows individuals to discover values for themselves, to experience them, to create new values. This, with all the 'intentionality' of mediation, is a unique and creative act. The mission of mediation in people's individual lives is thus more serious than it might at first appear. Mediation touches, or more accurately, can touch, on the very essence of human existence because it is not indifferent to what one believes and what one devotes one's strength and energy to. Mediation participants may thus ask questions about the essence and nature of man, his needs, possibilities, ideals and perspectives. However, deciding for oneself also brings many difficulties and obstacles. An individual acts at their own risk and danger with the constant possibility of individual failure. Every choice means engaging in human community, in a world of multiple polarities of personal tendencies and social norms. It is reasonable to assume that this is also the case in mediation. If a person succeeds in fulfilling one's life, they are happy. If they are limited to the minimum in this, if they fail to make it true to the extent they consider desirable and satisfactory, they experience a sense of life failure and unhappiness. They may transcend this vicious circle by their creative activity. We speak of transcendence of human subjectivity. Through it, man is more than he is. He transcends himself by creating. In the words of Antoine de Saint-Exupéry, man is one who carries within himself a being greater than himself. In a creative approach to conflict resolution, we discover new meanings of things and values around us. Virtually anything can be not only a source of joy, a sense of self-importance, abundance, enchantment but also a threat and hardship. In the process of mediation, a person discovers their possibilities and capabilities and develops their inner richness. As Kučerová writes, 'All human activity is nothing but the creation of values, their protection, the efforts to maintain them, to reproduce them, to develop them.'[46]

John Rawls draws on the concept of abstraction of the well-known social contract theory. He imagines justice as virtue and as decency. The concept reflects the idea of the original state of equality that '... no one knows his or her place in society, class position or social status, nor does any one know his or her fortune in the distribution of natural assets and abilities, nor his or her intelligence, level of strength, and the like'.[47] The state of equality of the parties to mediation can thus be explained by the fact that as parties to a contractual relationship, they are ignorant of everything, which ensures that neither one nor the other can be advantaged at anyone's expense. Even though each tends to favour itself to obtain a benefit, Rawls enunciates two principles to maintain the equality of the parties. The first is equality and preservation of fundamental rights and freedoms, which are equal for all citizens. The second is the equalisation of social and economic inequality among individuals. He refers to injustice simply as '... inequality that does not benefit everyone'.[48]

46. Stanislava Kučerová, *Hodnotová dimenze výchovy a globální výzva*, 3 Pedagogická orientace 14 (1993).
47. Rawls, *supra* n. 25, at 21–22.
48. *Ibid.*, 49.

It follows that justice is one of the basic prerequisites of democratic rule of law and civil society. Here we can see legal bases also for mediation because the principle of equality of parties, the development of civil society and the desire to improve citizens' access to justice, that is, to exercise their rights and freedoms more fully, are also applied in mediation.

§5.03 MEDIATION TO IMPROVE CITIZENS' ACCESS TO JUSTICE

To conceptualise mediation as improving citizens' access to justice, we shall begin with a brief historical excursus. In doing so, we will focus in particular on sociolegal aspects that we believe may have played an important role in this context. The second part of the subsection will be devoted to European efforts to find new forms of justice, and we will conclude with a social and restorative perspective on justice in mediation.

[A] A Short Historical Excursus

In order to achieve 'individual' justice in overburdened court systems and to resolve disputes more quickly and cheaply, groups of American reformers in the late 1970s proposed two possible approaches to achieve greater efficiency in court proceedings. The first was to choose the most appropriate approach to dispute resolution on an individual basis. In addition to litigation, this was the way of alternatives to litigation. This included mainly the methods of arbitration, negotiation and mediation. The aim was to encourage the parties to take responsibility for solving their problems and to participate more actively. The concept of the 'Multi-Door Courthouse', developed by Harvard Law Professor Frank Sander, was based on the idea that if presented with a range of different approaches in the courthouse, the parties to a dispute would choose one they consider most appropriate for them. They decide for themselves, figuratively speaking, which door in the courthouse they will enter. The US government then piloted funding for several local court systems to create such 'multi-door' courthouses.[49] Another group of reformers believed that effective tools were necessary to resolve disputes in an alternative manner. It built on the premise that there are many types of disputes that do not have simple solutions. The search for 'truth' and 'justice' was, in their view, complicated. They also believed that parties working together to find a solution could come up with a creative outcome that could not have been achieved through the standard judicial process. The courts, from their perspective, have only limited options to solve the problem. Typical examples are child-custody issues, healthcare disputes or intellectual property issues. This 'creative' approach to dispute resolution has then led to the work of specialists in designing appropriate procedures for different types of disputes. Comparing the two approaches to reforming

49. Carrie Menkel-Meadow, *The History and Development of ADR (Alternative/Appropriate Dispute Resolution)*, Voelkerrechtsblog (1 Jul. 2016), https://voelkerrechtsblog.org/the-history-and-development-of-a-dr-alternativeappropriate-dispute-resolution/.

the American justice system, it can be said that they were not contradictory but complementary.

From the 1970s onwards, the ADR movement developed as a social movement addressing civil rights and as judicial activities. In 1976, the Roscoe Pound Conference was convened by former Chief Justice of the US Supreme Court Warren Burger to search for the causes of public dissatisfaction with the administration of justice. It was with this conference that the modern history of dispute resolution in the USA began.[50] It resulted in the establishment of three experimental courts, where various forms of ADR, such as mediation, arbitration, and so on, were assigned to selected disputes. Since then, the ADR movement in the USA has developed rapidly from one-off experiments to large-scale programmes. This transition was also supported by US administrative rules and federal court proceedings. Institutions providing out-of-court dispute resolution are socially and legally encouraged to use these methods widely. They are seen as a means of solving complex individual and community problems, strengthening civic institutions, and educating for democracy and peace.

In the 1980s, a demand for out-of-court methods arose also in the commercial sphere. This led to their rapid development. As a result of a largely positive reception in both lay and professional circles, possibilities expanded for applying out-of-court methods to, for example, family conflicts, ecological conflicts, institutional conflicts, labour law, commercial and consumer disputes, healthcare disputes, political and international conflicts.

[B] European Efforts to Find New Forms of Justice

Amicable methods of conflict resolution expanded from the USA to Europe. The beginning of the twenty-first century in Europe can be described without exaggeration not only as a period of revolutionary political and economic changes but also, from a legal perspective, as a period of searching for new forms of justice to replace or at least complement some traditional, somewhat inflexible practices. In recent years, therefore, cooperative and amicable procedures have been increasingly applied in the field of dispute resolution in addition to standard court proceedings, the outcome of which is usually in favour of one party. These seek to take into account the interests of both parties and to reach a mutually acceptable outcome that the parties can identify with and implement. At the same time, there is a growing interest in legal regulation of these procedures, at both the international and national levels. The community thus underlines their legitimate acceptance. A proper and timely application of EU law in national law is also key to the success of the European integration process.[51] Out-of-court dispute resolution cannot replace an effective and fair justice system, but it should contribute to citizens' access to justice by using different methods and

50. Clifford J. Wallace. *Judicial Reform and the Pound Conference of 1976*, 80 Michigan Law Review 592–596 (1982).
51. Václav Stehlík, *Aplikace národních procesních předpisů v kontextu práva Evropské unie* 7 (Leges 2012).

procedures, and in particular, a different philosophy and approach to conflict resolution. Their purpose is to introduce consensual procedures of dispute resolution, which the parties can prefer. The right of access to justice, guaranteed constitutionally by the community and internationally, is not, and cannot be, affected by the use of out-of-court methods.[52] Out-of-court methods give the parties to a conflict different options and offer different values. They contribute to making proceedings more flexible while maintaining high standards of accuracy and fairness of decisions, and at the same time help understand the causes of violations of legal norms. As a result, it creates conditions not only for resolving conflicts that have already arisen but also for preventing future conflicts.

With the modernisation of judicial systems and the search for new forms of access to justice, amicable dispute resolution methods have been becoming increasingly available also in the EU.[53] Historically, the first significant step in efforts to institutionalise them in the field of law was the 1998 Action Plan of the Council of the EU and the European Commission,[54] followed up by the 1999 European Council summit in Tampere, Finland. The result of this summit was the report 'Alternative, extra-judicial procedures should also be created by Member States', recommending that the Member States, *inter alia,* introduce alternative, out-of-court dispute resolution procedures to support better access to justice.[55] This is a right required in accordance with Article 6 of the European Convention for the Protection of Human Rights and Fundamental Freedoms (published under No. 209/1992 Coll.) and in accordance with Article 47 *of the Charter of Fundamental Rights of the European Union* (2007/C 303/01) providing that 'everyone whose rights and freedoms guaranteed by the law of the Union are violated has the right to an effective remedy before a tribunal in compliance with the conditions laid down in this Article'. Rights of individuals in the EU have been established at different times, in different ways and in different forms. For this reason, the EU has decided to include them in a single document that has been drafted in the light of current social changes. The Charter of Fundamental Rights of the EU summarises all the personal, civil, political, economic and social rights that the EU confers on its citizens.[56] As its preamble states, among other things, the peoples of Europe are resolved to share a peaceful future based on common values. Based on their

52. František Zoulík, *Mediace jako alternativa soudního sporu*, 8 Bulletin advokacie 29 (2001).
53. Lenka Holá, Martina Urbanová & Martin Lakomý, *Informovanost o mediaci v evropském a českém kontextu*, 16 Scientia et Societas 94–105 (2020).
54. *Action plan of the Council and the Commission on how best to implement the provisions of the treaty of Amsterdam on an area of freedom, security and justice*, Council of the European Union (December 3, 2020), https://op.europa.eu/en/publication-detail/-/publication/4565d7d8-b5e4-4b4e-87ce-5f5e7f641383/language-en.
55. Specifically, in Part V of this document, the Council of Europe calls on the European Commission to set minimum standards for legal aid in cross-border disputes and to introduce simplified and expedited resolution of minor disputes. It also calls on member countries to introduce alternative out-of-court proceedings. *Tampere European Council 15 and 16 October 1999 Presidency Conclusions*, European Commission (15 Oct. 2020), https://www.ab.gov.tr/files/ardb/evt/1_avrupa_birligi/1_4_zirveler_1985_sonrasi/1999_10_tampere_zirvesi_baskanlik_sonuc_bildirgesi_en.pdf.
56. The EU's fundamental rights include the following: all rights arising from the case law of the Court of Justice of the EU; the rights and freedoms enshrined in the European Convention on

spiritual and moral heritage, what they consider common values are the values of human dignity, freedom, equality and solidarity. They place the individual at the centre of their activities and create a space of freedom, security and justice for them. The Union contributes to the preservation and development of these common values, while respecting the diversity of cultures and traditions of the peoples of Europe and striving to promote balanced and sustainable development. To this end, the EU considers it necessary to strengthen the protection of fundamental rights in the light of social evolution, social progress and scientific and technological development. The exercise of these rights entails responsibilities and obligations, both in relation to others and in relation to the human community and future generations.[57]

The outcome of the subsequent activities of the European Commission in the area of out-of-court dispute resolution was the Green Paper on ADR in civil and commercial law (hereinafter the 'Green Paper').[58] It expressed the conviction that the task of mediation and other ADR methods is not to remedy the shortcomings of individual court systems but to introduce more consensual ways of resolving disputes as opposed to court and arbitration procedures. The Green Paper defines what is meant by ADR procedures and encourages consulting on possible measures to promote the use of mediation. The same document stresses that mediation and other ADR procedures help promote quality access to justice for citizens. For this reason, the European Commission has advocated for the creation of databases of ADR procedures to facilitate citizens' access to ADR procedures in each Member State. The main philosophy of the Green Paper was to strike a balance between the two basic conditions of the ADR system, namely, the greatest possible degree of flexibility on the one hand and harmony between it and judicial proceedings on the other.[59]

Ensuring better access to justice is an objective that forms part of the EU's policy to create an area of freedom, security and justice and includes access to judicial and extrajudicial dispute resolution methods. Today, there is no doubt about the value equality of both approaches to justice – judicial and extrajudicial. However, in the area of practical application, there are still many obstacles to the equal use of out-of-court procedures.

§5.04 SOCIAL AND RESTORATIVE JUSTICE: A DIFFERENT VIEW OF THE SAME THING

So far, we have mainly examined mediation (more broadly, amicable dispute resolution procedures) through the lens of justice in the field of law. Even here we have not

---

Human Rights; other rights and principles arising from the EU's common constitutional traditions and other international instruments.

57. European Parliament, *Charter of Fundamental Rights of the European Union (2012/C 326/02)*, https://eur-lex.europa.eu/legal-content/EN/TXT/PDF/?uri=CELEX:12012P/TXT&from=EN.
58. European Commission, *Green Paper on alternative dispute resolution in civil and commercial law*, COM (2002) 196 final, https://eur-lex.europa.eu/legal-content/EN/TXT/HTML/?uri=CELEX:52002DC0196&from=EN.
59. Martin Svatoš, *Evropské aspekty mediace a dalších ADR*, ePravo.cz (6 Feb. 2013), https://www.epravo.cz/top/clanky/evropske-aspekty-mediace-a-dalsich-adr-88570.html.

avoided philosophical, ethical, social or psychological overlaps. Indeed, we consider these approaches relevant because the theory and practice of law are closely linked to social reality. Therefore, we will now enrich the theoretical and legal sources for the introduction of amicable procedures into legal orders with two additional perspectives on justice, namely, the social and the restorative perspectives.

Social justice represents one specific form of justice. It is also difficult to define; therefore, there is no universally valid and accepted definition. However, all its formulations have a common tendency to draw attention to critical elements of the social, political and economic conditions of society.[60] In general, social justice is seen as a process aimed at achieving a society in which human rights are respected, resources are allocated fairly and equal opportunities are provided to all members.[61] Therefore, it is characterised identically to mediation. According to some authors, this is an unattainable ideal but one that every modern and democratic society should strive towards.[62] Interestingly, in contrast to the history of mediation, social justice as a social, political and moral construct began to take shape roughly from the second half of the nineteenth century in Europe and only later in North America as a response to persistent sociopolitical tensions. More and more people yearned for a freer and more equal society.

The modern notion of social justice brings us back to the ideas of the American political philosopher John Rawls. His book *A Theory of Justice* (1971) can also be taken as the theoretical starting point for the concept of social justice.[63] For Rawls, the primary object of social justice is the basic structure of society and the ways in which the major social institutions distribute rights, duties and the benefits of social cooperation. The most important ideas of Rawls' conception of social justice were summarised by Schmidtz in three points. We will attempt to apply them to mediation: (1) all mediation participants should have equal access to justice and the broadest possible system of basic freedoms compatible with the freedoms of others; (2) the best form of such a system is a mediation community based on cooperation, bringing mutual benefit to all concerned; (3) the increasing benefits and gains from mediation should be equitably distributed among its participants.[64] According to these basic attributes, mediation can be seen as a tool for the application of social justice in society.

In order to take into account other dimensions of mediation through justice (besides legal dimensions, also psychological and social ones), we will also briefly consider mediation in the context of restorative justice. Restorative justice is the modern response to violations of rules, norms and laws. In its current form, it began to

60. David Vincent & Suzanne Marmo, *Commitment to Social Justice and Its Influence on Job Satisfaction and Retention of Nonprofit Middle Managers*, 42 Human Service Organizations: Management, Leadership & Governance 457–473 (2018).
61. *See*, e.g., Jeffrey S. Brooks et al., *Social justice* (Oxford University Press 2016); Dinesh Bhugra, *Social Discrimination and Social Justice*, 28 International Review of Psychiatry 336–341 (2016).
62. *See*, e.g., Cristina Balaceanu et al., *Sustainability and Social Justice*, 62 Procedia-Social And Behavioral Sciences 677–681 (2012); Tyler, *supra* n. 35; Allan C. Ornstein, *Social Justice: History, Purpose and Meaning*, 54 Society 541–548 (2017).
63. In this narrow sense, then, we could consider North America, not Europe, the cradle of the concept of social justice.
64. *See* David Schmidtz, *Prvky spravedlnosti* (Dokořán, 2015).

appear in the late 1980s in New Zealand, Australia, Canada and the US as an alternative to retributive justice.[65] Restorative justice is a concept, movement and modern vision of justice that says that crime does not primarily violate legal norms but causes harm and disrupts interpersonal relationships.[66] According to its founder, American criminologist Howard Zehr, restorative justice is a process that '... to involve, to the extent possible, those who have a stake in a specific offense and to collectively identify and address harms, needs, and obligations, in order to heal and put things as right as possible'.[67] If we view the above definition through the lens of mediation, mediation can also be said to involve the parties to the conflict to the maximum extent possible, to seek to restore their conflict-disturbed relationships, and to seek agreement on a balanced resolution of the dispute based on the identified needs and interests, which would be binding on the mediation participants. Zehr says restorative justice is not a map but a compass. Even mediation does not give guidelines on how to resolve the parties' dispute, but it helps them navigate the situation, take personal responsibility for its creation, and also resolve it responsibly. Mediation in the context of restorative justice is a change of perspective and approach to resolving a conflict situation. It is a way of finding justice by accepting personal responsibility. Finally, it offers ways of resolution in which there is a safe space for participation, dialogue and involvement of those who have been affected by the harm. As the term 'restorative' suggests, the primary effort is restoration. In Zehr's words, restorative justice comes with a new interpretation of how we can understand the concept of justice, how to put that justice into practice and how to make it accessible and understandable to all.[68] The goal of restorative justice is to agree on a solution to the situation and restore justice.[69]

It can be summarised that the concept of restorative justice provides a very suitable framework for mediation in two aspects. In the theoretical sense, the characteristics of restorative justice, as we have shown above, are consistent with those of mediation. In practical application, mediation is one of the most important tools of restorative justice,[70] and not only in the criminal field.

65. *See*, e.g., Masahiro Suzuki & William R. Wood, *Restorative Justice* 393–406 (Springer International Publishing 2017); Michael Wenzel & Tyler G. Okimoto, *Retributive Justice* 237–256 (Springer New York 2016); Michael Wenzel et al., *Do Retributive and Restorative Justice Processes Address Different Symbolic Concerns?,* 20 Critical Criminology 25–44 (2012).
66. Mark Umbreit & Marilyn P. Armour, *Restorative Justice Dialogue–An Essential Guide for Research and Practice* 2 (Springer Publishing Co. 2011).
67. Howard Zehr, *Changing Lenses: A New Focus for Crime and Justice* 271 (Herald Press 1990).
68. Harry Mika & Howard Zehr, *A Restorative Framework for Community Justice Practice* 135–152 (Kieran McEvoy & Tim Newburn eds., Palgrave Macmillan 2003).
69. Charlotte van Oyen-Witvliet et al., *Retributive Justice, Restorative Justice, and Forgiveness: An Experimental Psychophysiology Analysis*, 44 Journal of Experimental Social Psychology 10–25 (2008).
70. Pavel Štern et al., *Probace a mediace: Možnosti řešení trestných činů* 42 (Portál 2010).

§5.05 PARTIAL CONCLUSION

In conclusion, mediation can be seen in the context of law and justice from three perspectives: as a means of improving citizens' access to justice, as a means of applying social justice in society and as a means of restorative justice.

Justice is one of the basic prerequisites of democratic rule of law and a civil and socially just society. Here we can see legal bases also for mediation because the principle of equality of parties and their benefit, the efforts to improve citizens' access to a fuller exercise of their rights and freedoms, and the restoration of their social functioning are also applied in mediation. Law is part of the mediation reality. Whatever agreement is reached in mediation must stand before the law. On the other hand, mediation means taking the risk of entering a field of interests with a wide range of possible solutions. Rigid adherence to the legal framework can thus paradoxically complicate the practical implementation of the idea of mediation and create many professional and ethical dilemmas.

Reconciliation and agreement can be achieved in mediation if civic values are applied. The values are manifested in the way individuals balance their own needs with the needs of the whole. If, in accordance with amicable procedures, we want to create the reciprocity that conditions cooperative relations and a civil society, there should be shared values to which our society subscribes, also through its legal norms.

PART III

Systems of Approach to Mediation in the EU

Jan Holas

INTRODUCTION TO THE TOPIC

The third part of the book deals with systems of approach to mediation in the EU. The term 'system of approach to mediation' can be understood as the set of measures, factors and their interrelations that determine the possibilities for approaching mediation in a particular country. The most important measures that constitute the system of approach to mediation, and will be given the most attention, are usually enshrined in legislation (e.g., court-ordered mediation). However, the presented system of course also includes other non-legal factors influencing the approach to mediation (e.g., informal provision of information regarding the possibility of resolving disputes through mediation).

In Chapter 6, the reader is first introduced to the process of codification of mediation (or, more generally, incorporation of mediation into the legal system) in the European environment. This process reflects the course by which mediation is integrated into the legal systems of the Member States and the factors that have influenced it, which is of direct importance to the formation of the system of approach to mediation. It turns out that codification/incorporation of mediation has taken place in the Member States with very different results and that the systems of approach to mediation are often made up of different measures. Subsequently, the chapter charts the basic models that make up the systems of approach to mediation in particular Member States. These have been identified on the basis of generalisations of the types of measures used in the Member States and include mainly coercion-based models, motivation-based models, and models based on the provision of information on mediation. At this point, it is worth noting that the three models listed are only basic models in terms of frequency of use. However, they do not constitute an exhaustive enumeration. It is therefore possible that other models (such as measures of an informal nature) are represented in the system of approach to mediation in a Member State which, by their nature, could not be classified as either of the basic models.

Incorporation of measures forming a system of approach to mediation into the legal systems of the Member States can sometimes entail difficulties. If the measures being enshrined exceed certain limits due to their intensity of effect, they can negatively affect not only the concept of mediation but also, in the field of law, the concept of civil procedure and the fundamental guaranteed rights of the parties to the dispute. Chapter 7 of the book therefore examines the limits to introducing these measures into the legal systems of the Member States. These will primarily concern the limits to the measures introduced within the coercion model, as they in particular can act so intensely that they negatively affect the functioning of one of the concepts under investigation. On the contrary, measures within the models of motivation or provision of information on mediation do not usually produce such intense effects.

Since the specific rules contained in the legal systems of the Member States may differ from one another, I build on the principles of the concepts under investigation when identifying the basic limits of coercion. I understand principles as the starting points of a concept with a high degree of generality, which are of great importance in the development of legislation. Legislation should respect existing principles; otherwise, the concept of which the principle is typical could be distorted. In the context of the concept of mediation, the principle of voluntariness will be examined as a key limit to coercion; in the context of the concept of fundamental guaranteed rights, the right of access to the court will be examined; and in the context of the concept of civil procedure, the disposition principle, the obligation of the court to proceed ex officio, the principle of preference for amicable dispute resolution and the principle of procedural economy will be examined in particular. The subject of the analysis is to determine how intensive a limitation to a particular principle may be, not to have a negative impact on the concept examined.

CHAPTER 6

Development and Forms of Systems of Approach to Mediation in the EU

Jan Holas

In Europe, mediation began to develop to a greater extent in the late twentieth and early twenty-first centuries.[1] This development is evident both in the area of mediation practice[2] and at the level of theory and research of mediation.[3] Both of these aspects which have gradually led to the consolidation of mediation as a method of dispute resolution are closely related to the fact that this method of dispute resolution has been incorporated into the legal systems of the Member States in the years since.[4]

The term 'enactment of legislation on mediation' or 'codification of mediation' refers to the process by which mediation is integrated into the legal order, that is, the process by which mediation or its aspects become part of law. In this respect, mediation in Europe has already come a long way. In recent years, mediation has shifted considerably from a very little-known (in the European context) method of dispute resolution, and currently, there is some form of regulation in the legal systems of all Member States. However, this was not always the case.

1. *See* Nadja Alexander, *International and Comparative Mediation: Definitions and Developments* 53 (Nadja Alexander ed., Kluwer Law International 2009).
2. *See, e.g.*, Giuseppe De Palo, Mary B. Trevor et al., *EU Mediation Law and Practice* 5, 10 (Oxford University Press 2012).
3. *See, e.g.*, Nadja Alexander, et al., *EU Mediation Law Handbook: Regulatory Robustness Ratings for Mediation Regimes* (Kluwer Law International 2017); Matthias Wendland, *Mediation und Zivilprozess: dogmatische Grundlagen einer allgemeinen Konfliktbehandlungslehre* (Mohr Siebeck 2017), etc.
4. *See* Carrie Menkel-Meadow, *Variations in the Uptake of and Resistance to Mediation Outside of the United States*, SSRN, Research Paper No. 2015-80, 189 (4 Jan. 2021), https://papers.ssrn.com/sol3/papers.cfm?abstract_id=2658903.

§6.01 THE BEGINNINGS OF MEDIATION AND ITS MODERN INCARNATION

In an intuitive form, mediation as an amicable method of dispute resolution has been known for thousands of years,[5] and its history goes far back beyond today's judiciary systems.[6] Mediation – albeit in its simplest form – can be deemed to have existed from the very dawn of human society.[7] In many cultures, it represents or used to represent the original, natural way of resolving disputes between two or more parties based on their cooperation.[8] The first evidence of the existence of mediation dates back to the times of traditional communities. Despite the lack of a formalised state apparatus, it is possible to speak about a well-organised system for managing conflict resolution in families (clans) or tribes. Mediation was the preferred method of dispute resolution in these types of societies.[9]

In traditional cultures based on community, strong respect for social norms, cultural traditions and religious beliefs, a process was supported by which a third party with a high social status assisted in dispute resolution. These processes led not only to the resolution of disputes but also to the strengthening of social values and cohesion. Therefore, their function was also to maintain the social balance.[10]

However, the weakening of traditional societies was followed by other methods of dispute resolution which prevailed at different stages of societal development (especially violent, self-help or authoritative ways of dispute resolution).[11] At present, societal transformations[12] are accompanied by a rediscovery of mediation and its more frequent application in dispute resolution. This is referred to as incarnation of mediation,[13] modern mediation[14] or cognitive, scientific or Western mediation.[15] On a global scale, modern mediation began to appear in the 1970s and 1980s, especially in the US, Canada, Australia, New Zealand and the UK, and in the 1990s, it spread more significantly in continental Europe.[16]

5. *See* Carrie Menkel-Meadow, *The Future of Mediation Worldwide: Legal and Cultural Variations in the Uptake of or Resistance to Mediation* 29 (Ian Macduff ed., Kluwer Law International, 2016). *See also* Penny Brooker, *Mediation Law: Journey Through Institutionalism to Juridification* 1 (Routledge 2013).
6. *See* Inga Zaleniene & Agne Tvaronaviciene, *The Main Features and Development Trends of Mediation in Lithuania: The Opportunities for Lawyers*, 119 Jurisprudencija 229 (2010).
7. *See* David Spencer & Michael Brogan, *Mediation Law and Practice* 23 (Cambridge University Press, 2006).
8. *See* Jean Poitras, *A Study of the Emergence of Cooperation in Mediation*, 21 Negotiation Journal 281–300 (2005).
9. Spencer & Brogan, *supra* n. 7, at 23.
10. *Ibid.*, 23.
11. *See* Menkel-Meadow, *supra* n. 4, at 220.
12. *See* Part I.
13. Menkel-Meadow, *supra* n. 5, at 29.
14. *See* Nadja Alexander, *Global Trends in Mediation: Riding the Third Wave* 1 (Nadja Alexander ed., Kluwer Law International 2006).
15. Alexander, *supra* n. 1, at 53.
16. *Ibid.*, 53. *See also* Alexander, *supra* n. 14, at 1.

§6.02 THE EU AS A DRIVER IN THE FIELD OF MODERN MEDIATION

At the EU level, efforts to regulate alternative resolution of disputes date back to the 1990s.[17] The first mentions can be found in the 1993 Green Paper Regarding Consumer Access to Justice and the Settlement of Consumer Disputes in the Single Market, which aimed primarily at introducing out-of-court procedures for the resolution of consumer disputes. Mediation was explicitly mentioned as a special procedure for resolving these disputes.[18] The 1998 Vienna Action Plan[19] identified the development of mediation with a focus on family disputes as one of the priorities. The conclusions of the 1999 European Council meeting in Tampere, Finland,[20] called for the creation of alternative and out-of-court procedures in the Member States in order to improve access to justice in Europe. One year later in 2000, the European Council recommended, in its meeting in Lisbon,[21] promoting consumer confidence in e-commerce mainly through ADR systems. Following these initiatives, the Commission was tasked with drafting the Green Paper on ADR in Civil and Commercial Law (2002).[22]

First and foremost, the Green Paper states that forms of ADR are intended to contribute to wider access to justice.[23] However, they should be seen not only as a remedy for the difficulties associated with the judicial system but also rather as consensual methods that should lead to social harmony, in many cases in a more appropriate way than using judicial or arbitration proceedings. ADR brings the parties together to seek a solution to their dispute instead of standing against each other and ending their dispute in the positions of winner and loser.[24] Although it was a non-binding proclamation, the Commission clearly proposed and outlined the further direction of the European Community in the field of ADR, thus encouraging further discussion on this topic in Europe.

---

17. *See* Jacqueline M. Nolan-Haley, *Is Europe Headed Down the Primrose Path with Mandatory Mediation*, 37 North Carolina Journal of International Law and Commercial Regulation 989 (2012).
18. European Commission, *Green Paper on Access of Consumers to Justice and the Settlement of Consumer Disputes in the Single Market*, COM (93) 576 final, https://eur-lex.europa.eu/legal-content/EN/TXT/PDF/?uri=CELEX:51993DC0576&from=EN.
19. European Council and European Commission, *Action Plan on How Best to Implement the Provisions of the Treaty of Amsterdam on the Creation of an Area of Freedom, Security and Justice* (1998), https://eur-lex.europa.eu/legal-content/EN/TXT/HTML/?uri=CELEX:31999Y0123(01)&from=EN.
20. European Council, *Tampere European Council 15 and 16 October 1999, Presidency Conclusions* (1999), http://www.europarl.europa.eu/summits/tam_en.htm?textMode=on.
21. European Council, *Lisbon European Council 23 and 24 March 2000, Presidency Conclusions* (2000), http://www.europarl.europa.eu/summits/lis1_en.htm.
22. European Commission, *Green Paper on alternative dispute resolution in civil and commercial law*, COM (2002) 196 final, https://eur-lex.europa.eu/legal-content/EN/TXT/HTML/?uri=CELEX:52002DC0196&from=EN.
23. *Ibid.*, s. 1.2, at 5–13.
24. *Ibid.*, s. 1.2, at 10.

§6.03 EU DIRECTIVE AND MEMBER STATES' RESPONSES

An important milestone for a large part of Europe that followed on the previous developments outlined above was the issue of Directive 2008/52/EC of the European Parliament and of the Council of 21 May 2008 on certain aspects of mediation in civil and commercial matters (hereinafter 'EU Mediation Directive'). The main two objectives of the EU Mediation Directive are to:

(1) facilitate access to alternative methods of dispute resolution; and
(2) promote an amicable settlement of disputes.[25]

The objectives outlined above should be achieved especially by promoting the use of mediation and ensuring a balanced relationship between mediation and judicial proceedings.

The transposition of the EU Mediation Directive led to the creation of the first-ever legal regulations for modern mediation in some Member States, on the basis of which mediation began to be reflected in the legal normative system and constituted as a legal institution. This launched the process of codification of mediation in these countries.[26] The substantive scope of the EU Mediation Directive only included cross-border disputes.[27] However, there was nothing to prevent Member States from applying its provisions to national mediation proceedings, too.[28]

Under several provisions of the EU Mediation Directive containing mandatory rules, Member States were to implement and ensure enforceability of mediation agreements,[29] the effect of mediation on limitation and prescription periods,[30] and protection of confidentiality of mediation.[31] However, the EU Mediation Directive does not contain any specific requirements for approach to mediation. It only contains some other recommendations regarding the application of the provisions also to the resolution of national disputes,[32] enabling courts to refer parties to mediation,[33] anchoring

25. EU Mediation Directive, Art. 1.
26. It should be noted that legal regulation of mediation was already in place in the legal systems of many Member States before the adoption of the EU Mediation Directive, and the process of codification of mediation was already more advanced. This will be discussed in more detail below.
27. EU Mediation Directive, Art. 2.
28. This is also what most Member States did. According to the Study for an Evaluation and Implementation of the Mediation Directive, only four countries transposed the EU Mediation Directive solely in relation to cross-border disputes (Denmark, Ireland, the Netherlands, and the UK), and the existing regulation established before the issue of the EU Mediation Directive remained. *See* European Commission, *Study for an Evaluation and Implementation of Directive 2008/52/EC the 'Mediation Directive'*, Publications Office of the European Union 46 (2016), https://publications.europa.eu/en/publication-detail/-/publication/bba3871d-223b-11e6-86d0-01aa75ed71a1/language-en.
29. EU Mediation Directive, Art. 6.
30. *Ibid.*, Art. 8.
31. *Ibid.*, Art. 7.
32. *Ibid.*, Preamble, para. 8.
33. *Ibid.*, Art. 5.

informational meetings with mediators,[34] organisation of training and education of mediators,[35] use of mediator codes of conduct,[36] and dissemination of information on mediation to the general public.[37] In the aforementioned absence of specific provisions on the approach to mediation, regulation of mediation has developed very differently in each Member State.

According to the Study for an Evaluation and Implementation of the Mediation Directive,[38] fifteen Member States already had a comprehensive system of mediation at the time of the adoption of the EU Mediation Directive. In the case of these states, the EU Mediation Directive thus brought only minimal or even no changes to their system. The legal systems of four Member States contained only certain partial rules governing mediation or provided for mediation in the private sector on the principle of self-regulation. For these states, the obligation to transpose the EU Mediation Directive meant significant changes in the existing framework for the regulation of mediation. Finally, the remaining nine Member States adopted mediation legislation for the first time, given the obligation to transpose the EU Mediation Directive.

§6.04 FORMS OF SYSTEMS OF APPROACH TO MEDIATION

A gradual codification of mediation led to the creation of systems of approach to mediation in Member States. A system of approach to mediation is the set of measures, factors and their interrelations that determine the possibilities of approaching mediation in a particular state. Put simply, the term can be understood as a system composed of several subsets, that is, sub-models that determine the particular regime by which mediation is approached in a given state. Looking at the legislation of the Member States, I find that the regulation of the approach to mediation is highly diverse between various parts of Europe.[39] This heterogeneity is mainly due to the different processes of codification of mediation in the EU Member States.

A number of factors can be identified as to why codification of mediation (enactment of legislation on mediation) in Europe has proceeded in this direction. The most important factors that have led to the creation of different systems of approach to mediation include, in particular, the following:

- the different times at which legal regulation of mediation was established in the respective Member States – according to the Study for an Evaluation and Implementation of the Mediation Directive,[40] fifteen Member States already

34. *Ibid.*, Art. 5.
35. *Ibid.*, Art. 4.
36. *Ibid.*, Art. 4.
37. *Ibid.*, Art. 9.
38. European Commission, *supra* n. 28, at V–VI, 30 or 44–45.
39. *See*, e.g., Alexander, Walsh, Svatoš et. al., *supra* n. 3; Carlos Esplugues et al., *Civil and Commercial Mediation in Europe: National Mediation Rules and Procedures* (Intersentia 2013); De Palo, Trevor et al., *supra* n. 2; Klaus J. Hopt, et al., *Mediation: Principles and Regulation in Comparative Perspective* (Oxford University Press 2013).
40. European Commission, *supra* n. 28, at 30, 44.

had a comprehensive system of mediation regulation before the adoption of the EU Mediation Directive, while other Member States amended their regulations or created new ones following the issue of the EU Mediation Directive;
- the diversity of Member States' legal cultures and dispute resolution cultures[41] – given a large number of Member States, different legal traditions and the diversity of cultural roots among nations, it is natural that this factor has also contributed to the formation of different systems for how mediation operates;
- the differing situation in the judiciary – some states whose courts faced high levels of backlog sometimes tended to encourage the use of mediation to address this problem through widespread and intensified coercion into mediation;[42]
- the insufficient directive character of the EU Mediation Directive – the Directive does not lay down specific rules on measures aimed at coercing, motivating or informing about mediation that Member States would have to ensure; the provisions relating to this issue are rather of a recommendatory nature.[43]

The differences in the systems of approach to mediation are reflected in the model applied for coercing parties in civil proceedings into mediation. Here, in a comparative perspective, we are moving along a scale with legal systems of states that do not provide for any legal obligation in relation to mediation on one end and legislation mandating that parties to civil disputes use mediation on the other end. Legal regulations across the outlined scale are very often complemented by motivation elements. The function of motivation-based models is to make parties to civil disputes participate in mediation in an indirect manner – by favouring the parties in the event of their participation in mediation or, conversely, sanctioning them if they do not participate in mediation for stipulated reasons. Last but not least, systems of approach to mediation can be complemented by informational tools that can be used informally or based on a statutory obligation (Figure 6.1).

41. *Ibid.*, 71.
42. *See*, e.g., systems of approach to mediation in Italy, Greece and Romania presented below.
43. *See* §6.04.

Figure 6.1 Diagram of Systems of Approach to Mediation

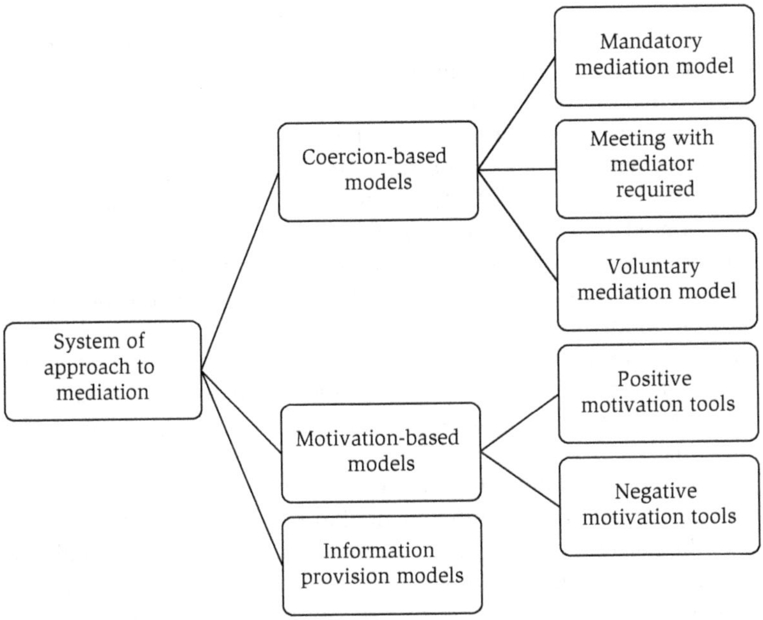

In addition to these three outlined basic sets of models (coercion-based models, motivation-based models, and models based on the provision of information on mediation), the system of approach to mediation in a particular state may be complemented by other models or other specific aspects typical of that state. In this respect, the outlined system by which mediation operates should be taken as simplified and focused in particular on the legal aspects.

§6.05 COERCION-BASED MODELS

The coercion-based model indicates the degree of direct coercion applied in a particular Member State and aiming to spur the initiation of mediation or participation in an informational meeting with a mediator. In a comparative perspective, we can distinguish several different groups of models by which parties to civil disputes are coerced into using mediation in the EU. These models are as follows:

(1) The mandatory mediation model – this model is characterised by the obligation to initiate mediation. Depending on how the obligation to initiate mediation is laid down, two subsets of mandatory mediation models can be distinguished:

(a) a general obligation to initiate mediation – there is a general legal obligation to initiate mediation within a defined range of disputes regulated by a legal regulation; this is a categorical[44] coercion;

(b) individual obligation to initiate mediation – in a particular case, the court or another authority may order the parties to the dispute to initiate mediation, or this obligation may be negotiated by the parties; this is usually a discretionary[45] coercion.

(2) Meeting with mediator required – in this model, parties to disputes are required to attend an informational meeting with a mediator in order to get acquainted with how mediation works. As a rule, the parties are offered an opportunity to initiate mediation and resolve their dispute in this way after the meeting. Again, the model has two variants depending on the form of the obligation imposed:

(a) a general obligation to attend an informational mediation meeting – the participation of the parties to the dispute in an initial mediation meeting is laid down by a legal regulation for a defined range of types of disputes; this is a categorical[46] coercion;

(b) an individual obligation to attend an informational mediation meeting – participation in an initial mediation meeting is individually imposed on the parties to the dispute by a decision of the court or another decision-making authority; this is usually a discretionary[47] coercion.

(3) Voluntary model – this model can be characterised by the fact that the legislation of a given state does not stipulate the obligation to initiate mediation or to attend a different kind of meeting with a mediator in a predetermined range of disputes, nor does it delegate to a decision-making authority the power to order parties to enter mediation in a particular case or order them to attend a different kind of meeting with a mediator. Direct coercion into mediation is absent here (Figure 6.2).

44. *See* Andreas Nelle, *Making Mediation Mandatory: A Proposed Framework*, 7 *Ohio State Journal on Dispute Resolution* 289 (1992).
45. *Ibid.*
46. *Ibid.*
47. *Ibid.*

Figure 6.2 Diagram of Models Based on Coercion into Mediation

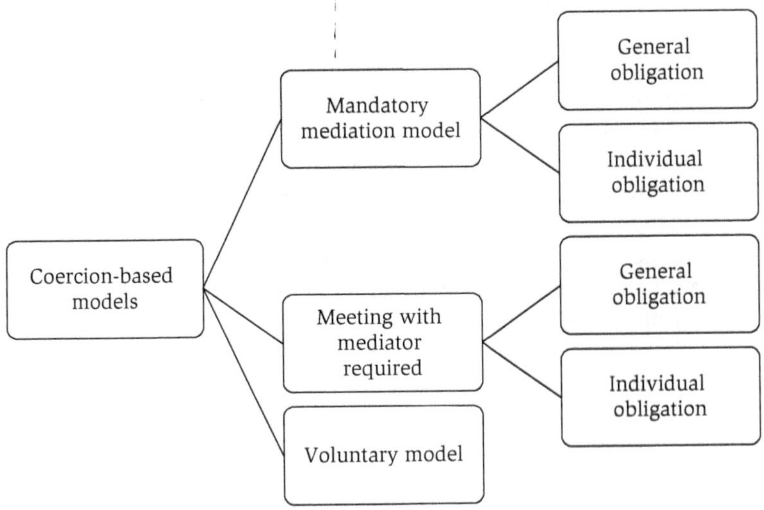

[A] Mandatory Mediation Model

The mandatory mediation model is applied in those Member States whose legal order allows obliging the parties to disputes to initiate mediation. However, in most cases, this does not mean that it is necessary to successfully terminate mediation in order to fulfil this obligation – that is, to resolve the dispute and conclude a mediation agreement. This aspect is usually left on a voluntary basis.[48] It is mandatory only to initiate mediation or to complete a certain part of the mediation process. The mandatory mediation model exists in three basic forms:

(1) mandatory pre-action mediation;
(2) ordering mediation in the course of judicial or other proceedings; and
(3) a mediation clause that derogates the court's power to rule on the case.

In the mandatory pre-action model,[49] initiation of mediation is a condition of access to court or, where appropriate, to another method of dispute resolution (e.g., arbitration). This type of mandatory mediation is characterised by a general obligation to initiate mediation. A legal regulation expressly stipulates cases in which a party to the dispute is obliged to initiate mediation first. Only after the end of mediation –

48. *See* Giuseppe De Palo & Leonardo D'Urso, *Achieving a Balanced Relationship Between Mediation and Judicial Proceedings. The Implementation of the Mediation Directive. WORKSHOP 29 November 2016* (EU Publication Office 2016), http://www.europarl.europa.eu/RegData/etudes/IDAN/2016/571395/IPOL_IDA%282016%29571395_EN.pdf.
49. Cf. Klaus J. Hopt & Felix Steffek, *Mediation: Comparison of Laws, Regulatory Models, Fundamental Issues* 24–26 (Klaus J. Hopt, Felix Steffek eds., Oxford University Press 2013).

whether successful or unsuccessful – can the action be admitted in court and can be heard.

In contrast, the use of the second variant – ordering mediation in the course of court proceedings – is characterised by an individual imposition of an obligation on specific parties. The court or other decision-making authority issues an order for the parties to initiate mediation. During mediation, the court usually does not take any action or stays the proceedings altogether. Failure to comply with the obligation to initiate mediation is usually associated with sanctions.

The parties themselves may also agree to settle the dispute through mediation by means of a mediation clause or, in general, an agreement to mediate.[50] However, only contractual arrangements by which the parties undertake to resolve their dispute through mediation and with which the legal order of the Member State associates the effect of derogating the power of the court to rule on the case until mediation is over will belong to the coercion-based mandatory mediation model. In countries where a dispute can be heard in court despite the conclusion of a mediation clause, this arrangement performs only a motivational function because its violation is often associated with sanctions.

[1] General Obligation to Initiate Mediation

The best known example of the use of the mandatory mediation model with a general obligation to initiate mediation in the EU was the system applied in Italy between 2011 and 2012.[51] Government Regulation No. 28/2010 was approved in response to the EU Mediation Directive transposition. It came into effect in March 2011.[52] Pursuant to the Regulation, mediation could be used as mandatory, voluntary, requested under a contractual arrangement or ordered by the court.[53] The Government Regulation made mediation mandatory for certain defined types of disputes. This included disputes concerning joint ownership, property rights, division, inheritance rights, family contracts, leases, loans-for-use, leases of businesses, compensation for damage resulting from vehicle and boat traffic, medical liability and defamation through the press and other media, or insurance, banking and financial contracts.[54]

Mediation had to be initiated before an action was filed in disputes involving such subject matter. As a result of this obligation, mediation became a condition for the

50. *Ibid.*, 29–31.
51. *See* Leonardo D´Urso, *Italy's Mediation Law: An Overview*, International Mediation Institute (22 Jun. 2017), https://imimediation.org/2017/06/22/italys-mediation-law-an-overview/. *See also* Martin Svatoš, *Mandatory Mediation Strikes Back*, Mediate.com (November 2013), http://www.mediate.com/articles/SvatosM1.cfm.
52. *See* Carlo Mastellone & Laura Ristori, *Chapter 17: Italy* 469 (Nadja Alexander, Sabine Walsh, Martin Svatoš eds., Kluwer Law International 2017). *See also* Nolan-Haley, *supra* n. 17, at 1004.
53. Mastellone, Ristori, *supra* n. 52, at 473.
54. *See* Tomaso Galletto & Richard L. Mattiaccio, *Mediation in Italy: A Bridge Too Far?*, 66 Dispute Resolution Journal (2011). *See also* Marcello Marinari, *Italy* 194 (Giuseppe De Palo & Mary B. Trevor eds., Oxford University Press 2012).

admissibility of an action.[55] The inadmissibility of an action could be objected to by the defendant or determined by the court of its own motion. If the court found that mediation had not been initiated or that an already initiated mediation had not yet ended, it would set a deadline for a mediation meeting. The condition was considered to be fulfilled if at least the first mediation meeting took place, even if it ended without agreement between the parties.[56]

In the event that an amicable agreement was concluded between the parties to the mediation, the mediator would take minutes, which were then annexed to the agreement. If no agreement was reached or the parties so requested, the mediator could draw up a draft reconciliation themselves. Where the parties did not agree even with such a proposal, the mediator would produce a report stating the mediator's proposal. In the event that in subsequent court proceedings the court ruled in accordance with the mediator's proposal set out in the report, the court ruled out the award of costs incurred by the successful party for the period following the proposal and ordered that party to pay the costs of the unsuccessful party for the same period, as well as to pay additional amounts equal to the court fee to the state. The Court of First Instance could rule out the award of costs even if the final judgment did not fully correspond to the content of the mediator's proposal if there were serious and exceptional reasons for doing so.[57] For most of the remaining disputes, mediation remained in the voluntary-use regime.

According to statistics of the Italian Ministry of Justice,[58] parties to disputes decided to proceed with mediation in 27% of cases. Agreement was reached in 43.9% of those cases. In 56.1% of the cases, no agreement was reached. It is obvious that the success rate of this mandatory mediation model may not be as high as that of voluntary mediation, for which the parties decide themselves.[59] The main reason for introducing mandatory mediation in the Italian circumstances was the intolerable workload of the courts. Before the introduction of mandatory mediation, they faced a backlog of almost six million cases.[60] While mandatory mediation helped solve this problem, it did put some strain on proceedings in which the parties did not want to resolve their dispute through mediation or tried to do so but mediation failed. The introduction of the obligation to initiate mediation could make resolution of such disputes lengthier and more expensive.

55. Svatoš, *supra* n. 51.
56. *See, e.g.*, Nolan-Haley, *supra* n. 17, at 1004–1005; Marinari, *supra* n. 54, at. 194. *See also* Ilaria Queirolo, Laura Carpaneto & Stefano Dominelli, *Italy* 268–270 (Carlos Esplugues, José Luis Iglesias, Guillermo Palao Moreno eds., Intersentia 2013).
57. *See* Giuseppe De Palo & Lauren Keller, *Mediation in Italy: Alternative Dispute Resolution for All* 671–682 (Klaus J. Hopt, Felix Steffek eds., Oxford University Press 2013). *See also* Queirolo, Carpaneto, Dominelli, *supra* n. 56, at 275–277.
58. Ministero della Giustizia – Dipartimento della organizzazione giudiziaria, del personale e dei servizi, Direzione Generale di Statistica, *MEDIAZIONE OBBLIGATORIA EX D.L. 28/2010, STATISTICHE AL 31 DICEMBRE 2012*, DG-Stat (27 Sep. 2017), https://webstat.giustizia.it/Analisi%20e%20ricerche/Mediazione%20civile%20-%20Anno%202012.pdf.
59. *See* Ch. 10.
60. Galletto, Mattiaccio, *supra* n. 54, at 80.

Recently, mandatory mediation has also been introduced in Greece. On 30 November 2019, Act No. 4640/2019 was published in the Greek Government's Gazette[61] under which the parties to the dispute are obliged to attend an initial meeting with a mediator in family disputes, except for matrimonial disputes pertaining to the divorce, the annulment of marriage, the recognition of the existence or non-existence of marriage and the parent-children relationships, such as the contesting of fatherhood or motherhood, and disputes heard in the ordinary course of proceedings before the Single-Member Court of First Instance, if the value of the claim exceeds the amount of EUR 30,000, and before the Multi-Member Court of First Instance, in accordance with the provisions of the Greek Code of Civil Procedure. Attending an initial mediation session is also a condition for action admissibility.[62] In the event that a party fails to participate in mandatory mediation, the court may impose a fine on that party.[63]

The general obligation to initiate mediation is not limited to only southern states whose judicial system is facing a high number of backlog cases. Mandatory mediation is applied, for example, in Austria, albeit to a much lesser extent. Mediation is generally voluntary there, but special laws provide for an obligation to attempt an out-of-court settlement of a dispute through mediation before bringing an action. These include, for example, disputes concerning genetic engineering, employment of persons with disabilities or neighbourly disputes over light and air pollution.[64]

[2] Individual Obligation to Initiate Mediation

In addition to the general obligation to initiate mediation, a model which allows imposition of an individual obligation to initiate mediation can also be encountered. That is to say, a model where a court or another authority may oblige particular parties to disputes to initiate mediation. There is such a system, for example, in Malta (in certain family disputes) or in Poland, unless the parties subsequently communicate their disagreement to the court.[65]

A possibility to individually negotiate an agreement to mediate or a mediation clause that derogates the court's power to rule on the case and establishes an obligation to attempt to resolve the case through mediation first also falls into this category.

61. *See* Vassiliki Koumpli, *Greece: Institutionalizing Mediation Through Mandatory Initial Mediation Session (Law 4640/2019)*, Kluwer Mediation Blog (20 Jan. 2020), http://mediationblog.kluwerarbitration.com/2020/01/20/greece-institutionalizing-mediation-through-mandatory-initial-mediation-session-law-4640-2019/. *See also* Olga Tsiptse, *Mediation in Greece*, Mediate.com (October 2020), https://www.mediate.com/articles/olga-mediation-greece.cfm; Nikos Anastopoulos, *Mandatory Mediation in Civil and Commercial Disputes by Virtue of Law 4640/2019*, Politis & Partners Law Firm (1 Dec. 2019), https://politispartners.gr/mandatory-mediation-in-civil-and-commercial-disputes-by-virtue-of-law-4640-2019/.
62. Tsiptse, *supra* n. 61; Anastopoulos, *supra* n. 61.
63. Koumpli, *supra* n. 61.
64. *See* Christina Lenz & Martin Risak, *Chapter 2: Austria* 33–58 (Nadja Alexander, Sabine Walsh, Martin Svatoš eds., Kluwer Law International 2017).
65. *See* Rafal Morek, *Chapter 24: Poland* 609 (Nadja Alexander, Sabine Walsh, Martin Svatoš eds., Kluwer Law International 2017).

[B] Informational Meeting with Mediator Required

Under this model, the parties to the dispute may be obliged to attend an informational meeting with a mediator. This meeting has mainly an informational function. The role of the mediator is to acquaint the parties with the operation of mediation, its principles and the advantages of amicable dispute resolution in general.[66] However, this procedure is not associated with an obligation to initiate mediation and usually not associated with an obligation to initiate mediation with the mediator the parties met in the initial meeting. However, imposing the obligation to attend such a meeting can have considerable psychological impact. The court – or legislator if the obligation to attend a meeting with a mediator is stipulated generally for certain types of disputes – thus makes the 'first step' for parties that would otherwise, as a result of their character or prolonged escalated conflict, never propose a solution to the dispute through mediation themselves, even if they would otherwise agree to amicable resolution of the dispute because they often perceive the willingness to reach an agreement as a sign of weakness.[67] After attending an informational meeting, the parties are usually offered an opportunity to initiate mediation. This type of coercion may occur in legal systems in similar forms as presented in the mandatory mediation model.[68]

[1] General Obligation to Attend an Informational Meeting with Mediator

A general obligation to attend a meeting before the initiation of court proceedings in resolving predetermined types of disputes has been used, for example, in Romania. This was on the basis of Act No. 115/2012 amending the Romanian Mediation Act. The amendment introduced a system of mandatory participation in informational meetings on mediation. It was therefore not an attempt to resolve the dispute through mediation itself but a mandatory meeting between the parties to the dispute with a mediator, with the purpose of explaining the benefits of mediation.[69] The sanction for not attending the meeting was a subsequent inadmissibility of the action. The change sparked debate about a possible restriction of the right of access to court. A later amendment No. 214/2013 extended the authorisation to carry out informational procedures to judges, attorneys and notaries.[70] The matter was eventually considered by the Romanian Constitutional Court, which concluded that the obligation to attend informational sessions and the sanctions in the form of inadmissibility of the action limited the

66. *See*, e.g., Monika Pauknerová, Magdalena Pfeiffer, *Mediation, More Particularly, Cross-Border and Judicial Mediation*, 5 The Lawyer Quarterly 123–124 (2015).
67. 'Especially in the countries where mediation does not have a very long tradition, the court can be very helpful.' *See* Martin Svatoš, *The Mediator-Judge Interaction: Does the Win-Win Approach Apply?* 219 (Alexander J. Bělohlávek, Naděžda Rozehnalová eds., Juris Publishing, 2015).
68. *See* §6.06[A] mandatory model.
69. *See* Constantin-Adi Gavrila & Christian Radu Chereji, *Don't Rush*, Mediate.com (February 2015), https://www.mediate.com/articles/CherejiGavrilaFutures.cfm.
70. *See* Constantin-Adi Gavrila & Sanda Elena Lungu, *Chapter 26: Romania* 641 (Nadja Alexander, Sabine Walsh, Martin Svatoš eds., Kluwer Law International 2017).

constitutionally protected plaintiff's right of access to court.[71] A system with a general obligation to attend an informational meeting with a mediator was introduced in Italy after abolition of the mandatory mediation model.[72]

[2] Individual Obligation to Attend an Informational Meeting with Mediator

A possibility for the court to individually order the parties to attend a meeting with a mediator exists, for example, in the Czech Republic. Where appropriate and useful, the judge may order the parties to hold a first meeting with a registered mediator totalling three hours and to suspend the proceedings for a maximum of three months. If the parties fail to agree on the person of the mediator without undue delay, the judge will select the mediator from a list maintained by the Ministry of Justice. After attending an informational meeting, the parties are offered an opportunity to initiate mediation. After three months at the latest (if mediation is not initiated), the court resumes the proceedings.[73] A similar system based on the possibility for the court to order the parties to attend an informational meeting with a mediator is used, for example, in Hungary.[74]

[C] Voluntary Model

This model in the coercion category is characterised by the absence of coercion to initiate mediation. In this system of approach to mediation, parties to disputes may use, in particular, private mediation[75] or they may decide to initiate mediation after a recommendation from a court or another authority. It is the parties to the dispute themselves who can agree to resolve the dispute through mediation.

There are advantages and disadvantages to this model. The advantage is that parties to disputes in this model want to reach an agreement and resolve their dispute through mediation, which in theory may imply a higher number of successful mediations and potentially concluded mediation agreements.[76] However, the disadvantage of this model, if applied absolutely (e.g., without motivational factors), can be seen – considering the low level of awareness of mediation – in the fact that the percentage of parties to disputes that initiate mediation will be rather lower.[77] Even if they knew about this possibility, both parties need to agree to initiate mediation.[78]

---

71. *Ibid.*
72. Act No. 69/2013 came into effect in Italy in September 2013.
73. *See* Martin Svatoš, *Chapter 7: The Czech Republic* 172–173 (Nadja Alexander, Sabine Walsh, Martin Svatoš eds., Kluwer Law International 2017). *See also* Pauknerová, Pfeiffer, *supra* n. 66, at 123–125; Svatoš, *supra* n. 67, at 224.
74. *See* Manuela Renáta Grosu, *Chapter 15: Hungary* 412–415 (Nadja Alexander, Sabine Walsh, Martin Svatoš eds., Kluwer Law International 2017).
75. Hopt, Steffek, *supra* n. 49, at 20.
76. *Ibid.*, 103.
77. *See* Part IV, explicitly Ch. 9.
78. Palo, D'Urso, *supra* n. 48, at 11–12.

However, in the course of a conflict, parties are often unable to even attempt an amicable resolution of the dispute without a third-party intervention. In principle, there is no need for specific legislation to use this model.

§6.06 MOTIVATION-BASED MODELS

In each of the outlined coercion-based models, additional tools may be used to encourage the parties to resolve their dispute through mediation. Their purpose is not to force the parties to disputes to participate in mediation by imposing obligations directly, but rather to promote dispute settlement through mediation indirectly through advantages or, conversely, sanctions. It thus performs the function of indirect coercion.

Motivation tools can be divided into two groups:

(1) Positive motivation tools: this group includes measures favouring parties that settled their dispute through mediation during already initiated court proceedings.
(2) Negative motivation tools: parties are penalised in court proceedings for not having resolved their dispute through mediation or for not having obeyed a call related to mediation.

[A] Positive Motivation Tools

Tools that may motivate parties to disputes to use mediation may include, for example, the possibility of using free mediation, that is, one financed by the state or another entity.[79] Other tools used include refund of the court fee paid, in whole or in part, if the parties manage to resolve their dispute through mediation after the initiation of court proceedings. Examples can be found in Bulgaria and Romania. In Bulgaria, parties successful in resolving a dispute through mediation may receive compensation equal to 50% of the court fee paid.[80] Romania is even considering a full exemption from the obligation to pay a fee.[81] However, given the relatively low amounts of court fees in these states, these motivational measures do not perform their function sufficiently.

[B] Negative Motivation Tools

A typical tool by which parties to disputes are penalised for not attempting to resolve their dispute through mediation or for not fulfilling another obligation relating to mediation is non-recognition of the costs of court proceedings in the event of a party's success in subsequent court proceedings. In the Czech Republic, this possibility is expressly provided for in §150 of the Code of Civil Procedure. It stipulates that exceptionally the court may not award costs in whole or in part if a party refuses to

79. *See, e.g.*, Lenz, Risak, *supra* n. 64, at 43; Mastellone, Ristori, *supra* n. 52, at 478.
80. Nolan-Haley, *supra* n. 17, at 1005.
81. *Ibid. See also* Gavrila, Lungu, *supra* n. 70, at 656.

attend the first meeting with a mediator ordered by the court without a serious reason.[82] A similar measure for failure to use mediation in a suitable case applies, for example, in Denmark.[83] The possibility for the court to impose a fine on a party that has not participated in mediation without a reason also acts as negative motivation in some Member States.[84]

§6.07 MODELS BASED ON THE PROVISION OF INFORMATION ON MEDIATION

In addition to the positive and negative motivation tools, legal systems contain tools whose function is 'mere' provision of information on the possibility of dispute resolution through mediation. These tools cannot be unambiguously classified as motivational because they do not meet all attributes of motivational tools. While they help parties resolve their disputes through mediation, they are generally not associated with any advantage or sanction.

The use of this model is very often grossly underestimated in practice, so there are often situations in individual EU Member States that mediators are highly skilled and the use of mediation is encouraged by the state, but there is a lack of interest of the public in resolving their disputes through mediation.[85] The public is not sufficiently informed about this method in some states. This was confirmed, for example, by recent empirical research in the Czech Republic. In November 2018, a public survey was conducted on a sample representing the Czech population. When asked 'What is mediation in your opinion?', only 33.6% of respondents selected the correct answer 'A way of out-of-court conflict solving'.[86]

Particular examples of these informational tools include, for example, a possibility for the court to recommend that the parties use mediation to resolve their dispute[87] or an obligation of a lawyer and other legal professional to acquaint their clients, before filing an action, with the possibility of resolving the dispute amicably through mediation.[88] Other tools may include inclusion of the topic of mediation in primary- and secondary-school educational programmes, information campaigns for the public[89] or anchoring of the obligation to indicate in an action being filed whether the

82. Svatoš, *supra* n. 73, 173.
83. *See* Louise Lerche-Gredal, *Chapter 8: Denmark* 197 (Nadja Alexander, Sabine Walsh, Martin Svatoš eds., Kluwer Law International 2017).
84. *See*, e.g., Svatoš, *supra* n. 73, 186; Grosu, *supra* n. 74, 414; Gavrila, Lungu, *supra* n. 70, 644.
85. European Parliament, *Resolution on the Implementation of Directive 2008/52/EC of the European Parliament and of the Council on certain aspects of mediation in civil and commercial matters* (2016/2066(INI)), https://eur-lex.europa.eu/legal-content/EN/TXT/HTML/?uri=CELEX:52017IP0321&qid=1614194030734&from=CS.
86. *See* Martina Urbanová, Lenka Holá & Martin Lakomý, *Mediation in the Context of Law Acquaintance*, 11 DANUBE 9 (2020).
87. *See*, e.g., Evgeni Georgiev, *Chapter 4: Bulgaria* 101 (Nadja Alexander, Sabine Walsh, Martin Svatoš eds., Kluwer Law International 2017); Boris Jukić & Anamarija Milanović, *Chapter 5: Croatia* 131 (Nadja Alexander, Sabine Walsh, Martin Svatoš eds., Kluwer Law International 2017); Delphine Wietek, *Chapter 12: France* 324 (Nadja Alexander, Sabine Walsh, Martin Svatoš eds., Kluwer Law International 2017); Tatiana Hambalkova, František Kutlik & Alexandra

parties have attempted to settle the dispute amicably, which is currently being applied in Poland.[90]

§6.08 PARTIAL CONCLUSION

A systematic review of the application of mediation in EU Member States has shown that the way in which the applied systems of mediation operate is quite diverse. The process of codification of mediation has undoubtedly had a significant influence on the emergence of such a wide variety of possible setups for the system of approach to mediation, as in each Member State this process took different course and there were no strong unifying elements.

The EU Mediation Directive can be seen as a step in the right direction in the European environment, although it has not had a significant impact on the unification of systems of approach to mediation. It has contributed to the development of systems of approach to mediation in many Member States and thereby, in part, to the development of the mediation culture. The Directive also raises national legislators' awareness of the existence of mediation, and for some Member States, it has been a substantial incentive to start working on a legal framework for mediation. However, this is still one of the initial steps that have not yet met the EU's expectations and original ambitions.[91] Although the system of application of mediation is different in each Member State, mediation has not yet become mainstream in any Member State and its frequency remains far from that of court proceedings.[92]

Kapišovská, *Chapter 28: Slovak Republic* 706–707 (Nadja Alexander, Sabine Walsh, Martin Svatoš eds., Kluwer Law International 2017).

88. *See*, e.g., Johan Billiet & Dilyara Nigmatullina, *Chapter 3: Belgium* 70 (Nadja Alexander, Sabine Walsh, Martin Svatoš eds., Kluwer Law International 2017); Gavrila, Lungu, *supra* n. 70, at 643.
89. *See*, e.g., George Mountis & Victoria-Zoi Papagiannis, *Chapter 6: Cyprus* 148 (Nadja Alexander, Sabine Walsh, Martin Svatoš eds., Kluwer Law International 2017).
90. Morek, *supra* n. 65, at 609.
91. European Parliament, *supra* n. 85.
92. *Ibid. See also* Part IV.

CHAPTER 7

Limitation of Coercion to Use Mediation in the EU

Jan Holas

The integration into the legal systems of the Member States of measures constituting the system of approach to mediation is associated with a risk of distorting the foundations on which mediation is built and which allow mediation to provide its characteristic outcomes. As a result, legal regulation can impact the entire concept of mediation and its use. Moreover, in addition to distorting the concept of mediation, the measures being integrated may also have a negative impact on the area of court dispute resolution and its functioning. It is appropriate, therefore, to reflect in these efforts on the limits of legislative activity and the way that the system of approach to mediation is set up in a given Member State.

Chapter 6 presented three basic models for the system of approach to mediation in a particular Member State. These were the coercion-based model, the motivation-based model, and the model based on the provision of information on mediation. While most tools and measures falling under the motivation-based model (except for some of the tools of negative motivation) and the model based on the provision of information on mediation do not usually have a major impact on the functioning of mediation and civil procedure, this is not the case for some of the measures and tools of the coercion-based model (e.g., the obligation to initiate mediation or to attend an informational meeting with a mediator). Those tools carry an element of direct coercion which may significantly restrict the autonomy of the parties to choose mediation or, conversely, court proceedings to resolve their dispute. The limits of coercion to use mediation will therefore be examined, as this coercion may result in a significant distortion of the concept of mediation and court proceedings.

Limits on coercion to use mediation can be seen as boundaries that the legislation should not exceed so that the values and principles of the concepts concerned are not unduly interfered with (Figure 7.1). In identifying concepts that could be affected by regulating the approach to mediation, account must be taken of both potentially affected areas – the area of mediation and the legal area. This is because legal regulation of mediation – in particular by enshrining the legal obligation to use mediation in the legal order – that exceeds certain limits may undermine the functioning of both the mediation itself and the civil procedure, including the related constitutionally guaranteed fundamental rights of the parties to the dispute (e.g., the right of access to court).

Figure 7.1 Basic Limits on Coercing Parties to Disputes to Use Mediation

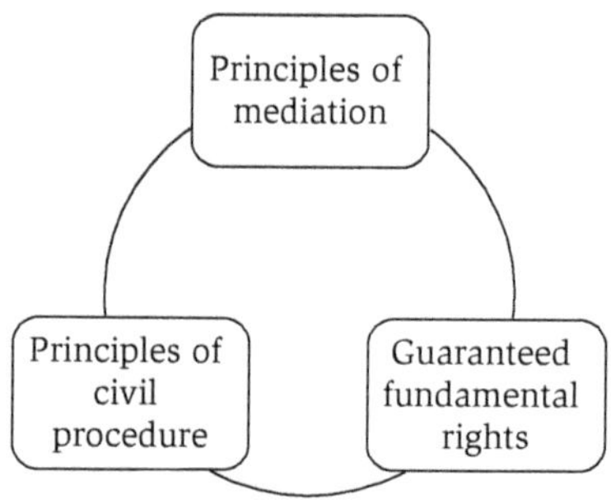

The concepts of mediation, civil procedure and constitutionally guaranteed fundamental rights are aimed at a specific objective and are built on certain principles that form their material basis. The word 'principle' is based on the Latin word '*principium*', which means a beginning, origin or basis. Principles thus form the basic premises, assumptions and starting points of any concept or theory, and should be distinguished from the objectives of concepts. While objectives represent the endpoints to be achieved in the development process, the principles of the process can be imagined as prerequisites or paths to achieve these objectives.

This chapter will be devoted to identifying the basic principles of potentially affected areas that may be impacted by coercion towards mediation, and examining the effect of obliging the parties to participate in mediation or attend an informational meeting with a mediator on these principles. The aim is to identify the degree of coercion towards mediation that can generally still be considered permissible so as not to constitute an insurmountable barrier to the normal functioning of the area. This means a degree of coercion that will not limit the principles of the concepts under examination to an extent that the objectives of concepts as their endpoints would no longer be achieved. In ensuring limits on coercion towards mediation, principles are used because specific rules may vary from one European country to another. However, principles, because of their generality, should play a unifying role across these states and predetermine the direction of legislation.

§7.01 PRINCIPLES OF MEDIATION (PRINCIPLE OF VOLUNTARINESS)

For some time now, mediation can no longer be seen as a uniform way of resolving disputes. Within mediation, various mediation styles[1] can be distinguished, which significantly predetermine the form of the mediation process. Each of these styles is built on specific principles, is characterised by certain mediation techniques and leads to the desired objective of the mediation style. Regardless of the differences outlined, however, basic principles common to all mediation styles can be identified. Charlton speaks of five basic philosophical foundations of mediation.[2] These are:

(1) voluntariness;
(2) confidentiality;
(3) empowerment;
(4) neutrality; and
(5) a unique solution.[3]

To proceed further, I start from the above paradigm: the principles of a particular concept are the basic premises and starting points. The aim of a concept is the endpoint to be achieved in a particular process. A principle can therefore be likened to a path that leads to the achievement of the objective of a particular concept. In this sense, the defined principles forming the material basis of the theory of mediation should always be faithfully mirrored in its legal regulation because the objectives of mediation can be achieved only by respecting these basic premises. If any of the assumptions put forward were to be tossed aside or unduly restricted, there is a risk that the original concept could be distorted because mediation would lose its characteristic form.

If we build on this paradigm and acknowledge that the basic objective of mediation is to reach an agreement,[4] or, depending on the chosen mediation style[5] and other circumstances, to reach, e.g., the satisfaction of the parties with the mediation process and the outcome of the conflict resolution or improvement of relations and

1. The best known mediation styles include facilitative mediation; evaluative mediation – *see*, e.g., Susan H. Blake, Julie Browne & Stuart Sime, *A Practical Approach to Alternative Dispute Resolution* 216–218 (Oxford University Press 2nd ed. 2012), Harold I. Abramson, *Mediation Representation* 101–102 (Oxford University Press 2nd ed. 2011); transformative mediation – Robert A. Baruch Bush & Joseph P. Folger, *The Promise of Mediation: Responding to Conflict Through Empowerment and Recognition* (Jossey-Bass 1994); and narrative mediation – John Winslade & Gerald D. Monk, *Narrative Mediation: A New Approach to Conflict Resolution* (Jossey-Bass 2000).
2. Ruth Charlton, *Dispute Resolution Guidebook* 14–15 (LBC Information Services 2000).
3. Other authors agree. *See* David Spencer & Michael Brogan, *Mediation Law and Practice* 85 (Cambridge University Press, 2006).
4. *See*, e.g., Directive 2008/52/EC of the European Parliament and of the Council of 21 May 2008 on certain aspects of mediation in civil and commercial matters (hereinafter 'EU Mediation Directive'), Art. 3. *See also* Stella Vettori, *Mandatory Mediation: An Obstacle to Access to Justice?*, 15 *African Human Rights Law Journal* 257 (2015). Blake, Browne & Sime, *supra* n. 1, at 200.
5. *See supra* n. 1.

communication between the parties to the dispute,[6] then we can understand the principles of mediation as tools through which such objectives can be achieved.

When confronted with possible coercion to participate in mediation, the principle of voluntariness may be the most affected of the five defined essential principles that guarantee mediation its characteristic form.[7] Voluntariness contributes to satisfaction with the process and the results of mediation, to higher settlement rates, and to better compliance with the agreement concluded.[8] It is this principle that is significantly reflected in the level of the permissible level of coercion and thus constitutes an important potential limit on the coercion of the parties to use mediation. However, in order to draw further conclusions, it is first of all appropriate to examine the principle of voluntariness in a broader context and try to define it theoretically. On the basis of the clarified content of the principle of voluntariness, its importance can then be inferred in legislative considerations on the appropriateness of specific measures or in further considerations concerning the setting up of a system of approach to mediation.

If we look at the etymological meaning of the word '*voluntariness*', it is clear that a certain will of the parties to resolve their dispute in mediation will be required - in a general sense this will be a consensus of the parties[9] - and that, on the contrary, involuntariness, or an element of a certain degree of coercion, will be inadmissible. However, it is not possible to infer the scope of application of the principle under examination from such a generalised definition. Thus, the subject of further research must be the extent of the required voluntariness, as it is not clear from the concept itself whether it is necessary to apply the principle of voluntariness fully in all phases of mediation or only in some of them in order to fulfil the characteristic objectives of mediation.

In the literature, a definition of the principle of voluntariness was attempted, for example, by Wolski.[10] Wolski originally defined it by the following four attributes:

(1) the parties' voluntary entry and participation in mediation;
(2) the absence of pressure to resolve the dispute;

6. *See*, e.g., Bush & Folger, *supra* n. 1, Winslade & Monk, *supra* n. 1.
7. Coercion towards mediation has some overlap with other principles of mediation, especially the principle of empowerment, under which the right to self-determination is also subsumed. Cf., e.g., Robert A. Baruch Bush & Joseph P. Folger, *Reclaiming Mediation's Future: Re-focusing on Party Self-Determination*, 16 Cardozo Journal of Conflict Resolution 742 (2014). *See also* Jacqueline Nolan-Haley, *Self-Determination in International Mediation: Some Preliminary Reflections*, 7 Cardozo Journal of Conflict Resolution 278–280 (2006). There is also an overlap to the principle of confidentiality. *See* Vettori, *supra* n. 4, at 358–359. This also entails the potential risk of misuse of information obtained in mediation by a disputant who is not in good faith in subsequent court proceedings. *See also* Dorcas Quek, *Mandatory Mediation: An Oxymoron? Examining the Feasibility of Implementing a Court-Mandated Mediation Program*, 11 Cardozo Journal of Conflict Resolution 492–493 (2010).
8. *See* Timothy Hedeen, *Coercion and Self-Determination in Court-Connected Mediation: All Mediations Are Voluntary, But Some Are More Voluntary than Others*, 26 Justice System Journal 275 (2005).
9. Spencer, Brogan, *supra* n. 3, at 87.
10. *See* Bobette Wolski, *Voluntariness and Consensuality: Defining Characteristics of Mediation?*, 15 Australian Bar Review 213–214 (1997).

(3) the parties define the subject matter and the form of the dispute outcome; and
(4) the ability of the parties to refuse to agree and the ability to accept or reject a particular outcome.

However, the thus defined pure conception of the principle of voluntariness was later revised by the author.[11] After a deeper examination of the cultural and historical context of mediation, Wolski began to distinguish degrees of voluntariness. She acknowledged there was a distinction between coercion into mediation and coercion within mediation.[12] While coercion into mediation is applied mainly before the mediation starts and is aimed at its commencement, coercion within mediation is applied when the mediation has already started and is aimed mainly at a successful conclusion of the mediation, that is, in most cases at the conclusion of a mediation agreement. Wolski reduced the principle of voluntariness to the parties' ability to accept or reject the outcome of the mediation, which is reflected in the lack of the mediator's power to decide authoritatively on the dispute. On the contrary, she does not subsume the entry of parties into mediation under the principle of voluntariness, as this is regularly associated with some form of coercion. Nor does she see as problematic the pressure on dispute resolution exerted by the mediator in his/her position of expert.

One can fully agree with the outlined view in relation to the aforementioned coercion within mediation. The principle of voluntariness should be preserved in the course of mediation. Coercion should not be used when the parties decide whether or not to continue with mediation nor in relation to their ability to accept or reject a particular solution to the dispute. Otherwise, the consensuality of the concept would be negated.[13] A related point is that private-law relationships are based on the principle of autonomy of will.[14] This is not procedural law, the public-law nature of which is, conversely, characterised by a third party acting in a position of authority deciding on the rights and obligations of the parties to disputes.[15] In mediation, the will of the parties to agree on a solution is therefore decisive. The mediator's pressure on dispute resolution and on the parties to remain in mediation can only be accepted to the extent that the pressure constitutes a mediation technique to promote an effective resolution of the dispute.[16] Pressure that exceeds this level (e.g., coercion to reach an agreement) is not acceptable.

In relation to the coercion into mediation, or the need to preserve the principle of voluntariness when initiating mediation, taking a clear position is more problematic. While such coercion does not usually prevent the parties from terminating mediation at any time after it has been initiated (thus preserving the imaginary cornerstone of the principle of voluntariness – the possibility to refuse to resolve the dispute or to accept

11. *Ibid.*, 227.
12. *See* also Hedeen, *supra* n. 8, at 275. Quek, *supra* n. 7, at 485. Sometimes also referred to as 'coercion to enter' and 'coercion to settle'. Cf. Vettori, *supra* n. 4, at 358.
13. *See* Ch. 3.
14. *See*, e.g., Beata Gessel-Kalinowska vel Kalisz, *The Legal, Real and Converged Interest in Declaratory Relief* Ch. 5 145, 177 (Kluwer Law International 2019).
15. *See* Ch. 7, §7.02[B][2].
16. Cf. Blake, Browne, Sime, *supra* n. 1, at 49.

a particular solution), it may, on the other hand, entail a potential risk of negatively affecting the concept of mediation and its success.

In a comparative perspective, several methods of coercion into mediation can be distinguished. Tools of coercion can be divided into direct and indirect ones. Tools of direct coercion aim directly at the initiation of mediation. In contrast, tools of indirect coercion are more likely to be factors motivating the parties to the dispute to initiate mediation.

Nelle defined basic forms of direct coercion through legal tools.[17] Among those relevant to the civil law legal culture, he includes coercion by:

- law (an obligation established by a generally binding rule);
- judicial decision (an obligation created by an individual legal act); and
- contract (an obligation created by the will of the parties, most often in the form of a mediation clause).

In addition, non-legal forms of coercion to initiate mediation can also be encountered.

Direct coercion is usually categorical or discretionary.[18] Categorical coercion is characterised by an across-the-board acting towards a predetermined set of cases. An example would be the imposition of a statutory obligation to initiate mediation prior to the filing of a motion to initiate proceedings in family matters. In contrast, discretionary coercion is based on the discretion of an entity to impose a duty on the parties to initiate mediation. For example, it may be a model in which a judge is empowered to impose an individualised duty to initiate mediation on litigants if certain conditions are met.

Indirect tools of coercion into mediation are not aimed at imposing an obligation to initiate mediation. Their purpose is primarily to encourage or support the parties to choose mediation as a means of dispute resolution themselves. The intensity of their actions varies. This group includes especially negative motivation tools – for example, penalising a party by not awarding the costs of proceedings if mediation is not attempted.[19] Last but not least, this includes imposing an obligation to attend an informational meeting with a mediator,[20] the purpose of which is to provide the parties with a qualified introduction to mediation and to offer them the possibility of resolving their dispute in mediation.

Tools of coercion into mediation should be used in such a way that they contribute to increasing the frequency of use of mediation, but at the same time do not unduly hinder the achievement of mediation objectives and do not reduce the success of mediation as a result of excessive coercion. The essence of mediation should therefore not be lost. In particular, mediation should not constitute inclusion of another step on the long way to access to justice, which will only bring the parties further delay

17. *See* Andreas Nelle, *Making Mediation Mandatory: A Proposed Framework*, 7 Ohio State Journal on Dispute Resolution 289 (1992).
18. Quek, *supra* n. 7, at 481.
19. *See* Ch. 6. §6.06.
20. *See* Ch. 6. §6.05[B].

in resolving the dispute and extra costs.[21] This may be particularly so in extreme forms of direct coercion in the form of mandatory mediation based on categorical, random ordering of mediation, disproportionate sanctions for refusal to mediate, and excessive supervision of participation in mediation.[22]

However, to a reasonable extent, coercion into mediation can be seen as encouragement and support to resolve the dispute in this way,[23] which gives the parties a real opportunity to overcome their prejudices against ADR.[24] It need not have a substantial negative effect on the form of mediation (e.g., it may be a tool of indirect coercion into mediation). Moore[25] reaches the same conclusion in other words: voluntary participation in mediation does not mean that there must not be certain pressure on the parties to try mediation, but this must not be confused with forcing the parties to reach an agreement. In considering how to set up a system of approach to mediation, it is therefore possible to build on a modified conception of the principle of voluntary mediation, that is, a conception in which there is room for a certain degree of coercion into mediation. However, in a particular system of approach to mediation applied in a particular state, this level should not exceed a boundary beyond which mediation would lose its form and cease to serve the characteristic objectives of this concept.

§7.02 GUARANTEED FUNDAMENTAL RIGHTS (RIGHT TO ACCESS TO COURT)

Initiatives to use mediation in the European context have so far been top-down, that is, in the form of legislative acts,[26] rather than from the bottom up, stemming from the will of the parties themselves.[27] Therefore, in some Member States, elements of coercion in relation to mediation are being incorporated into the legal order (in particular through the imposition of legal obligations) to increase the number of disputes resolved in mediation. At the extreme end of the spectrum is the introduction of mandatory mediation, a form of coercion in which participation in mediation is a condition for the admissibility of an action or in which the parties to disputes are obliged to participate in mediation in the course of court proceedings.[28] Its introduction, particularly in the

21. *See* Vettori, *supra* n. 4, at 357–358.
22. Quek, *supra* n. 7, at 490–492.
23. Hedeen, *supra* n. 8, at 278.
24. *See* Matthias Wendland, *Mediation und Zivilprozess: dogmatische Grundlagen einer allgemeinen Konfliktbehandlungslehre* 575 (Mohr Siebeck 2017).
25. *See* Christopher W. Moore, *The Mediation Process: Practical Strategies for Resolving Conflict* 20 (Jossey-Bass 3rd ed. 2003).
26. *See* Ch. 6, §6.02.
27. The parties to the dispute in some Member States are not even sufficiently informed of mediation. *See* Ch. 6, §6.07. This is also indicated by the low ratio of disputes settled in mediation to court disputes. *See* European Parliament, *Resolution on the Implementation of Directive 2008/52/EC of the European Parliament and of the Council on certain aspects of mediation in civil and commercial matters* (2016/2066(INI)), https://eur-lex.europa.eu/legal-content/EN/TXT/HTML/?uri=CELEX:52017IP0321&qid=1614194030734&from=EN.
28. *See* Ch. 6, §6.05[A].

European environment long oriented towards the protection of human rights, raises a number of questions, among the most important of which is the legal question of whether coercion towards mediation may constitute an unduly restriction of the right of access to court.

In this context, the principles guaranteed by the constitutional law of the Member States and other documents[29] may be considered another potential limit to coercion towards mediation, as they may be unduly interfered with by obligations imposed on the parties to the dispute to participate in mediation. Attention should be paid to the right of access to court, or to justice,[30] as coercion of the parties to participate in mediation or attend a different kind of meeting with a mediator may, in some jurisdictions, be a condition for the initiation (admissibility) of court proceedings or cause their stay for the duration of the mediation or a different kind of meeting with a mediator.[31]

The question of whether mediation can fulfil the right of access to justice has been debated in the literature. In fact, countless court systems are dealing with the problems of high costs, delays in proceedings and the associated uncertainty of the parties.[32] Depending on their intensity, these factors may lead to a limitation or even a denial of the right of access to justice. In such cases, mediation could be a way of overcoming these problems and ensuring access to justice.[33] In connection with this subject, opinions have been expressed that mediation is one of the ways to access justice as well as opinions that it is not, and that ADR, unlike civil justice, does not fulfil this right but, on the contrary, may even limit it.

[A] Right of Access to Justice Versus Right of Access to Court

In their study of access to justice,[34] Cappelletti and Garth presented three basic waves of a global legal reform. The third wave was intended to be a systematic reform of the legal system through greater access to justice primarily through ADR. This view is also shared by the EU, which in its documents[35] subordinates mediation to the concept of justice, specifically viewing it as an alternative form of justice.

On the other hand, there are also sceptical views. Genn points out that the civil justice system is a public good and that access to justice is linked to the concept of the

29. *See*, e.g., European Convention on Human Rights (ECHR) and Charter of Fundamental Rights of the European Union (EU Charter of Fundamental Rights).
30. *See* Art. 6 of the ECHR and Art. 47 of EU Charter of Fundamental Rights.
31. *See* systems of approach to mediation in Ch. 6.
32. *See*, e.g., European Union Agency for Fundamental Rights and Council of Europe, *Handbook on European law relating to access to justice* 111–148 (Publications Office of the European Union 2016).
33. *See* Vettori, *supra* n. 4, at 356.
34. Mauro Cappelletti & Bryant Garth, *Access to Justice: The Newest Wave in the Worldwide Movement to Make Rights Effective*, 27 Buffalo Law Review 222 (1978).
35. Cf., e.g., the preamble of the EU Mediation Directive, para 5. *See also* European Commission, *Green Paper on alternative dispute resolution in civil and commercial law*, COM (2002) 196 final, s. 1.2., https://eur-lex.europa.eu/legal-content/EN/TXT/HTML/?uri=CELEX:52002DC0196&from=EN.

rule of law. While it is often argued in the literature that, although ADR is private in nature, the shift of legal disputes away from litigation towards mediation is a strategy that actually increases access to justice, in Genn's view, the argument outlined requires closer examination. She believes that mediation does not contribute to access to courts and justice as mediation requires the parties to disputes to abandon the idea of rights and instead attempt to resolve a common problem. Mediation is merely a private dispute resolution process that results in an agreement between the parties, not a decision under public law.[36] Vettori stated the same in different wording.[37] The primary objective in mediation is dispute resolution, not justice. By contrast, in the civil court system, in Vettori's view, the primary objective is not dispute resolution but justice.

Critics further argue that mediation does not provide the procedural safeguards of a court and therefore offers 'second-class' justice.[38] This is particularly noticeable in cases of unequal bargaining power of the parties involved in mediation.[39] The argumentation outlined above is reinforced in some systems based on mandatory mediation, as in these systems, the parties are forced into a method of resolution lacking the procedural guarantees offered by a court. Moreover, in many cases, the parties have to pay for the mandatory mediation,[40] which may also have a negative impact on the property rights of the parties.

With respect to the arguments put forward by the opponents, it can be said that although mediation can be very effective in resolving a dispute, there is no guarantee that the dispute will always be resolved. It is well known that certain types of disputes are not suitable for mediation.[41] In civil court proceedings, by contrast, an authoritative decision on the merits, in accordance with the prohibition of *denegatio iustitiae*, is ensured in all cases. As Vettori states, while the focus of mediation is on agreement, the focus of the judicial process is on achieving justice. Where the parties do not have the will to resolve the dispute or there is no prospect of a successful resolution, mediation will not be an appropriate tool to resolve the dispute.[42] And it is the limited usability of mediation that may constitute an argument for not classifying it as a form of exercise of the right of access to justice.

---

36. *See* Hazel Genn, *What Is Civil Justice For? Reform, ADR, and Access to Justice*, 24 Yale Journal of Law & the Humanities 397, 411 (2012).
37. Vettori, *supra* n. 4, at 360.
38. Cf. Craig A. McEwen & Laura Williams, *Legal Policy and Access to Justice Through Courts and Mediation*, 13 Ohio State Journal on Dispute Resolution 865 (1998). *See also* Nadja Alexander, *Global Trends in Mediation: Riding the Third Wave* Ch. 1, 10 (Nadja Alexander ed., Kluwer Law International 2006).
39. *See* Lorna McGregor, *Alternative Dispute Resolution and Human Rights: Developing a Rights-Based Approach Through the ECHR*, 26 The European Journal of International Law 609 (2015).
40. *See* Alexander, *supra* n. 39, at 10.
41. *See*, e.g., Alex Bevan, Guy Hollebon & Lucinda Bromfield, *Mediation: A Practical Guide* 16–24 (Thorogood 2010).
42. Vettori, *supra* n. 4, at 357.

Alexander[43] distinguished between access to justice and access to the courts and further explained that access to justice[44] goes beyond the concept of access to the courts as it involves the ability of parties to overcome procedural, economic and organisational barriers to justice.[45] However, the conclusion that mediation does not fulfil the right of access to the courts is determinative of the limits on coercion towards mediation. This is evident both from the above arguments and from a simple glance at Article 6 of the European Convention on Human Rights (ECHR) or Article 47 of the EU Charter of Fundamental Rights and the related case law of the courts. It is clear from the wording that a narrower concept of access to justice is required, namely, access to court. It must be an independent and impartial court established by law, its judgments must be pronounced publicly, and other requirements specified in the case law must be met – in particular, requirements for the court and the judge, requirements for the proceedings or requirements for a reasonable length of proceedings.[46] It is clear that mediation does not meet the standards of an independent and impartial court, public hearing or other procedural safeguards and therefore cannot fulfil the public right of access to court under the cited obligations. On the contrary, it may constitute a factor that will limit this right. It is therefore necessary to further examine how the right of access to court limits the possibilities of coercion towards mediation.

[B] Coercion Towards Mediation as a Limit to the Right of Access to Court

Although mediation may contribute to access to justice, it does not meet the requirements of access to court. In such a case, mediation, or coercion to use mediation, may constitute a barrier to access to court. This may be manifested in a pressure to settle and a burden on the parties (costs of mediation, time spent in mediation, etc.). Several cases have already been dealt with in Europe in which coercion to mediate has been examined as a possible barrier to access to justice, at both a national and transnational level.

[1] Selected Cases in European Countries

[a] England

Mediation was no longer a novelty for England at the time Directive 2008/52/EC was issued.[47] The question of the use of mandatory mediation had already been discussed

43. Alexander, *supra* n. 39, at 9–10.
44. *See* European Commission, *supra* n. 36, p. 1.2. For possible inclusion of mediation under the concept of access to justice *see, e.g.*, McGregor, *supra* n. 40, at 626–634.
45. In her view, by using mediation, one can avoid a formally established judicial procedure, incurrence of costs of proceedings, etc.
46. *See* Ch. 7, §7.02[B], [2].
47. *See* Ch. 6, §6.01.

in the years following the introduction of a civil justice reform.[48] In England, a court cannot formally order parties to mediate without their consent. However, parties will often use mediation on their own or on the advice of counsel as they risk incurring costs if they refuse it without justification at the suggestion of the other party or the court. The court may stay the proceedings while mediation is taking place.[49]

The issue of the compatibility of the right of access to court and mandatory mediation was considered by the Court of Appeal in the joined cases of *Halsey v. Milton Keynes General NHS Trust* and *Steel v. Joy*.[50] In its decision, the Court concluded that requiring an unwilling party to mediate their dispute based on an imposed obligation violated the litigant's fundamental right of access to the courts under Article 6 of the ECHR.[51] The conclusion was reasoned by the fact that mandatory mediation would achieve nothing except increase the parties' costs, shift the time at which the court would conclude the proceedings and damage the perceived effectiveness of forms of ADR.[52]

In the already cited decision in the joined cases *Halsey v. Milton Keynes General NHS Trust* and *Steel v. Joy*, the Court of Appeal found, in light of the potential negative consequences of mandatory mediation in relation to the limitation of the right to a fair trial, that while forcing parties to engage in mediation is unacceptable, it is the role of the court to encourage the choice of mediation.[53] Accordingly, the court further held that parties, even successful litigants, that unreasonably withhold consent to mediation may be liable for the costs of proceedings. In the court's view, the burden is on the unsuccessful party to prove that there is an exception to the general rule that the unsuccessful party bears the costs.[54]

In the decision, the court provided a demonstrative list of factors that may be considered in determining whether a party's refusal to participate in mediation is justified:[55]

- the nature of the dispute;
- the merits of the case;
- other settlement methods have been attempted;
- the costs of mediation would be disproportionately high;
- delay;
- whether the mediation had a reasonable prospect of success.

---

48. *See* Genn, *supra* n. 37, at 407.
49. *See* Bill Marsh, Alexander Oddy & Jan O'Neill, *England and Wales* Ch. 9, 215–220 (Nadja Alexander, Sabine Walsh & Martin Svatoš, eds., Kluwer Law International 2017).
50. *Halsey v. Milton Keynes General NHS Trust* and *Steel v. Joy* [2004] EWCA Civ 576.
51. *Ibid.*, para. 9.
52. *Ibid.*, para. 10.
53. *Ibid.*, para. 11.
54. *Ibid.*, para. 13. *See also* Jacqueline M. Nolan-Haley, *Is Europe Headed down the Primrose Path with Mandatory Mediation?*, 37 North Carolina Journal of International Law and Commercial Regulation 1000 (2012).
55. *Halsey v. Milton Keynes General NHS Trust* and *Steel v. Joy* [2004] EWCA Civ 576, paras. 17–23.

However, in some subsequent decisions, the Court of Appeal expressed greater support for mediation. These included *Faidi v. Elliot Corporation*,[56] in which the Court of Appeal expressed dismay that the parties to a neighbour dispute had not attempted to resolve the dispute in mediation, or *Wright v. Michael Wright Supplies Ltd & Anor*,[57] in which the Court of Appeal asked whether it was time to reconsider the conclusion of *Halsey v. Milton Keynes General NHS Trust* and *Steel v. Joy* regarding breach of Article 6 of the ECHR.

[b] Italy

One of the countries where mandatory mediation was introduced across the board in a wide range of civil disputes was Italy.[58] This 2011 legislative change was mainly justified by the overload of Italian courts, which were faced with a backlog of almost six million civil cases.[59] However, shortly after the introduction of mediation, the Italian Constitutional Court abolished the provision requiring initiation of mediation as a condition for the admissibility of a lawsuit in 2012.[60] However, the reason for the abolition of the set model was not the unconstitutionality of the established concept of compulsory mediation but the lack of power of the government to issue an act regulating this procedure.[61] In 2013, the obligation was reintroduced, but this time in the form of a law, and it was directed only to participation in an informational meeting with a mediator operating on an opt-out basis. After the meeting, the potential plaintiff did not have to continue mediation and the condition for filing a lawsuit was fulfilled.[62]

[c] Romania

Romania was another country to introduce a general obligation related to the use of mediation. This was on the basis of Act No. 115/2012 amending the Romanian Mediation Act.[63] The amendment introduced a system of general (across-the-board) mandatory attendance at informational meetings with a mediator. It was therefore not an attempt to resolve the dispute through mediation itself but a mandatory meeting between the parties to the dispute with a mediator, with the purpose of explaining the benefits of mediation.[64] The sanction for not attending the meeting was a subsequent inadmissibility of the action. The change sparked debate about a possible restriction of

56. *Faidi v. Elliot Corporation* [2012] EWCA Civ 287.
57. *Wright v. Michael Wright Supplies Ltd & Anor* [2013] EWCA Civ 243, para. 3.
58. *See* Decreto legislativo 4 marzo 2010, n. 28. *See also* Ch. 6, § 6.05 [A], [1].
59. Cf., e.g., Nolan-Haley, *supra* n. 55, at 982.
60. *See* Carlo Mastellone & Laura Ristori, *Chapter 17: Italy* 469–470 (Nadja Alexander, Sabine Walsh, Martin Svatoš eds., Kluwer Law International 2017).
61. *See* Martin Svatoš, *Mandatory Mediation Strikes Back*, Mediate.com (November 2013), https://www.mediate.com/articles/SvatosM1.cfm.
62. *See* Mastellone & Ristori, *supra* n. 61, at 465–492. The Court of Justice of the EU has also commented on this system in terms of fundamental rights; *see* below §7[B][2].
63. Act No. 192 of 16 May 2006.
64. *See* Constantin-Adi Gavrila & Christian Radu Chereji, *Don't rush*, Mediate.com (February 2015), https://www.mediate.com/articles/CherejiGavrilaFutures.cfm.

the right of access to court. A later amendment No. 214/2013 extended the authorisation to carry out informational procedures to judges, attorneys and notaries. The matter was eventually considered by the Romanian Constitutional Court, which concluded that the obligation to attend informational sessions and the sanctions in the form of inadmissibility of the action limited the constitutionally protected plaintiff's right of access to court.[65]

In its decision,[66] the Constitutional Court concluded that this established procedure not only restricted the right of access to court but also denied it. The plaintiff is not given the opportunity to decide whether or not they need the information provided. Any restriction of the right of access to court must be justified and analysed to determine whether the possible disadvantages outweigh the advantages of the measure. Therefore, the Constitutional Court considered the mandatory information procedure on the benefits of mediation an obstacle to claiming rights in court. Moreover, it held that Directive 2008/52/EC only stipulates that the parties have a possibility, not an obligation to use mediation and that the introduced system of provision of information on mediation rebuts the presumption *nemo censetur ignorare legem*, that is, that ignorance of the law excuses no one.

[d] Summary

It can be concluded from the above examples and attitudes towards the imposition of obligations in relation to mandatory mediation or other related obligations that this is a topical issue in the European context that Member States are facing and will probably continue to face in the future. It can be inferred that mediation in the European environment continues to be a new phenomenon which is difficult to integrate, in the legislative process, into the concept of civil procedural law or generally settlement of private-law disputes. There is no settled opinion as to whether mediation should be a full-fledged part of the system of access to justice or merely an aid for resolving disputes outside that system to which reference can ideally be made in certain cases.

[2] Supranational Level

Cases of conflict between the right of access to court and the obligation to participate in mediation or an information meeting with a mediator (or another kind of ADR) have already been addressed at the supranational and EU level in the case law of the Court of Justice of the European Union (CJEU) and, marginally, of the European Court of Human Rights.

The right of access to court according to the case law of these courts is not absolute and can therefore be limited.[67] However, the relevant question is to what

---

65. *See* Constantin-Adi Gavrila & Sanda Elena Lungu, *Chapter 26: Romania* 641 (Nadja Alexander, Sabine Walsh, Martin Svatoš eds., Kluwer Law International 2017).
66. Decision No. 266 of the Romanian Constitutional Court of 7 May 2014.
67. European Union Agency for Fundamental Rights and Council of Europe, *supra* n. 33, at 28.

extent. The assessment of the conflict between coercion to settle a dispute out of court and the right of access to court has already been addressed by the CJEU in its judgment of 18 March 2021, C317/08 to C320/08, in the case *Rosalba Alassini and Others v. Telecom Italia SpA*.[68] In that case, the issue was whether it was possible to bring an action in a situation where the plaintiffs in the original proceedings had not first made the obligatory attempt to settle the dispute out of court.[69]

The conflict between coercion to mediate and the right of access to court was later addressed by the CJEU in its judgment of 14 June 2017, C75/16, in the case *Menini and Rampanelli v. Banco Popolare Società Cooperativa*.[70] In the case at hand, the Italian banking institution sought an order for payment against L. Menini and M. A. Rampanelli for an amount corresponding to the value owed to it by them under a contract concluded for the purpose of opening a current account. The debtors opposed the order. However, under the national law applicable *ratione temporis*, such opposition proceedings were admissible only on the condition that the parties had attempted to resolve the dispute in mediation prior to those proceedings.[71]

In that case, the CJEU explained that mediation may be initiated by the parties to disputes or may be proposed or ordered by a court, but it may also be provided for by the law of a Member State. Therefore, national legislation making the use of mediation compulsory need not be assessed as inappropriate. The Court pointed out that the voluntary nature of mediation does not lie in the freedom of the parties to use such proceedings but in the fact that the parties are responsible for them, can organise them as they wish and can terminate them at any time.[72] The CJEU has previously held that such an 'additional stage of access to court' may also pursue legitimate objectives of general interest such as speedy and low-cost resolution of disputes as well as reducing the burden on the courts.[73] This applies, however, on the condition that such legislation does not prevent the parties from exercising their right of access to court. It is not important whether the mediation system is compulsory or optional but what matters is that the parties' right of access to court is preserved.[74]

The CJEU has therefore reached the same conclusion that I have reached on the basis of theoretical considerations.[75] The imposition of an obligation to mediate, although generally pursuing the common interest, does not fulfil the right of access to court but may, on the contrary, restrict it.

68. Court of Justice of the EU, Joined Cases C317/08 to C320/08, *Rosalba Alassini v. Telecom Italia SpA, Filomena Califano v. Wind SpA, Lucia Anna Giorgia Iacono v. Telecom Italia SpA* and *Multiservice Srl v. Telecom Italia SpA*, 18 Mar. 2010.
69. *Ibid.*, paras 18–20.
70. Court of Justice of the EU, C75/16, *Livio Menini and Maria Antonia Rampanelli v. Banco Popolare – Società Cooperativa*, 14 Jun. 2017, paras 63–65.
71. *Ibid.*, paras 19–25.
72. *Ibid.*, paras 49–52.
73. Court of Justice of the EU, Joined Cases C317/08 to C320/08, *Rosalba Alassini v. Telecom Italia SpA, Filomena Califano v. Wind SpA, Lucia Anna Giorgia Iacono v. Telecom Italia SpA* and *Multiservice Srl v. Telecom Italia SpA*, 18 Mar. 2010, paras 62, 64.
74. *Ibid.*, paras. 49–51.
75. *See* §7.02 [A].

Moreover, the CJEU set out conditions under which the operation of mandatory mediation does not exceed a reasonable degree of restriction of the right of access to court and the principle of effective judicial protection is preserved:[76]

– Mediation must not lead to a decision that is binding on the parties

Quasi-judicial procedures can provide a less formal, faster and cheaper alternative to court proceedings. However, non-judicial bodies do not in principle have the power to issue decisions binding on the parties to the dispute.[77] In the view of the European Court of Human Rights, non-judicial bodies can be considered a court if they perform judicial functions and provide the procedural guarantees required by Article 6 of the ECHR.[78] In addition to the power to issue binding decisions, the essential characteristics of a court are usually considered to be independence,[79] impartiality,[80] establishment by law,[81] competence to decide[82] and sometimes a statutory judge (not a random assignment of a judge to a case).[83] In the case law of the CJEU, we find as basic conditions the legal basis of the authority, its permanence, the binding nature of its jurisdiction, contentious nature of the proceedings, application of the law by the authority as well as its independence.[84] If the non-judicial body does not meet these criteria, it must be subject to the supervision of a judicial body which has full jurisdiction and meets the requirements of Article 6 of the ECHR or Article 47 of the EU Charter of Fundamental Rights.[85]

– Mediation does not lead to a substantial delay in bringing the action to court

Justice delayed may be justice denied.[86] As noted above, the right of access to court is not absolute. It may therefore be restricted to some extent.[87] However, such a

76. Court of Justice of the EU, Joined Cases C317/08 to C320/08, *Rosalba Alassini v. Telecom Italia SpA, Filomena Califano v. Wind SpA, Lucia Anna Giorgia Iacono v. Telecom Italia SpA* and *Multiservice Srl v. Telecom Italia SpA*, 18 Mar. 2010, para. 61.
77. European Union Agency for Fundamental Rights and Council of Europe, *supra* n. 33, at 49.
78. *Ibid. See* also European Court of Human Rights, *Oleksandr Volkov v. Ukraine*, No. 21722/11, 9 Jan. 2013, paras 88–91.
79. *See* European Court of Human Rights, *Bryan v. the United Kingdom*, No. 19178/91, 22 Nov. 1995, paras 88–91. *See also* European Union Agency for Fundamental Rights and Council of Europe, *supra* n. 33, at 35–37.
80. *See* European Court of Human Rights, *Kyprianou v. Cyprus*, No. 73797/01, 15 Dec. 2005, para. 119. *See* also European Union Agency for Fundamental Rights and Council of Europe, *supra* n. 33, at 37–39.
81. Cf., e.g., European Court of Human Rights, *Findlay v. the United Kingdom*, No. 22107/93, 25 Feb. 1997.
82. European Court of Human Rights, *Sramek v. Austria*, No. 8790/79, 22 Oct. 1984, para. 36.
83. European Court of Human Rights, *DMD Group, a. s. v. Slovakia*, No. 19334/03, 5 Oct. 2010.
84. Cf., e.g., Court of Justice of the EU, *Synetairismos Farmakopoion Aitolias & Akarnanias (Syfait) and Others v. GlaxoSmithKline plc, GlaxoSmithKline AEVE, formerly Glaxowellcome AEVE*, No. C-53/03, 31 May 2005, para. 29.
85. European Union Agency for Fundamental Rights and Council of Europe, *supra* n. 33, at 49.
86. Cf., e.g., European Court of Human Rights, *Papachelas v. Greece*, No. 31423/96, 25 Mar. 1999, partly concurring and partly dissenting opinion of Judge Zupančič. European Court of Human Rights, *Doroshenko v. Ukraine*, No. 1328/04, 26 May 2011, partly dissenting opinion of judge Yudkivska joined by Judge Zupančič.
87. Cf., e.g., European Court of Human Rights, *Harrison Mckee v. Hungary*, No. 22840/07, 3 Jun. 2014.

restriction, in the form of an obligation to attend mediation or a different kind of meeting with a mediator, either before the initiation of the court proceedings as a condition for the hearing of the case or during the court proceedings, must meet certain criteria. The restriction must have a legitimate aim, be PDR and not undermine the very essence of the right of access to court.[88] In the above-mentioned case of *Rosalba Alassini v. Telecom Italia SpA*,[89] the CJEU found Italian measures conditioning the admissibility of an action on an out-of-court attempt at settlement to be legitimate and PDR as they were aimed at a quicker and cheaper amicable settlement of the dispute and at relieving the overburdened Italian judicial system.

– Mediation stays the limitation period of the rights in question

If an attempt to resolve the dispute in mediation fails, the parties to the dispute should have the option of going to court or using arbitration. This procedure should not be prevented by the legal rules on limitation or prescription of the rights in question.[90] For this reason, the Member States should ensure that parties which choose mediation in an attempt to settle a dispute are not prevented from later initiating court or arbitration proceedings on the same matter by the lapse of the limitation or prescription period during the mediation procedure.[91] That measure is, *inter alia*, a protection against feigned negotiation, that is, a situation where a party to a dispute participates in mediation only to cause lapse of the limitation or prescription periods for the rights in question and inability of the other party to successfully assert those rights in court after the unsuccessful termination of mediation.

– Mediation does not result in costs for the parties or its costs are insignificant for the parties

Just as the right of access to court may be unduly restricted by disproportionately high court fees,[92] an obstacle to access to court may also be an obligation to pay disproportionate costs for ordered mediation or a different kind of meeting with a mediator.

– Electronic form is not the only way of accessing mediation

E-justice is a concept based on the use of electronic means (videoconferencing, email, electronic payment order, etc.) to increase the efficiency of court proceedings and facilitate access to justice.[93] However, it cannot be assumed that every individual has

88. European Union Agency for Fundamental Rights and Council of Europe, *supra* n. 33, at 113.
89. Court of Justice of the EU, Joined Cases C-317/08 to C-320/08, *Rosalba Alassini v. Telecom Italia SpA, Filomena Califano v. Wind SpA, Lucia Anna Giorgia Iacono v. Telecom Italia SpA* and *Multiservice Srl v. Telecom Italia SpA*, 18 Mar. 2010, paras 63–65.
90. EU Mediation Directive, para. 24.
91. *Ibid.*, Art. 8.
92. *See* European Union Agency for Fundamental Rights and Council of Europe, *supra* n. 33, at 117–119. *See also* Court of Justice of the EU, C530/11, *European Commission v. the United Kingdom of Great Britain and Northern Ireland*, 13 Feb. 2014.
93. European Union Agency for Fundamental Rights and Council of Europe, *supra* n. 33, at 177–178.

access to the internet and the necessary technology. In view of this, the CJEU states that procedures should not be accessible only through electronic means.[94]

– In exceptional cases where the urgency of the situation so requires, preliminary rulings may be issued

A preliminary ruling is a means of protection of rights used to provisionally regulate circumstances or to avert harm caused by the impossibility of future successful execution.[95] Its purpose is thus to ensure the effectiveness of judicial protection. In cases where the parties to the dispute are forced to participate in mediation instead of court proceedings, it is appropriate that a party to the dispute whose rights or satisfaction may be jeopardised during the mediation should be allowed to protect their rights in this way during that period.[96]

The conditions thus defined can be understood as particular manifestations of limitation of coercion of the parties to use mediation. However, the set-up of each system of approach to mediation in a given state will need to be examined individually and in a broader context. Courts will generally weigh conflicting principles and values in each particular case.

In the same way as making participation in mediation a prerequisite for the admissibility of an action, in relation to the right of access to court, it may also imply a limitation of the right of access to court by suspending the ongoing court proceedings. The court may stay the proceedings in connection with the ordering of mediation or an informational meeting with a mediator. This will be particularly problematic in cases where the parties to the dispute do not agree with this procedure. This may result in delays in the proceedings and unnecessary costs. The assessment of such cases should always be carried out comprehensively, that is, in the light of the specific circumstances of the case. There is greater space for staying proceedings in family-law cases, for example. According to the European Court of Human Rights, mediation can be an effective tool for the implementation of the rights protected by Article 8 of the ECHR.[97] Therefore, the fulfilment of the right stipulated in Article 8 of the ECHR could compensate for the limitation of the right of access to court in Article 6 of the ECHR in these cases. A different view should probably be taken especially in cases where there is an unreasonably long stay of the proceedings for the purpose of carrying out mediation or familiarisation with mediation with which the parties to the dispute do not agree, and it is already apparent before the stay that the dispute will not or cannot be resolved in mediation.

---

94. Court of Justice of the EU, Joined Cases C317/08 to C320/08, *Rosalba Alassini v. Telecom Italia SpA, Filomena Califano v. Wind SpA, Lucia Anna Giorgia Iacono v. Telecom Italia SpA* and *Multiservice Srl v. Telecom Italia SpA*, 18 Mar. 2010, para. 67.
95. Cf. Peter L. Murray & Rolf Stürner, *German Civil Justice* 433–442 (Carolina Academic Press 2004).
96. Court of Justice of the EU, Joined Cases C317/08 to C320/08, *Rosalba Alassini v. Telecom Italia SpA, Filomena Califano v. Wind SpA, Lucia Anna Giorgia Iacono v. Telecom Italia SpA* and *Multiservice Srl v. Telecom Italia SpA*, 18 Mar. 2010, paras 59–60.
97. European Court of Human Rights, *Kacper Nowakowski v. Poland*, No. 32407/13, 10 Jan. 2017.

Beyond the above, the property rights of the parties to the dispute protected by Article 1 of the Protocol to the ECHR or Article 17 of the EU Charter of Fundamental Rights can be seen as a limit to coercion to mediate. These may be limited in particular if the parties are forced to use mediation they have to pay for themselves, and unlike in court proceedings, there is no possibility of fee exemption.

§7.03 PRINCIPLES OF CIVIL PROCEDURE

Another area in which limits to the possible coercion of parties to private-law disputes to use mediation can be sought is civil procedure. Mediation and civil procedure are two separate methods of dispute resolution. While mediation is based on consensus and cooperation between the parties to disputes[98] and usually leads to the conclusion of a mediation agreement,[99] in civil procedure, the court makes an authoritative decision on the subject matter of the dispute[100] and issues a binding decision on the parties.[101] In practice, however, the two methods of dispute resolution may be intertwined, precisely when imposing obligations aimed at the use of mediation in the course of civil procedure.[102] Such imposition of obligations, however, carries the risk of limiting the fundamental principles underlying the concept of civil procedure. For this reason, it is appropriate to examine whether, or to what extent, coercion into mediation can be used to interfere in this area.

As the vast majority of the legal systems of the Member States are currently based on civil law,[103] the following text will focus on the functioning of civil procedure in the civil law legal system. The legal and social function of civil procedure in many states whose legal system is based on civil law is to re-establish or preserve the legal peace.[104] In this system, civil procedure thus represents a means of ensuring the prevention of arbitrariness (self-help), which may otherwise disturb the social order.[105] In practice, this function is fulfilled primarily by the state providing a procedure in which a right or obligation is declared or constituted (trial proceedings) and, where applicable, subsequent enforcement by power (enforcement proceedings).[106]

To set limits in civil procedure in relation to the imposition of the obligation to mediate or to attend an informational meeting with a mediator, it is possible – in a generalised perspective of the functioning of civil procedure in civil law – to build on

98. *See* Vettori, *supra* n. 4, at 358. *See also* Ch. 3.
99. *See*, e.g., Henry J. Brown & Arthur L. Marriott, *ADR: Principles and Practice* 143–149 (Sweet and Maxwell 1993).
100. *See* Walter H. Rechberger, *Civil Procedure in Austria* 16 (Kluwer Law International 2nd ed. 2016).
101. *Ibid.*, 49–52.
102. Cf. Ch. 6, §6.05 [A].
103. The common-law legal system is used in Ireland and partially also in a former Member State, Great Britain. Cf. American Law Institute & International Institute for the Unification of Private Law, *Principles of Transnational Civil Procedure* 5–6 (Cambridge University Press 2006).
104. *See* Konstanze Plett, *Civil Justice and Its Reform in West Germany and the United States*, 13 Justice System Journal 197 (1988). *See also* Rechberger, *supra* n. 101, at 16.
105. *Ibid.*
106. Murray & Stürner, *supra* n. 96, at 4.

the rule that once civil procedure has been initiated, the court proceeds in it without further motions[107] in order to hear and decide the case as quickly as possible.[108] In doing so, it seeks primarily to resolve the dispute amicably.[109] This set-up suggests that, when examining the limits in the context of the principles of civil procedure, it will be necessary to focus on three aspects in particular:

(1) the disposition principle and the ex officio procedure of the court;
(2) the principle of preference of an amicable dispute settlement; and
(3) the principle of procedural economy.

[A] The Disposition Principle and the Ex Officio Procedure of the Court

The disposition principle (referred to as *Dispositionsmaxime* in German and Austrian legal theory) and – its opposite – the principle of officiality answer the question of who initiates civil proceedings, defines their subject matter and may dispose of the proceedings and their subject matter.[110] The application of the disposition principle is characteristic of contentious proceedings, in which the parties to the dispute have the status of mutual opponents (adversarial status). In these proceedings governed by the disposition principle, the parties to the dispute have the power to decide on the issues outlined above.[111] This does not apply to non-contentious proceedings, as is often the case in the civil procedural law of European civil law states, for example, in succession proceedings, guardianship proceedings, proceedings concerning custody of minors or proceedings concerning commercial registers.[112] In those proceedings, the parties are not adversarial[113] and the public interest prevails.[114] In such proceedings, the court may exercise wider control over the definition of the subject matter of the proceedings and their initiation and termination.[115]

The disposition principle, which applies principally in contentious proceedings, is manifested by the fact that the parties are granted the power to dispose of the contents and course of the proceedings as a whole.[116] Given that it is up to each

107. Rechberger, *supra* n. 101, at 19.
108. Murray & Stürner, *supra* n. 96, at 165.
109. Murray & Stürner, *supra* n. 96, at 153.
110. Murray & Stürner, *supra* n. 96, at 154–157. *See also* Jiří Valdhans, David Sehnálek & Petr Lavický, *Evidence in Civil Law – Czech Republic* 1–2 (Lex localis 2016). Rechberger, *supra* n. 101, at 18.
111. Murray & Stürner, *supra* n. 96, at 156.
112. *See* Murray & Stürner, *supra* n. 96, at 442–443. *See also* Juan Montero Aroca et al., *Derecho jurisdiccional II: Proceso civil* 776 (Tirant Lo Blanch 17th ed. 2019).
113. Murray & Stürner, *supra* n. 96, at 157.
114. Alan Uzelac, *Goals of Civil Justice and Civil Procedure in the Contemporary World* Ch. 1, 17 (Alan Uzelac ed., Springer 2014).
115. Murray & Stürner, *supra* n. 96, at 157.
116. The disposition principle is applied in civil contentious proceedings across Member States' legal systems based on civil law. *See*, e.g., Germany – Murray & Stürner, *supra* n. 96, at 156–158; Austria – Rechberger, *supra* n. 101, at 18–19; Czech Republic – Alena Winterová, Alena Macková et al., *Civilní právo procesní* 75–77 (Leges 9th ed. 2018); *see also* Valdhans, Sehnálek & Lavický, *supra* n. 111, at 1–2; Polsko – Joanna Studzińska & Paweł Cioch, *Poste*

individual to decide whether and how to exercise their rights, this autonomy must also enable them to decide freely whether or not to use the relevant institutions of the state judicial system. Their freedom, however, only concerns the contents, initiation, course and termination, not the structural design of civil procedure and its principles. Once they have decided to select a certain procedure, they must comply with the relevant principles and 'rules of the game' for the procedure laid down in the Code of Civil Procedure.[117]

At first glance, in contentious proceedings associated with the disposition principle, it may seem inappropriate for the court to order mediation or an informative meeting with a mediator and to stay the proceedings for this purpose without a motion by the parties. In contrast, in non-contentious proceedings governed by the principle of officiality, and particularly in proceedings concerning custody of minors,[118] it seems to be considerably less problematic to order the parties to attend mediation or to meet with a mediator because it is the court that disposes of the proceedings.

However, this view can be somewhat confusing. Not only in non-contentious proceedings but also in phases of contentious proceedings that do not depend on the dispositive acts of the parties, the court proceeds ex officio, that is, of its own motion.[119] This is sometimes referred to as the judge's duty to structure the proceedings.[120] According to this theory, the judge is to conduct the proceedings in accordance with the procedural rules even in the absence of motions by the parties to the dispute so that the case is heard and decided as quickly as possible.[121] Given that the ordering of mediation or an informational meeting with a mediator does not change the subject matter of the proceedings, the imposition of such an obligation could be seen more as a procedure of the court in the proceedings that as such does not violate the disposition principle in civil procedure.

On the other hand, it should be taken into account that ordering mediation or an informational meeting with a mediator may limit the parties' ability to dispose of the proceedings – the proceedings should generally be stayed by the court for the duration of the mediation or informational meeting, which may already appear to be in tension with the disposition principle. Moreover, in its ex officio activity, the court should (*de lege ferenda*) aim to hear and decide the case within the civil proceedings in question

---

powanie cywilne 70 (C.H. Beck 5th ed. 2017); *see also* Katarzyna Bagan-Kurluta, Piotr Konrad Fiedorczyk, *Evidence in Civil Law – Poland* 1-3 (Lex localis 2015); Spain – Sonia Calaza López, *Principios rectores del proceso judicial español*, 6 Revista de Derecho UNED 61-63 n. 8 (2011); *see also* Núria Mallandrich Miret, *Evidence in Civil Law – Spain* 2 (Lex localis 2015); France – Martin Oudin, *Evidence in Civil Law – France* 1-2 (Lex localis 2015), etc.

117. Wendland, *supra* n. 25, at 600.
118. Moreover, this may be underlined by the purpose of proceedings aimed at protecting the interests of the child.
119. American Law Institute & International Institute for the Unification of Private Law, *supra* n. 104, at 6. *See also* Uzelac, *supra* n. 115, at 17-18. Christian Koller, *Civil Justice in Austrian-German Tradition* Ch. 2 44 (Alan Uzelac ed., Springer 2014).
120. Murray & Stürner, *supra* n. 96, at 165.
121. *Ibid.* The judge's duty to structure the proceedings includes preparation of the hearing, setting the date of the hearing, managing the course of evidence taking, proposing a settlement, etc.

rather than referring the parties to other dispute resolution procedures, especially against their will.

Nevertheless, it can be taken into account that, if used appropriately, mediation is a procedure that can contribute to an early conclusion of the case by concluding a court settlement or, alternatively, withdrawing the action if the parties to the dispute are satisfied with the mediation agreement. This is also close to the social concept of civil procedure,[122] which is characterised by strengthening of judicial power and limitation of the freedom of the parties so that the court can actively intervene in the course of the proceedings, although its normal task is not to order the use of another method of dispute resolution. According to this view, civil procedure should not only serve to promote the individual interests of the parties and the dispute should not be regarded as a private matter of the parties in which the state should not interfere. The aim of civil procedure should also be to implement social objectives.[123] Therefore, although the court's duty to proceed ex officio to hear and decide the case may be interfered with and the disposition principle limited, it may be a limitation that is proportionate to the priority given to other values and principles.

Civil procedure should be understood in a broader social context. It is intended to contribute to the protection of not only the legal peace but also the social peace. It may therefore be considered that the dispositional principle need not in certain cases create difficulties when mediation or a meeting with a mediator is ordered, or that this principle need not necessarily be unduly restricted by the imposition of such obligations. The situation would be different, however, if coercion towards mediation in this form would not serve its purpose; that is, mediation or different kinds of meetings would be overused, ordered in inappropriate cases, would lead to delays in proceedings due to the low success rate, etc. In such cases, the court would not proceed in such a way as to guide the proceedings towards a decision (here, the conclusion of a settlement) and the disposition principle could be unduly restricted and the court's ex officio procedure undermined. Conceptually, it is not common for a civil court to order parties to use another dispute resolution method against their will.

[B] The Principle of Preference of an Amicable Dispute Settlement

In the theory of civil procedural law, the preference for an amicable dispute settlement is not usually explicitly formulated as a principle, although this requirement can usually be identified in legal regulations. It follows, for example, from the Principles of Transnational Civil Procedure.[124] The literature also often explicitly refers to the obligation of courts to guide the parties towards settlement.[125] The preference for an

122. Uzelac, *supra* n. 115, at 26.
123. Uzelac, *supra* n. 115, at 6, 26.
124. American Law Institute & International Institute for the Unification of Private Law, *supra* n. 104, at 44–45.
125. Murray & Stürner, *supra* n. 96, at 486. *See also* Koller, *supra* n. 120, at 53.

amicable outcome can be seen as beneficial not only economically[126] but also socially.[127]

The court should seek settlement at all stages of civil procedure.[128] The court may also structure the proceedings in order to encourage the parties to reach a settlement.[129] Nevertheless, one can agree with the view that the parties should not be forced into settlement.[130] This position, however, is not always negated by the nature of the obligation imposed to enter into mediation or to attend an informational meeting with a mediator.[131] The parties are encouraged to familiarise themselves with mediation and also with the advantages and the environment in which they can resolve their dispute consensually. However, after this familiarisation, they have the option not to initiate or continue mediation and proceed with court proceedings instead. The parties are thus only encouraged by the common authority, which in this case is the court, to resolve the dispute amicably, which can be seen as a procedure consistent with the aforementioned principle of civil procedure, provided that the measure serves its purpose, that is, that it is an effective measure for achieving amicable settlements.

[C] The Principle of Procedural Economy

Another principle of civil procedural law undoubtedly not irrelevant for the assessment of the appropriateness of a measure relating to coercion towards mediation is the principle of procedural economy. This principle is intended to ensure the effective protection of rights in civil proceedings.[132] In accordance with this principle, the court should proceed in civil proceedings in such a way as to deal with the dispute not only thoroughly but also in the shortest possible time.[133] In addition to the speed of proceedings, the principle of procedural economy also implies that the lowest possible costs should be incurred in the course of the proceedings.[134] These aspects can also be

---

126. Conclusion of an amicable settlement is usually economically advantageous for the parties to the dispute as well as to the state. Cf. Michael Berlemann & Robin Christmann, *Determinants of in-Court Settlements: Empirical Evidence from a German Trial Court,* 15 Journal of Institutional Economics 143–162 (2019).
127. An amicable settlement contributes in particular to creating a culture of amicable dispute resolution and to holding litigants socially accountable by leaving the responsibility for resolving the dispute in their hands. *See*, e.g., Neil Andrews, *The Modern Civil Process: Judicial and Alternative Forms of Dispute Resolution in England* 193 (Mohr Siebeck 2008). *See also* Ch. 4.
128. Murray & Stürner, *supra* n. 96, at 487.
129. *Ibid.*, 492.
130. American Law Institute & International Institute for the Unification of Private Law, *supra* n. 104, at 44–45. *See also* Murray & Stürner, *supra* n. 96, at 490.
131. *See* § 7.01. Coercion within mediation or coercion to conclude a mediation agreement is not permissible.
132. Koller, *supra* n. 120, at 44.
133. Murray & Stürner, *supra* n. 96, at 165.
134. *Ibid.*, 613–614. *See also* Lucie Zavadilová, *The Principle of Procedural Economy in the Context of the Taking of Evidence in the European Area of Justice* 1106–1108 (Eva Kovářová, Lukáš Melecký & Michaela Staníčková eds. 2016).

drawn from the documents guaranteeing fundamental rights.[135] Coercion towards mediation can have an impact on the length and cost of court proceedings.

At first glance, it could seem that imposing an obligation to enter into mediation or to attend a different kind of meeting with a mediator will generally make the court proceedings more expensive (i.e., incur additional costs, in particular payment to the mediator) and longer. This may be the case if the parties decide not to initiate mediation after the initial meeting or if mediation is not successful.[136] If mediation does not result in an agreement, it will often be an extra step on the path to the goal.[137] This may be the case if mediation is ordered across the board.[138] In these cases, one can speak of limiting the principle of procedural economy.

On the other hand, if mediation is successful, the dispute can be resolved significantly cheaper and faster than if the court proceedings continued, including any subsequent appeals. In order to maintain some proportionality between procedural economy and the pursuit of an amicable settlement, it is therefore desirable to monitor and examine more closely the rate of dispute resolution in mediation and the effectiveness of mandatory mediation in a given state.[139] In particular, the success rate of mediation will determine its impact on the cost-effectiveness of the proceedings.

§7.04 PARTIAL CONCLUSION

The analysis conducted has shown that forcing parties to civil disputes to mediate has its limits. These limits have been identified in three basic areas that may be negatively impacted by imposition of an obligation to initiate mediation or attend an informational meeting with a mediator, primarily by compromising the value or principle underlying the examined concept.

However, the presented limits define only the framework within which legal regulation of coercion towards mediation can operate so as not to limit the principles of mediation in question, constitutionally guaranteed fundamental rights of the parties to the dispute and the principles of civil procedural law. The question for the next part of the book is to identify a specific place within the thus defined framework that will constitute the most appropriate and effective form of a functioning system of approach to mediation with minimal restriction of the principles of the three areas under scrutiny.

In general terms, the limits were defined as follows.

135. *See* Art. 6 of ECHR, Art. 47 of EU Charter of Fundamental Rights. *See also* European Union Agency for Fundamental Rights and Council of Europe, *supra* n. 33, at 119, 133–148.

136. However, even if attempted mediation ends in these ways, it does not always mean failure of mediation. For example, in custody cases, professional interventions of a mediator, even if the mediation does not result in an agreement between the parties, may lead to subsequent more constructive cooperation between the parties in court proceedings on the regulation of the custody of minors and to better reaching an agreement in those proceedings.

137. Cf. Vettori, *supra* n. 4, at 362.

138. *Ibid.*, 358.

139. A publication on the topic has been published in the Czech Republic: Lenka Holá, Martina Urbanová et al., *Mediace v praxi optikou empirického výzkumu* (Wolters Kluwer 2020).

The aspect of mediation: in principle, a certain degree of coercion to enter into mediation or an informational meeting with a mediator (as opposed to coercion within mediation) need not unduly limit the principle of voluntary mediation. As a rule, it does not necessarily have a significant negative impact on the functioning of mediation. The exceptions are, in particular, a direct form of coercion based on categorical, random ordering of mediation, disproportionate sanctions for refusal to mediate, and excessive supervision of participation in mediation or other measures that undermine the principle of voluntariness (or other principles of mediation, if applicable) to such an extent that the objectives inherent in mediation are no longer achieved.

The aspect of constitutionally guaranteed fundamental rights: mediation alone does not fulfil the right of access to court; on the contrary, this right may be infringed by forcing the parties to enter mediation or attend an informational meeting with a mediator. However, it must be examined in each individual case whether the interference is disproportionate. This may be the case, in particular, if mediation would lead to a decision that would be binding on the parties, if it would constitute a substantial delay in bringing an action before the court, if it would not stay the limitation period for the rights in question, if it would entail significant costs for the parties, if it could not be conducted otherwise than in electronic form, and if it would not be possible to issue preliminary rulings during the mediation. Another risk may be undue delays in the proceedings related to the stay of the proceedings during ordered mediation or an informational meeting with a mediator.

The aspect of civil procedure: coercion to initiate mediation or attend an informational meeting with a mediator in a contentious proceeding, and, in particular, the associated stay of proceedings, may limit the disposition principle and in conceptual terms also the court's obligation to conduct the case ex officio towards a decision. However, in a functional system of approach to mediation, this may be balanced by the fulfilment of the principle of preference for an amicable settlement of the dispute. At the same time, in a dysfunctional system of mediation provision, the principle of procedural economy may be restricted due to prolongation and increased costs of the proceedings. In contrast, a functional system largely leading to dispute resolution in mediation may contribute to the fulfilment of procedural economy.

These limits should be considered in legislative activities related to coercion towards mediation, but always taking into account the specific legal order and other relevant circumstances in the country in question.

PART IV

A Spatiotemporal Analysis of the Rate of Mediation Use in Individual EU Countries

David Fiedor & Lenka Holá

INTRODUCTION TO THE TOPIC

In the context of global support for a wider use of mediation, the EU has also focused on research on mediation itself and the conditions for the quality of mediation provision in its Member States.[1] The first studies, carried out from the 1980s to approximately the middle of the first decade of the twenty-first century, focused on research into the effectiveness of mediation as opposed to standard court proceedings and the use of mediation in various application areas.[2] These studies focused mainly on the outcome of mediation and the factors that influence mediation itself, but they have neglected broader, contextual determinants.[3]

Research studies focusing on the cultural aspects of mediation and examining the effectiveness of mediation from the mediator's perspective[4] constitute a certain thematic transition to research studies of the last decade, which reflect especially societal events in the context of international conflict and the migration crisis. For

1. Lenka Holá, David Fiedor & Martina Urbanová, *První setkání se zapsaným mediátorem na základě prostorové analýzy míry jeho využívání v České republice*, 9 Právník 876–886 (2019).
2. *See*, e.g., Kenneth Kressel & Dean G. Pruitt, *Mediation Research* (Jossey-Bass 1989); Enid O. Cox & Ruth J. Parsons, *Senior-to-Senior Mediation Service Project*, 32 The Gerontologist 420–422 (1992); Howard H. Irving & Michael Benjamin, *An Evaluation of Process and Outcome in a Private Family Mediation Service*, 10 Mediation Quarterly 35–55 (1992); Douglas A. Henderson, *Mediation Success: An Empirical Analysis*, 11 Ohio State Journal on Dispute Resolution 105–147 (1996).
3. James A. Wall, Jr. et al., *Mediation: A Current Review and Theory Development*, 45 Journal of Conflict Resolution 370–391 (2001).
4. *See*, e.g., Stephen K. Bell et al., *The Effectiveness of Peer Mediation in a Low-SES Rural Elementary School*, 37 Psychology in the Schools 505–516 (2000); Lorig Charkoudian, *A Quantitative Analysis of the Effectiveness of Community Mediation in Decreasing Repeat Police Calls for Service*, 23 Conflict Resolution Quarterly 87–98 (2005).

example, Bergmann and Niemann examined the effectiveness of the EU as a mediator of peace negotiations using the conflict between Serbia and Kosovo as a case study.[5] Salmon et al. examined the cultural aspects of mediation and the influence of mediation style on the effectiveness of intercultural conflict resolution, noting that very few studies have examined these factors.[6] Mediation in a national and international (European) context is also addressed by Matefi.[7]

The last important area of research on mediation is investigation of the conditions and quality of mediation provision in EU countries. One of the first studies is that by De Palo and Trevor. It responds to an urgent demand for relevant and up-to-date information in this area. The study shows, among other things, that there are significant differences in the quality of mediation and that mediation is still very underused. The study stresses the need for a uniform European concept of mediation while at the same time promoting its adaptation to the specific conditions of each country.[8] The role of the EU was assessed by the Member States as important for the development of an effective European mediation policy. An important document in this respect was Directive 2008/52/EC of the European Parliament and of the Council on certain aspects of mediation in civil and commercial matters (hereinafter also the 'Mediation Directive'). Its aim is to harmonise the understanding of mediation and its principles and to set minimum quality standards. At the same time, it does not aim to create a uniform regulation of mediation across the EU. The Directive puts pressure on the Member States to provide legislative, professional and qualification conditions for the use of mediation and to ensure its quality. The implementation deadline for Member States expired on 21 May 2011. In 2013, the European Commission commissioned a study to assess the impact of the Mediation Directive and its implementation in each EU Member State. The study also showed that the extent of the impact of the Directive varies considerably from country to country, depending on the existing national mediation system.[9] Fifteen Member States already had a comprehensive mediation system in place before the adoption of the Mediation Directive. In these countries, the Mediation Directive brought only limited changes to the system or none at all. In nine Member States, the rules governing mediation were either inconsistent or based on self-regulation in the hands of the private sector. In these countries, the implementation of the Directive led to the adoption of substantial changes to the existing mediation system. Four Member States adopted mediation systems for the first time as a result of the implementation of the Directive. In these Member States, the

5. Julian Bergmann & Arne Niemann, *Mediating International Conflicts: The European Union as an Effective Peacemaker?*, 53 Journal of Common Market Studies 957-975 (2015).
6. Elizabeth D. Salmon et al., *Cultural Contingencies of Mediation: Effectiveness of Mediator Styles in Intercultural Disputes*, 34 Journal of Organizational Behavior 887-909 (2013).
7. Roxana Matefi, *Mediation – in National and International Context*, 2 Journal of Social and Legal Studies 11-16 (2015).
8. Giuseppe De Palo, Mary B. Trevor et al., *EU Mediation Law and Practice* (Oxford University Press 2012).
9. European Commission, *Study for an evaluation and implementation of Directive 2008/52/EC* (30 Apr. 2021), https://www.observatoiredesmediations.org/Asset/Source/refBibliography_ID-37_No-01.pdf.

Directive led to the establishment of appropriate legislative frameworks governing mediation.[10]

The European Commission study was partly followed up by a study by the European Parliament.[11] It was based on a questionnaire survey, which received 562 responses from interested professionals - mediators, judges, lawyers, other legal practitioners, academics, organisations, public authorities and Member States across the EU.[12] The majority agreed that the unconvincing results of the Mediation Directive so far were due to its insufficient transposition into national law and the lack of motivational and promotional tools to increase the use of mediation. The study was also critical of the low use of mediation in dispute resolution.[13]

A recent important contribution to research on mediation in the EU is the *EU Mediation Law Handbook*.[14] It analyses each of the legal frameworks of the national jurisdictions of EU Member States relevant to mediation (including statutes, case law, practice guidelines, codes of ethics, standards of conduct and other regulatory instruments). The handbook also analyses the choices between court and out-of-court (specifically mediation) procedures. It asks the important question of which jurisdiction offers the 'best' legal framework to promote effective dispute resolution. This book, which identifies the potential strengths and weaknesses of regulatory mediation regimes, is unique in its approach. It provides a basis for Member States' policies to develop appropriate legislative strategies to increase the attractiveness and wider application of mediation in practice. Therefore, in the context of a spatiotemporal analysis of the use of mediation, we do not cite specific legislation on mediation in individual EU Member States, as full reference can be made to this detailed publication.

In European countries, the issue of mediation is mainly discussed in connection with the question of the extent to which it is used in practice and is closely linked to the development of mediation application across the EU. Despite European harmonisation tendencies, which give legislative and organisational frameworks to mediation systems at the national level, each country approaches the issue individually.[15] It is thus clear that an international comparison of the rate of mediation use is very difficult in view of

---

10. European Commission, *Report from the Commission to the European Parliament, the Council and the European Economic and Social Committee on the Application of Directive 2008/52/EC of the European Parliament and of the Council on certain aspects of mediation in civil and commercial matters. COM/2016/0542 final*, https://eur-lex.europa.eu/legal-content/EN/TXT/?uri=CELEX%3A52016DC0542.
11. European Parliament, *'Rebooting' the Mediation Directive: Assessing the Limited Impact of its Implementation and Proposing Measures to Increase the Number of Mediations in the EU*, https://www.europarl.europa.eu/thinktank/en/document.html?reference=IPOL-JURI_ET(2014)493042.
12. The questionnaire survey was carried out from 18 Sep. 2015 to 18 Dec. 2015 and took the form of a public online consultation.
13. *See*, e.g., European Parliament, *Resolution on the Implementation of Directive 2008/52/EC of the European Parliament and of the Council on certain aspects of mediation in civil and commercial matters* (2016/2066(INI)), https://eur-lex.europa.eu/legal-content/EN/TXT/HTML/?uri=CELEX:52017IP0321&qid=1614194030734&from=CS.
14. Nadja Alexander et al., *EU Mediation Law Handbook: Regulatory Robustness Ratings For Mediation Regimes* (Kluwer Law International 2017).
15. *Supra* n. 10.

the legislative arrangements of each EU country. Nevertheless, such a comparison is necessary and important with a view to the further development of mediation. In addition, the spatial aspect offers a completely different perspective on the data, which makes it possible to see the connections hidden at first sight in the data.

The fourth part of the book builds smoothly on the previous part aimed at presenting EU countries' approaches to mediation and seeks to analyse the available data. Chapter 8 will first present the EU as a whole and the use of mediation to resolve civil, family and criminal disputes in their Member States. This will be followed by Chapter 9, which will limit itself to the post-socialist states of the Visegrad Group. These are characterised by a relatively similar starting position, where alternative conflict resolution was not encouraged by the previous regime (until the early 1990s). Therefore, based on the analysis of national data on mediation, we will conduct a spatiotemporal analysis of the extent of mediation use in the EU countries and compare them. This will show to what extent mediation is used in each country and how this phenomenon changes over time. We want to focus in greater detail on the V4 countries, as they can be assumed to stand in cultural, political and economic proximity, which could shed more light on the obstacles that hinder an increased use of mediation in litigation in the Central European area. The last chapter, Chapter 10, presents possible perspectives for the further development of mediation in the EU based both on the theoretical concepts applied by individual states in the field of mediation and on the results of research on its actual use.

The research provides one of the first comprehensive insights into the use of mediation in litigation in individual EU states. A spatiotemporal analysis of the extent of use of mediation in a region as geographically large and at the same time diverse as the EU has not been carried out before. The analysis provides specific statistical data, compares the rate of mediation use between countries, reveals possible obstacles to its wider application and at the same time reveals the scope for improving the EU's support to its individual Member States in the field of mediation.

CHAPTER 8

Rates of Mediation Use in Individual EU Countries

David Fiedor & Lenka Holá

The chapter is based on an analysis of data provided by individual EU countries. After presenting the publicly available data and the methods of collecting and processing the primary data, three agendas are defined that can be identified within each legal system: civil, family and criminal. The aim of the chapter is to analyse the rate of mediation use in each EU country in the monitored agendas for the years 2017, 2018 and 2019.

§8.01 DATA AND METHODS

The analysis of the rate of mediation use in each EU country depends on the available data on mediation. We first attempted to obtain these data from publicly available sources. In particular, the Council of Europe and its European Commission for the Efficiency of Justice (CEPEJ) play a very important role here. The Commission brings together experts from all forty-seven Council of Europe countries. It collects data on mediation through a questionnaire survey every two years (most recently for 2018). In some form (not all agendas are filled in), data on the number of cases resolved by mediation for thirteen EU countries can be found there. In addition to this source, data can also be drawn directly from the official websites of each country. It should be noted here that the quality of publicly available data varies considerably from one EU country to another. On the one hand, it is possible to find countries with detailed information on litigation mediation (e.g., Italy, Poland or Slovakia), while on the other hand there are EU countries that collect and publish virtually no data on mediation or litigation (e.g., Ireland, Austria or Sweden).

For the sake of comparability and accuracy of data, we decided to approach all EU countries with a request for data through an official enquiry. The Czech Ministry of Justice, with which Palacký University in Olomouc has concluded a memorandum of cooperation on scientific and research activities in the field of mediation for the purposes of the research project, coordinated the outreach to individual states. The request for data was forwarded to the Permanent Representation of the Czech Republic to the EU through the Legislative Section for International Agenda of the Ministry of Justice of the Czech Republic. The Councils for the Judiciary of the Member States were requested to cooperate through this representation.[16] The Councils for the Judiciary were contacted during January 2021 and had two months to comment, as the deadline for sending the documents was the end of March 2021.

Most Member States (twenty-three) responded to the request, although four of them do not collect this type of information at a central level (Austria, Denmark, Latvia and Sweden). Four countries have not responded to repeated calls for assistance, namely, Cyprus, Greece, Ireland and Luxembourg. Unfortunately, we do not have any data from these eight countries to carry out a spatiotemporal analysis.

Therefore, the dataset on which the analyses in this chapter are based was prepared in early April 2021. In some cases (Italy, Spain), all we got in response instead of data provided was references to yearbooks or other files publicly available on the website of the particular institution of the country in question. It should be noted that in such cases we tried to track down the data ourselves, but this was not always possible due to language barriers (especially for technical terminology in the official language of the country) or other problems.

As the numbers of cases in which mediation was recommended or initiated are relatively low in each country, we looked at data for a three-year period, that is, 2017, 2018 and 2019. The data we requested included information on the number of mediations carried out and the number of all legally concluded disputes in each year for courts of first instance, broken down by three agendas: civil, family (custody) and criminal. Aware of the different categorisation of court disputes and the manner they are reported in the court statistical sheets, we defined these three agendas as broadly as possible in order to eliminate the risk of misclassification of a given type of dispute under a given agenda. The agendas will be defined in more detail at the beginning of each of the sections below.

Absolute numbers of disputes where mediation was used would not in themselves be meaningful, as different countries have different population sizes and different numbers of litigation, which would lead to different results. Therefore, the proportion of the number of mediated lawsuits concluded in a given year to the total number of lawsuits concluded in that year was chosen as the basic comparator. Information on the total number of disputes settled in individual EU countries can also be obtained from the European Statistical Office (Eurostat), but it only distinguishes between civil and/or commercial; administrative and criminal agendas.[17] While for some countries the data provided to us agree with those reported by Eurostat, for others

16. We obtained data for the Czech Republic directly, in the civil and family agenda from the Ministry of Justice of the Czech Republic and in the criminal agenda from the Probation and Mediation Service of the Czech Republic.
17. *Legal cases processed in first instance courts by legal status of the court process*, Eurostat (April 30, 2021), https://appsso.eurostat.ec.europa.eu/nui/submitViewTableAction.do/.

they differ, in some cases very significantly. These differences are then probably related to potentially differently defined agendas, between which no further adjustment and recalculation of the data are possible. In addition to the relative expression of mediation use as a proportion of mediated disputes in the total number of disputes in a given agenda, other possibilities can be used. This is used, for example, by CEPEJ, where the number of mediated disputes is given relative to thousand inhabitants of mean population.[18] As part of the analysis, we will also attempt to compare these two relative expressions by graphically plotting the two relative values in a correlation array chart. This is a dot chart from which the relationship between the two variables can be read. In addition, map outputs in the form of a cartogram will be used to show the relative values of the indicator, in this case the proportion of the number of disputes in which mediation has been recommended or used to the total number of disputes.

§8.02 CIVIL AGENDA

What we consider civil agenda is all private-law (*ius privatum*) disputes except family-law disputes. Data from sixteen EU countries have been collected as part of the civilian agenda, with Table 8.1 capturing the absolute and relative position of mediation in those countries. It shows the number of disputes for each year of the period 2017–2019 that have been recommended for mediation or in which mediation has been used as part of a judicial settlement.

Before analysing the rate of mediation use in each EU country, two points should be noted. The first is the specific national features of the conduct of the judicial agenda. Not all EU countries separate the civil and family agendas in the data, as the family agenda is part of the civil agenda there. This applies, for example, to Italy and Slovenia. In Germany, disputes where mediation was used are not separated from all disputes where one of the ADR methods was used (cf. § 278 III 2 of the German Civil Procedure Code – ZPO). Second, we are aware of the difference between 'recommending' a dispute for mediation and 'using' mediation. Recommending mediation to the parties to a dispute while respecting their freedom of decision does not a priori mean that the parties will use mediation. This is a limit imposed by the different models of the degree of coercion to mediate, as discussed in Part III of this book, and by the different forms of incorporation of mediation into national legal orders. However, for the purposes of our analysis, we have included both of these cases in the same category of 'use' of mediation, particularly because recommending and raising awareness of mediation significantly increases the motivation and potential for litigants to use it as well.[19] At the same time, by identifying a case suitable for mediation (and recommending

18. Mean population is calculated as the average population living in a given territory. In the case of one year, it is usually calculated as an average of the population at the beginning and end of the reference year.
19. In this context, Press, an American author, noted in her article on the institutionalisation of mediation more than twenty years ago that no one can make an informed decision about the use of mediation if they do not know that this option exists. Sharon Press, *Institutionalization: Savior or Saboteur of Mediation?*, 24 Florida State University Law Review 903–917 (1997).

mediation), the court also creates the preconditions for its use now or in the future. The vague statement that the table shows the number of cases where mediation has been recommended (the Czech Republic, Slovakia, France) or used is also slightly misleading. In international comparisons, it is important to note these differences. However, the mere fact that mediation is recommended by the courts can be seen positively as raising awareness of this out-of-court method of dispute resolution, as mentioned above.

Table 8.1 Absolute Numbers of Disputes for Which Mediation Was Recommended or Used in the Civil Agenda in 2017, 2018 and 2019, Supplemented by the Relative Importance of Mediation[20] in the Total Number of Disputes

EU 27 Countries	*2017*		*2018*		*2019*	
	abs.	*rel. (%)*	*abs.*	*rel. (%)*	*abs.*	*rel. (%)*
Austria			*not available*			
Belgium	7,851	3.79	7,098	3.95	5,896	3.52
Bulgaria	89	0.03	158	0.05	136	0.04
Croatia	498	0.42	403	0.34	430	0.42
Cyprus			*no answer*			
Czech Republic	872	0.24	1,227	0.32	1,250	0.33
Denmark			*not available*			
Estonia			*not available*			
Finland	7,920	1.92	7,388	1.59	7,063	1.63
France	1,201	0.08	1,319	0.10	1,626	0.12
Germany	14,841	1.10	13,700	1.04	13,578	0.99
Greece			*no answer*			
Hungary	655	0.33	791	0.44	765	0.48
Ireland			*no answer*			
Italy	155,457	N/A	144,934	N/A	140,137	N/A
Latvia			*not available*			
Lithuania	312	0.18	229	0.15	243	0.17
Luxembourg			*no answer*			
Malta	1	0.05	N/A		1	0.04
Netherlands	232	N/A	215	N/A	198	N/A
Poland	3,822	0.11	3,776	0.12	4,627	0.17
Portugal			*not available*			

20. We consider the relative importance of mediation in a given country to be the rate of its use, that is, the proportion of disputes in which it has been used to the total number of disputes. The rate of use is an indicator of the importance of mediation and its legitimisation in a given court system. Similarly in Table 8.2 and Table 8.3.

EU 27 Countries	*2017*		*2018*		*2019*	
	abs.	*rel. (%)*	*abs.*	*rel. (%)*	*abs.*	*rel. (%)*
Romania	414	0.04	328	0.03	297	0.03
Slovakia	7,442	2.98	5,294	2.94	3,662	2.58
Slovenia	2,470	N/A	2,451	N/A	2,414	N/A
Spain	4,024	0.18	3,695	0.15	5,040	0.19
Sweden	*not available*					

Sources: questionnaire survey; own processing.

Country-specific notes in addition to the information provided by each respondent:

- Bulgaria: The total number of resolved cases entering the calculation of the rate of mediation use includes dismissed cases;
- Germany: Data refers to cases handled by conciliation judges;
- Italy: Data retrieved from external source;[21]
- Malta: During the years 2017–2019, no mediations in the civil field were held with respect to court orders, while a voluntary mediation was held in 2017 and another one in 2019. An agreement was reached on all the disputed issues in both cases;
- The Netherlands: 'Civil' concerns commercial matters and subdistrict court cases (e.g., certain claims up to the amount of EUR 25,000, employment cases, cases regarding rent and consumer sale);
- Latvia: In response to your request, the Ministry of Justice of Latvia would like to explain that in 2015 Latvia has implemented court-annexed mediation. Civil Procedure Law lays down the obligation for a judge to propose mediation to the parties to be used in a dispute resolution at the initiation of a civil case as well as at other stages of litigation. However, it is up to the parties whether to choose mediation or not. There are no statistical data on the use of mediation after the litigation has been initiated nor on cases where the court proceedings have been terminated because the parties have reached an agreement through mediation;
- Lithuania: Please note that according to the laws of the Republic of Lithuania, mediation is not applicable in certain cases, when settlement agreement cannot be arranged according to the requirements specified in the Civil Code of the Republic of Lithuania. For example, mediation is not applicable in adoption cases, cases of paternity affiliation, cases of restriction of parental authority, etc. Therefore, the number of above-mentioned cases is excluded from the data of legally settled civil and family cases (2017 – 4,682 cases when

21. *Mediazione Civile*, Ministero della Giustizia: Direzione Generale di Statistica e Analisi Organizzativa (30 Apr. 2021), https://webstat.giustizia.it/SitePages/StatisticheGiudiziarie/civile/Mediazione%20Civile.aspx/.

mediation is not applicable; 2018 – 4,743 cases when mediation is not applicable; 2019 – 4,393 cases when mediation is not applicable).

Table 8.1 shows that most states experienced fluctuations in both absolute and relative rates of mediation use over the three-year period. Thus, only France, Hungary, Poland and the Czech Republic show a gradual increase. Although this is not usually a significant increase (this can probably only be said in the case of Hungary, which saw a decrease in the absolute number of mediated disputes in 2018), a positive trend can be reported. In contrast, a gradual decline in the use of mediation in the civil agenda can be observed in Germany and Slovakia in this period. It can be seen that only these six countries have seen some growth or decline over the three-year period, while the trend could not be traced for the rest of the countries. For this reason, it is more appropriate for international comparison to use the average rate (i.e., the rate determined as the ratio of the average number of mediated disputes in the period 2017–2019 to the average number of disputes over the same time period) of mediation use. Figure 8.1 shows that mediation is used to the greatest extent in Belgium and Slovakia (here, however, it should be taken into account that this is a rate of mediation use based on the number of recommended mediations). Finland has almost one percentage point less, while Germany is also above the one-percentage-point mark.

Figure 8.1 Percentage of Civil Cases for Which Mediation Was Recommended or Used Out of the Total Number of Disputes per EU Country During 2017–2019

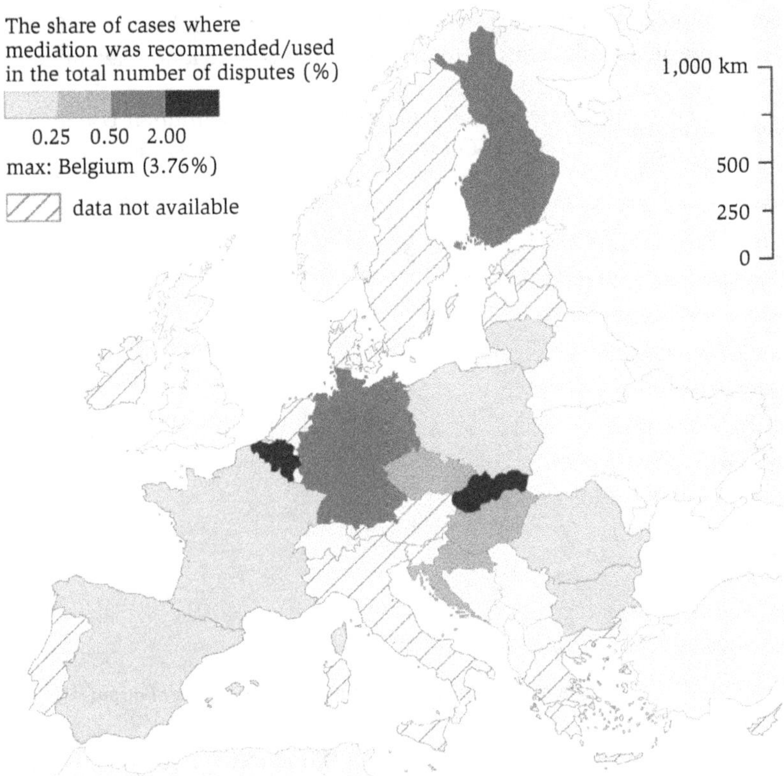

So far, only countries that provided both the number of mediated disputes and the total number of civil-agenda disputes in the survey have been compared. In order to also assess the position of states that provided only numbers of mediated disputes, we have used a relative expression of the number of mediated disputes per thousand inhabitants of mean population. In this indicator, Finland (1.35 mediated disputes per thousand inhabitants) is the best performer among the compared states, followed by Italy (1.27), Slovenia (1.18), and Slovakia (1.00). As already mentioned, this indicator is also used, for example, by the European Commission for the effectiveness of justice. Therefore, it is possible to compare the two relative indicators (Figure 8.2). Finland's first position in the number of mediated disputes per thousand inhabitants, together with its 'merely' third position in the share of mediated disputes in all civil disputes, can be attributed to the relatively high number of disputes (during the period 2017–2019 it is an annual average of about 438,000 disputes per 5.5 million inhabitants). Therefore, it is clear that the higher the number of lawsuits, the more they should be mediated. To this we can add that the more litigation a country has (in absolute terms, that is, the number), the more likely it is that the number of mediated disputes will also be higher. Therefore, Finland has a higher number of disputes in this indicator. Even though the relative importance of mediation may not be high, the absolute number of mediated disputes is high, which is why it is higher per thousand inhabitants. Italy, where mediation has even been compulsory in the past for civil disputes, is next, followed by Slovenia and Slovakia (where again only referrals to mediation are counted, not mediation as such).

Figure 8.2 Relationship Between the Relative Rates of Mediation Use in the Civil Agenda Across EU Countries for the Period 2017–2019

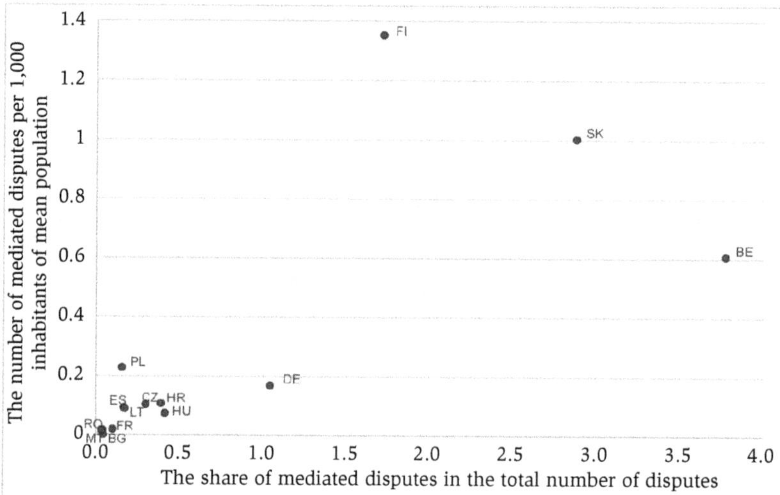

The use of mediation in civil matters may be influenced to some extent by public awareness of ADR methods and their promotion. The results can thus be easily compared with the evaluation 'Promotion of and Incentives for Using ADR Methods in Civil and Commercial Disputes'.[22] In this evaluation of promotion, Hungary and Germany ranked best in the civil agenda (12 points). Of the countries surveyed, Spain, Poland and Croatia came next (all 11 points); followed by Belgium, Bulgaria, Finland and Slovenia (10 points); the Netherlands, Lithuania and Malta (9 points); France, Belgium, Romania and Italy (8 points); the Czech Republic (6 points); and Slovakia (5 points). Interestingly, the countries that did not even respond to our request are generally at a very low level of promotion of and incentives for ADR methods (Greece with 8 points; Ireland with 5 points; Luxembourg with 4 points; and Cyprus with 3 points).

22. European Commission, *EU Justice Scoreboard 2020* (30 Apr. 2021), https://ec.europa.eu/info/sites/info/files/justice_scoreboard_2020_en.pdf.

§8.03 FAMILY AGENDA

What we consider the family agenda is all private-law disputes arising out of family-law relationships. Data from sixteen EU countries have been collected as part of the family agenda, with Table 8.2 capturing the absolute and relative rate of mediation use in those countries. It shows the number of disputes for each year of the period 2017–2019 that have been recommended or in which mediation has been used as part of settlement. Overall, much higher rates of mediated cases than civil cases can be observed. In five countries, there was a gradual, constant increase over the three-year period under review, namely, Bulgaria, the Czech Republic, Finland, Lithuania and Portugal.

Table 8.2 Absolute Numbers of Disputes for Which Mediation Was Recommended or Used in the Family Agenda in 2017, 2018 and 2019, Supplemented by the Relative Importance of Mediation in the Total Number of Disputes

EU 27 Countries	*2017*		*2018*		*2019*	
	abs.	*rel. (%)*	*abs.*	*rel. (%)*	*abs.*	*rel. (%)*
Austria			*not available*			
Belgium	N/A		652	1.88[23]	1,221	1.75
Bulgaria	111	0.89	134	1.05	139	1.08
Croatia			*not available*			
Cyprus			*no answer*			
Czech Republic	157	0.14	199	0.17	245	0.21
Denmark			*not available*			
Estonia	56	6.22	54	7.73	43	6.85
Finland	3,469	9.71	3,580	9.74	3,415	9.98
France	3,030	0.76	2,763	0.78	2,036	0.58
Germany	3,197	0.52	3,077	0.52	2,989	0.51
Greece			*no answer*			
Hungary	645	1.31	772	1.73	742	1.64
Ireland			*no answer*			
Italy			*not available*			
Latvia			*not available*			
Lithuania	207	1.51	223	1.61	290	2.12

23. A new code in the IT system of the family court to register (direct) conciliations was created on 1 Jun. 2018. Before this date, conciliations were registered under the civil court. Conciliations in the family court are thus counted in the category 'civil' until 1 June 2018. For this reason, the number of disputes has been multiplied by two so that the share of disputes corresponds to the whole of 2018.

EU 27 Countries	*2017*		*2018*		*2019*	
	abs.	*rel. (%)*	*abs.*	*rel. (%)*	*abs.*	*rel. (%)*
Luxembourg			*no answer*			
Malta	1,705	64.85	1,883	66.77	1,705	57.58
Netherlands	1,523	N/A	1,565	N/A	1,403	N/A
Poland	6,575	1.01	6,985	1.09	7,993	1.22
Portugal	288	0.38	254	0.39	330	0.54
Romania	607	0.50	436	0.35	397	0.30
Slovakia	1,770	1.38	1,326	1.00	N/A	
Slovenia			*not available*			
Spain	5,563	N/A	4,937	N/A	4,769	N/A
Sweden			*not available*			

Sources: questionnaire survey; own processing.

Country-specific notes in addition to the information provided by each respondent:

- Bulgaria: The total number of resolved cases entering the calculation of the rate of mediation use includes dismissed cases;
- Croatia: In family disputes, mediation takes place at social welfare centres, not at the courts, so we do not have data for that reason;
- Estonia: According to §563 of the Code of Civil Procedure, the court conducts a compulsory conciliation procedure in case of violation of agreement or order regulating access to child. We can provide the number of proceedings conducted according to §563;
- France: Custody procedures are exempted (there are no data for this);
- Germany: Our data refer to cases handled by conciliation judges. That means that the case numbers in our answer do not refer to mediation (only), but rather all methods of conflict resolution that may be used (cf. §278 III 2 of the - ZPO);
- Malta: Prior to commencing a family court litigation, one has to go through the mediation procedure. Only when the mediation process does not reach an agreement, one may file a court case. Settled Court Disputes statistics include both mediation and court terminated cases.

During the three-year period under review, mediation in family matters was used most in Malta (62.9% of disputes), followed by Finland (9.8%) and Estonia (6.9%) by a wide margin (Figure 8.3). Compared to other countries, the incredible proportion of mediated family-law disputes in Malta is due to legislation. In family-law matters, mediation is mandatory, especially in cases concerning divorce, contact with the child, child custody and maintenance for children and/or spouse. Of the European countries surveyed, mediation in family matters is least used in the Czech Republic. However, this is largely due to the fact that, according to statistical reporting, only the number of custody disputes was listed under this agenda (the definition is therefore narrower than the definition of the entire family agenda).

Figure 8.3 Percentage of Family Cases for Which Mediation Was Recommended or Used Out of the Total Number of Disputes per EU Country During 2017–2019

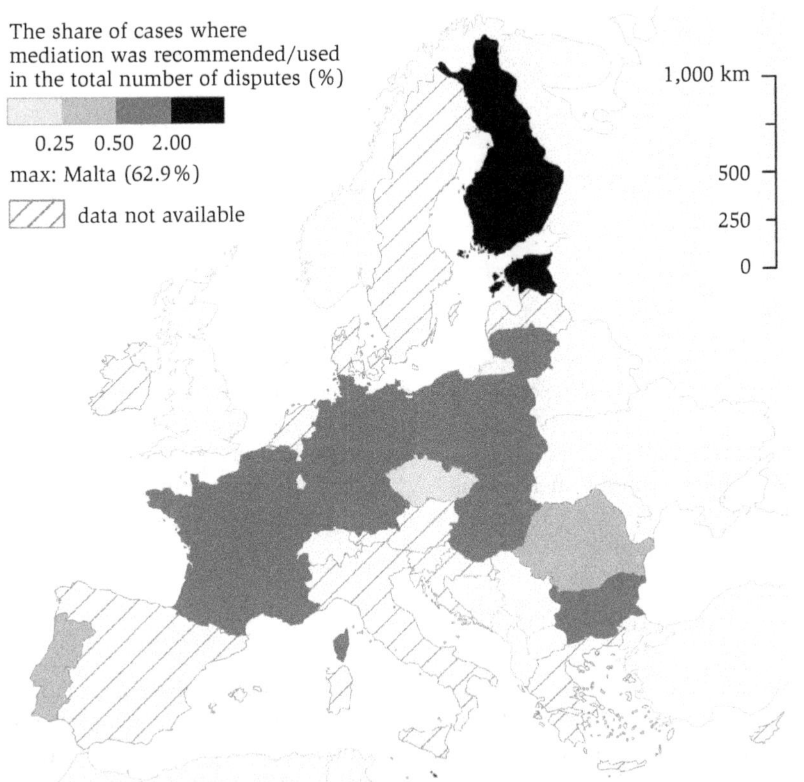

Estonia's position in this respect is somewhat striking. While the country ranks third in terms of the share of mediated cases, it ranks tenth in terms of the number of mediated cases per thousand inhabitants. It is even behind Spain, for which we do not know the total number of disputes, and thus it is not possible to calculate the proportion of mediated disputes. Part of the answer can be found in the very low total number of disputes (on average 742 family disputes resolved in one year in Estonia's population of 1.32 million).

Figure 8.4 Relationship Between the Relative Rates of Mediation Use in Family Agenda Across EU Countries for the Period 2017–2019

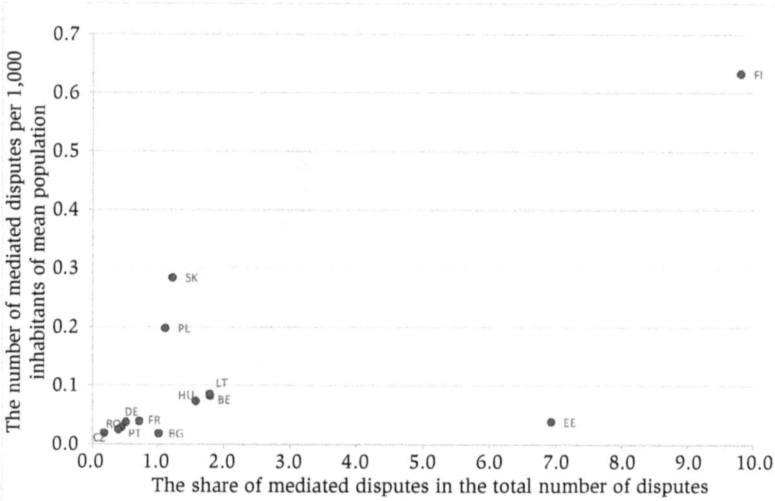

Note: Malta is not shown in Figure 8.4 due to very different figures (the proportion of mediated family disputes in Malta is 62.9%; the number of mediated disputes per thousand inhabitants is 3.63, which is three percentage points higher than in the second country, Finland).

§8.04 CRIMINAL AGENDA

What we consider criminal agenda is all public-law disputes where a socially harmful act (crime) has occurred. Within the criminal agenda, we received complete responses from only six countries (moreover, from the Netherlands, we received only data on the number of mediated disputes). For those countries that responded but did not provide data, the explanation is twofold. Either they do not have the possibility of mediation in the criminal field enshrined in law or they do not record it statistically. The specific values (absolute and relative) are shown in Table 8.3. An increase can be observed for the Czech Republic and Slovakia, while for Spain we see a decrease in the already low values.

Table 8.3 Absolute Numbers of Disputes for Which Mediation Was Recommended or Used in the Criminal Agenda in 2017, 2018 and 2019, Supplemented by the Relative Importance of Mediation in the Total Number of Disputes

EU 27 Countries	*2017*		*2018*		*2019*	
	abs.	*rel. (%)*	*abs.*	*rel. (%)*	*abs.*	*rel. (%)*
Austria			*not available*			
Belgium	2,661	N/A	2,752	N/A	2,386	4.88
Bulgaria	6	0.00	14	0.01	7	0.00
Croatia			*not available*			
Cyprus			*no answer*			
Czech Republic	637	0.83	675	0.92	768	1.04
Denmark			*not available*			
Estonia	834	N/A	792	N/A	792	N/A
Finland			*not available*			
France			*not available*			
Germany			*not available*			
Greece			*no answer*			
Hungary			*not available*			
Ireland			*no answer*			
Italy			*not available*			
Latvia			*not available*			
Lithuania			*not available*			
Luxembourg			*no answer*			
Malta			*not available*			
Netherlands	597	N/A	829	N/A	817	N/A
Poland	4,364	0.21	3,973	0.21	4,272	0.23
Portugal			*not available*			
Romania			*not available*			
Slovakia	1,100	1.52	1,105	1.59	1,118	2.00
Slovenia			*not available*			
Spain	3,843	0.12	2,718	0.09	2,650	0.08
Sweden			*not available*			

Sources: questionnaire survey; own processing

Country-specific notes in addition to the information provided by each respondent:

- Bulgaria: The total number of resolved cases entering the calculation of the rate of mediation use includes dismissed cases;
- Croatia: In criminal proceedings, in accordance with Article 527 of the Criminal Procedure Code, when it comes to proceedings on private lawsuits, the parties are given the opportunity to resolve their dispute by conciliation, but in practice this does not apply and we do not have relevant data;
- Finland: Criminal cases are not mediated in the courts;
- Lithuania: Please note that according to the laws of the Republic of Lithuania, mediation is not applicable in penal (criminal) cases;
- Portugal: void results or under statistical confidentiality (if one or two).

Given the small number of countries (six) for which we have complete data, in our opinion, it does not make sense to create a map output analysing the spatial differentiation of the rate of mediation use by individual EU countries in the criminal field. Instead, the relationship between the number of mediated criminal cases per thousand inhabitants and the proportion of mediated cases in the total population will be directly compared (Figure 8.5). There is a very large difference between Belgium and Slovakia in the proportion of mediated cases, while the number of cases per thousand inhabitants in both countries is very similar. Last but not least, it is worth noting the practically zero values in the case of Bulgaria.

Figure 8.5 Relationship Between the Relative Rates of Mediation Use in Criminal Agenda Across EU Countries for the Period 2017–2019

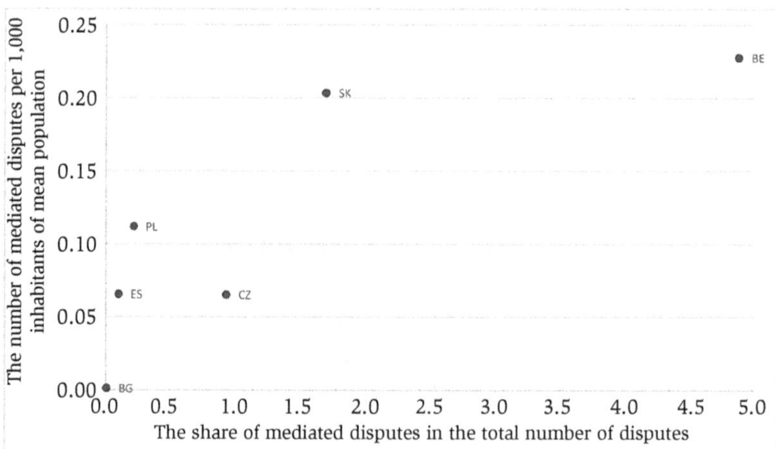

§8.05 PARTIAL CONCLUSION

There is no doubt that the rate of use of mediation varies widely across the EU and is difficult to compare. The data collected and published by the individual states are often not compatible, inasmuch as they do not have the same definition of judicial agendas or they record different data in relation to mediation (e.g., the number of disputes in which mediation was recommended, in which an informational meeting with a mediator was ordered or in which a mediation agreement was approved), but not the number of court cases actually resolved by mediation. Even so, at least a partial comparison can be made.

Within the civil agenda, mediation is relatively most used in Belgium, followed by Slovakia (here, however, the data are affected by the fact that Slovakia records only court-recommended mediations). In the family agenda, the case of Malta dominates, where more than 60% of family proceedings are mediated, mainly because the parties are obliged to first try to resolve the dispute through mediation. In the family agenda, mediation is used the least in the Czech Republic.

Data for the criminal agenda were obtained from only seven EU countries, and complete data from only five EU countries (the Netherlands did not provide the total number of disputes). Fifteen states did not record data, and four states did not respond to the request for data. The unavailability of data stems from the fact that mediation is not used in this area or there is a lack of statistical data on it. For a detailed description of the integration of mediation into the legal systems of each EU country and an analysis of the legal conditions for its practice, *see* the publication by Alexander et al., which we refer to in this respect.[24]

When comparing EU countries across agendas, the Visegrad Four countries (the Czech Republic, Slovakia, Poland and Hungary) form an interesting profile. In the assessment of the rate of mediation use within the civil agenda, almost all of them are marked in a different colour in the cartogram (Figure 8.1); that is, they fall into different categories defined on the basis of the relative rate of mediation use (only the Czech Republic and Hungary are in the same category, but these two countries differ substantially from each other in the family agenda). However, their historical development and context are very similar and it can be said that they had relatively the same starting position in the application of alternative methods of resolving court disputes. Therefore, the next chapter will follow up the analysis of the extent of the use of mediation in each EU country with a more detailed analysis of these four countries.

24. Alexander, Walsh & Svatoš eds., *supra* n. 14.

CHAPTER 9

The Rate of Mediation Use by Courts of First Instance in the Visegrad Four Countries

David Fiedor & Lenka Holá

The Visegrad Four (V4) is a regional grouping of four Central European post-socialist states (the Czech Republic, Slovakia, Poland and Hungary) established in 1991. All four states then joined the EU together on 1 May 2004. However, the grouping has not disappeared but continues to strive for joint action and cooperation within the EU. In our spatiotemporal analysis of the rate of mediation use in the EU, the use of mediation in the countries of this Central European community appears to be an interesting and unexplored topic. Considering that previous studies have tended to focus on the developed Western democratic countries, where mediation has the longest tradition and experience with mediation is greatest, the authors of this book consider it appropriate to analyse more closely the rate of mediation use in these post-socialist countries, where mediation has only been establishing itself in the last three decades or so. The topic has attracted the interest of experts in Europe and especially in other parts of the world more distant from Europe. The impact of the EU's tendency to harmonise the conditions for the use of mediation is distinctive in the post-socialist countries of Central Europe due to their different cultural, social, political and economic backgrounds.

In this chapter, we therefore first focus on the basic characteristics of the post-socialist countries and their transition to democracy. The purpose is to highlight their sociopolitical and cultural specificities which, as we have already pointed out several times, play an essential role in efforts to introduce mediation and increase its use. In preparing this section, we drew mainly on domestic sources and those of experts from the V4 countries, as their analyses are based on a more detailed knowledge of the environment. This will be followed by a discussion of the readiness of post-socialist countries to use amicable procedures as a theoretical starting point for a spatiotemporal analysis of the rate of mediation use in the Visegrad Four (hereinafter 'V4') countries. After a closer presentation of the data and the methods of data processing, the V4 as a whole will be presented; subsequently, the individual countries will be discussed separately and, where possible given the available data, the different agendas will be distinguished again as in the previous chapter (civil, family and criminal). The chapter is based on a more detailed analysis of the data provided by these countries - specifically data on the use of mediation in court disputes at the level of individual courts of first instance. The aim of the chapter is thus to analyse the level of mediation use by individual courts of first instance in the V4 Member States.

§9.01 POST-SOCIALIST COUNTRIES AND THEIR TRANSITION TO DEMOCRACY

Post-communism is the period of political, economic and social change following the collapse of communist regimes. The term 'post-socialism' refers to the historical period that followed socialism and is associated with a dynamic transformation of post-socialist countries.[1] It includes geographical, political and economic connotations that refer to the transition from totalitarianism to democratic rule and from central planning with its rejection of market mechanisms to a neoliberal market economy.[2] The phenomenon of the post-socialist environment differs mainly in the conditions that have prevailed in the various continents. Post-socialism in Central and Eastern Europe should be seen differently from the Asian countries that were once part of the Soviet Union or China. In order to understand the historical aspects in the Central European space and their influence on the conditions for the application of conciliatory procedures in dispute resolution with an emphasis on mediation, we will briefly focus on the analysis and interpretation of the sociocultural development of former socialist societies after 1989.

[A] Democratisation in Central Europe: Between Socialism and Post-socialism

Democratisation was made possible by the loss of legitimacy of communist regimes. Having exhausted their ideological legitimacy, these countries could not justify their existence with anything else, not even, for example, with economic success. In the countries of Central and Eastern Europe, different types of opposition began to form, reflecting the loss of functionality of the socialist regimes. An essential impetus for democratic processes was a change in the policies of external actors. In particular, it

1. Barbora Půtová, *Similarities and Connections Between Postsocialism and Postcolonialism: Analysis of Postsocialist and Postcolonial Countries*, 7 Anthropologia Integra 61 (2016).
2. Hana Červinková, *Postcolonialism, Postsocialism and the Anthropology of East-Central Europe*, 48 Journal of Postcolonial Writing 155–163 (2012).

was the attitude of the Soviet Union, which decided not to interfere in the situation of its own countries and favoured political and economic liberalisation.[3]

The transition of socialist regimes into democratic ones is referred to as the third wave of democracy. It took place differently in each of the countries we have studied (the Czech Republic, Slovakia, Poland and Hungary). In Hungary, it took the form of a transformation (transition) that could be described as democratisation from above. The people in power gradually eliminated the undemocratic regime until democracy was established. The transformation was peaceful. However, the former socialist rulers went unpunished because they had participated to some extent in the democratisation process and managed to secure advantageous positions in the new regime. In Poland and the former Czechoslovakia,[4] democratisation took place through transplacement. The socialist government decided on a slight liberalisation of the regime and easing restrictions of political freedoms, which, however, were not yet constitutionally guaranteed. This led to the strengthening of the opposition and its protests. Repression to maintain order ensued, leading to a stalemate followed by negotiations. These were attended by representatives of both sides, who were able to reach roundtable agreements on the shape of the electoral and political system in the years to come. Also with this type of democratisation, the communist elites went unpunished as they purposely ensured their representation in the already democratically elected parliaments via the proposed electoral system.[5]

Democratisation was gradual. Poland inspired and stimulated other countries, especially Hungary and Czechoslovakia. The quick and relatively easy overthrow of communism was replaced by a long and difficult process of introducing democracy and a free-market economy.[6] The transition to democracy was successful for most countries but its consolidation was not.

[B] Post-socialism: A New Type of Social Change

After the fall of the socialist regime in the countries of Central and Eastern Europe, we could see a certain 'void' that could not be easily filled by democracy. As Dahrendorf writes, 'Each country in East Central Europe has its own history and political culture. One of the delights of 1989 is the rediscovery of these differences. Thus, every country's attempt deserves its own explanation.'[7] The hope of a return to Europe was a reaction to the trauma caused by socialism. Part of the concept of post-socialist normalisation was the restoration of geographical continuity and the reunification of

3. Vladimír Nálevka, *Světová politika ve 20. století* 271 (Nakladatelství Aleš Skřivan 2000).
4. The division of Czechoslovakia and the creation of two separate states, the Czech Republic and Slovakia, took place on 1 Jan. 1993.
5. Michal Kubát, *Postkomunismus a demokracie: politika ve středovýchodní Evropě* 14 (Dokořán 2003).
6. Jadwiga Staniszkis, *Postkomunismus: zrod hádanky* 121–122 (Centrum pro studium demokracie a kultury 2006).
7. Ralf Dahrendorf, *Reflections on the Revolution in Europe: In a Letter Intended to Have Been Sent to a Gentleman in Warsaw* 15–16 (Random House 1990).

Europe.[8] However, the bureaucratic normalisation of the new Europe clashed with the traditional culture of the post-socialist countries.[9] The people of Central and Eastern Europe had old working habits, different attitudes to food and health, different ways of communicating, a different view of what constitutes a good life and different values. Efforts by the Western European countries to promote common, universally valid normative practices of unification and standardisation in the post-socialist countries also met with resistance. In the post-socialist countries, there has been disappointment and the opposite reaction, i.e., a new desire for difference and authenticity.[10]

The post-socialist transformation thus represents a new type of qualitative social change. This is particularly true for the post-socialist countries that have become new members of the EU.[11] The process of transformation has consisted of two phases. The first phase involved a transition to a democratic political system coupled with rapid and radical economic changes. The second phase was influenced by the integration of the post-socialist countries into the EU and the increasing economic cooperation with developed European countries.[12] Thus, young democratic systems are still developing an appropriate political culture and seeking a balance between administrative regulation and civil society.[13] According to Svensson, the liberalisation dimension is still more important than the participation dimension.[14]

§9.02 MEDIATION IN POST-SOCIALIST COUNTRIES

The possibilities of using mediation are related to the values of the respective society and its preferred methods of conflict resolution. By this we mean the cultural background of conflicts. We have dealt with this in more detail in Chapter 3 of this book. At this point, we can summarise, in agreement with Ross, that cultures represent a very good background for the use of mediation or participatory methods of conflict resolution when they have a constructive approach to conflict resolution and the following common features: low levels of inclination towards aggression and violence, strong links between the interests of individuals and the community, a preference for self-determination and a desire for control over dispute resolution, the availability of third-party assistance (helping to resolve the conflict, not making decisions for the disputants), an interest in peacemaking or cooperation and the possibility to withdraw if an acceptable solution cannot be reached.[15]

8. Karl-Rudolf Korte, *Die Wiederkehr Europas*, 2 Beilage der Süddeutsche Zeitung 10 (1990).
9. Půtová, *supra* n. 1, at 63.
10. *See*, e.g., Chamsy El-Ojeili, *Beyond Post-Socialism: Dialogues with the Far-Left* (Palgrave Macmillan 2015); Maja Zehfuss, *Constructivism in International Relations: The Politics of Reality* (Cambridge University Press 2002).
11. Půtová, *supra* n. 1, at 63.
12. Gil Eyal et al., *Making Capitalism Without Capitalists: The New Ruling Elites in Eastern Europe* (Verso 2000).
13. Milan Tuček et al., *České elity po patnácti letech transformace* 40 (Sociologický ústav Akademie věd ČR 2006).
14. Palle Svensson, *Teorie demokracie: Brněnské přednášky* 262–263 (Centrum pro studium demokracie a kultury 1995).
15. Marc H. Ross, *The Management of Conflict* (Yale University Press 1993).

What are post-socialist societies like in this respect? The social and cultural conditions created for mediation will match the extent to which these societies value togetherness, natural human ties, traditions, customs, reciprocity and solidarity. The decision to resolve conflict amicably is not a matter of law or a primarily legal decision. The choice between mediation and litigation is a demonstration of cultural maturity and individual maturity. It is also interesting to think in the opposite direction, that is, what is the importance of mediation for culture and society? And how do they influence individuals through society? Is the introduction of mediation as a common method of conflict resolution in a given society and its support by the state an expression of the values that a given society recognises or, more accurately, prefers?

Therefore, we must also look at the conditions of mediation in the light of developments and social events. In this sense, the research of Lakis is very inspiring, as he observed how the social events of the transformation of the post-socialist society influence the quality of the social environment. He has separately analysed the legal, cultural, organisational and educational conditions for the development of cooperation and how these conditions retrospectively influence the quality of the social environment.[16] The topic was dealt with in the period of post-socialist transformation in Lithuania. Radical political and economic changes and turbulence of cultural and ethical norms created a state of fragile stability, competition, social clashes and conflicts. The main question of his research was what contributed to the constructive course of reforms, what methods of conflict resolution were effective so as to maintain social stability and sustain social dialogue. He examined these issues in four areas, namely, legal, organisational, cultural and educational. There he assumed that there were numerous social interactions and first attempts to apply alternative methods of dispute resolution, namely, negotiation and mediation. He found that the conditions for the application of participation are influenced by three factors, namely, the manifestation of conflicts, the institutionalisation of conflicts and the management of conflicts.

According to many other authors, the choice of method and style of conflict resolution depends primarily on the cultural tradition and legal environment of a given society.[17] To this end, Kazan describes three models of conflict resolution, namely, harmonisation, confrontation and regulation, which he identifies in different cultures.[18] Kazan then focused his interest on conflict resolution in socialist and Post-Communist countries where centralised power exercised tight control over conflicts in

16. Juozas Lakis, *Conflicts and Cooperation in the Shifting Social Environment (The Case of Lithuania)* 617–626 (Management, knowledge and learning – International Conference 2012).
17. *See*, e.g., Marc H. Ross, *Creating the Conditions for Peacemaking: Theories of Practice in Ethnic Conflict Resolution*, 23 Ethnic and Racial Studies 1002–1034 (2000); Zhenzhong Ma, *Conflict Management Styles as Indicators of Behavioral Pattern in Business Negotiation: The Impact of Contextualism in Two Countries*, 18 International Journal of Conflict Management 260–279 (2007); Elizabeth Salmon et al., *Cultural Contingencies of Mediation: Effectiveness of Mediator Styles in Intercultural Disputes*, 34 Journal of Organizational Behavior 887–909 (2013).
18. Kamil M. Kazan, *Culture and Conflict Management: A Theoretical Framework*, 8 International Journal of Conflict Management 338–360 (1997).

an effort to suppress or prevent their public resonance. Such a sociocultural environment demotivates people from resolving conflicts through their own efforts.[19] They delegate their lives and decision-making to the 'authorities'. People lack individual and group capacities. The sense of social integrity was distorted, people's interactions frustrated by a lack of personal responsibility. Cooperation and competition were out of balance or did not develop from below.[20] Similar results were reached in research by Schwartz et al., where the countries of Central and Eastern Europe were characterised as having high levels of conservatism.[21] On this basis, one can then consider that there is a tendency to avoid conflict and change, to be conformist, to maintain social order and externally ordered relationships, as well as the attitude of being dependent on the opinions of others.[22]

It is probably here that we can see the reasons for the low readiness of post-socialist countries to use participatory practices in conflict resolution. These are the limits imposed by history.[23] Opportunities are conditioned by gradual cultivation and emancipation at both the individual and societal levels. It is a process of several generations.

§9.03 DATA AND METHODS

The previous chapter described the method of approaching individual EU countries to obtain data. The V4 countries were asked for more detailed data at the level of courts of first instance. We obtained these data for the Czech Republic, Slovakia and Poland but unfortunately not for Hungary. For Hungary, the competent authority (the Ministry of Justice) provided only basic data in the structure provided by the other EU countries, that is, only at the level of the whole country without distinguishing between individual courts of first instance. Therefore, the intended detailed spatiotemporal analysis of the rate of use of mediation for the years 2017–2019 could not be carried out for Hungary. For the other states (the Czech Republic, Slovakia and Poland), cartographic outputs were produced, namely, maps showing the relative rate of use of mediation, that is, the proportion of the number of disputes in which mediation was recommended or used in relation to the total number of disputes. Here, it is also important to point out a certain discrepancy in the 'mediation' data from the statistical records of the states. The Czech Republic records the number of initial meetings with a registered mediator for civil and custody disputes, which is not mediation but an informative meeting that the parties to the dispute are obliged to attend on the basis of

19. Miloslav Petrusek, *Společnosti pozdní doby* (Sociologické nakladatelství 2006).
20. *See*, e.g., Philip Kotler et al., *The Marketing of Nations: A Strategic Approach to Building National Wealth* (Free Press 1997). Leszek Balcerowicz, *Socjalizm, kapitalizm, transformacja* (Wyd PWN 1997).
21. Shalom H. Schwartz et al., *Value Adaptation to the Imposition and Collapse of Communist Regimes in East-Central Europe* 217–237 (Stanlye A Renshon & John Duckitt eds., Springer 2000).
22. Vladimír Labath, *Kontext uplatňovania mediácie* 74–94 (Lenka Holá, Michal Malacka et al., Leges 2014).
23. Petrusek, *supra* n. 19, at 244–245.

a court decision. In criminal matters, it records the number of mediations carried out. Slovakia recorded the number of referrals to mediation in civil and custody disputes. However, there has been a change in the family agenda and as of 2019, Slovakia records the numbers of approved mediation agreements. In addition, within the civil agenda, Slovakia also records the number of cases in which at least one type of claim was settled by conciliation. In the criminal agenda, similar to the Czech Republic, the numbers of mediations carried out are recorded. Therefore, Slovakia alone shows four different categories of data in relation to mediation. Poland is the most consistent in the data provided and has provided data on the number of mediations for all agendas (civil, family and criminal). When comparing the three countries, it is therefore clear that the best comparable data are in the area of the criminal agenda, as they relate to the number of mediations carried out in all three countries. For the sake of simplicity (while remaining aware of these differences), we will hereinafter refer to recommended or used mediations.

In addition to maps, common methods of descriptive and inferential statistics were used. Specifically, the Spearman's rank correlation coefficient was used to capture the strength of association between two variables. A positive value indicates a direct dependence, while a negative value indicates an indirect dependence.

The spatial distribution of the jurisdiction of each Court of First Instance plays an important role in spatial analyses of the use of mediation. This is different in the countries analysed (the Czech Republic, Slovakia and Poland) from the way the territorial units are defined administratively. While the Czech Republic is administratively divided into 76 districts (LAU 1) and the territory of the Capital City of Prague, there are 86 judicial districts (territorial jurisdiction of courts of first instance) in the Czech Republic, as the Capital City of Prague is divided into 10 districts of municipal courts and these have the same powers and duties as district courts, whose seats are located in all district towns (the boundaries of administrative and judicial districts are therefore different). There are 8 superior courts (regional courts) in the Czech Republic. Slovakia is administratively divided into 79 districts (LAU 1) as administrative units, whereas there are only 54 district courts in Slovakia. It follows that each district town is not the seat of a district court. The boundaries of the superior courts do not exactly follow the administrative boundaries of the regions (NUTS 3 units), although only the classification of two specific districts in neighbouring regions (Šala and Levoča) is different. There are 8 superior courts (regional courts) in Slovakia. In Poland, the same problem is encountered, as there are 379 districts as administratively defined units (LAU 1), while there are 'only' 318 district courts. There are 45 superior courts (regional courts) in Poland. The aggregate level of regional courts will be used to compare the relative level of use of mediation in the V4 countries (section §9.04), while the analysis of the spatial differentiation of the level of use of mediation in each country (sections §9.05–§9.07) will be carried out at the level of individual district courts. Therefore, in addition to the data, it was also necessary to obtain a layer (.shp) of the spatial delineation of the jurisdiction of each court from each state, without which the analysis could not be performed.

§9.04 VISEGRAD FOUR (V4) COUNTRIES

The Visegrad Four (V4) is the unofficial name of a regional grouping of four Central European post-socialist states: the Czech Republic, the Slovak Republic, the Republic of Poland and the Republic of Hungary.[24] Historically, these countries have always been part of one civilisation sharing cultural and intellectual values and common roots of religious traditions.

This regional grouping was formed in 1991 with the signing of a declaration by the V4 Member States on close cooperation on their path towards European integration.[25] After the fall of the communist regimes, such cooperation between the countries was important for their transition from totalitarian systems to free, pluralistic and democratic societies. The V4 group was not created as an alternative to the efforts for pan-European integration, nor does it seek to compete with the functional Central European structures. On the contrary, it seeks to promote optimal cooperation with all countries, especially neighbouring countries, and is interested in the democratic development of all parts of Europe.[26] Following the accession of the V4 countries to the EU in 2004, the V4's foreign policy activities have increased significantly. The group has focused on promoting cooperation and stability in the wider Central European region. Within the framework of the Regional Partnership, the V4 cooperates with Austria and Slovenia, and within the framework of the V4 + programme, it cooperates with other Central and Eastern European countries.

V4 activities cover all areas of public life, especially not only public administration but also culture, science and education. For example, in December 2016, a conference titled 'the Good Governance Forum' was held in Warsaw with the participation of representatives of the individual V4 members as well as representatives of Romania and Bulgaria. The conference was organised by the Polish V4 Presidency and focused on three themes: cooperation between central government and local government, reform of administrative procedures and user-friendly services. Although mediation was not explicitly the topic of the meeting, we could still see it in a broader sense as a tool to increase the efficiency of public administration. Conversely, improving and streamlining administrative procedures is a means of creating conditions for wider use of mediation.

During the thirty years of its existence, V4 cooperation has undergone various shifts: from the euphoria of the early days to the decline at the end of the 1990s, to the

24. Originally, the group of countries was called the Visegrad Three. The name Visegrad Four is a consequence of the division of the Czechoslovak Federal Republic into two separate states, the Czech Republic and Slovakia, in 1993. The grouping got its name during a meeting between the President of the Czechoslovak Republic Václav Havel, the Prime Minister of Hungary József Antall and the President of Poland Lech Wałęsa held in the northern Hungarian city of Visegrad on 15 Feb. 1991. The city of Visegrad was not chosen at random. In 1335, its castle, then the seat of the Hungarian kings, was the scene of negotiations between the Polish, Czech and Hungarian kings. Here the rulers agreed to work closely together on political and commercial issues, inspiring the founding of this modern Central European initiative.
25. *Visegrad Declaration 1991*, Visegrad Group (30 Apr. 2021), https://www.visegradgroup.eu/documents/visegrad-declarations/visegrad-declaration-110412-2/.
26. *About the Visegrad Group*. Visegrad Group (30 Apr. 2021), https://www.visegradgroup.eu/.

accession to North Atlantic Treaty Organization (NATO) and the EU and the search for a new format of coexistence. The big turning point was the stance on the European migration crisis in 2015 and the axis between Warsaw and Budapest. The Group's cooperation has always been characterised by fluctuations that depended on the extent to which the interests and political preferences of the four governments were aligned.[27] Asked what not only unites but also divides the Czech Republic, Slovakia, Poland and Hungary, Jiří Pehe, a Czech political scientist, expressed a more critical view. He said that he did not consider the V4 to be a natural but essentially an artificial alliance. He believes that today it serves politicians mainly to justify provincial populism and nationalism. Currently, we are more and more often seeing a Visegrad 2 + 2 formation, with the Czech Republic and Slovakia resisting the Orbanisation of the V4 on the one hand and Poland and Hungary promoting their interests together on the other. Even so, the main objective of the V4 remains the same, i.e., to cooperate and promote common interests. As Szicherle writes, 'Central Europe is still a place that has consumed more history than it has been able to digest. And occasionally, because of this, we get caught up in some pains that we like to share together. But alongside this, we are also united by the story of unprecedented cooperation and integration that we have achieved by joining the EU.'[28]

When comparing the extent of the use of mediation in the V4 countries in the area of civil matters, it was clear from the previous chapter that the overall proportion of disputes resolved by mediation varies from country to country. A closer spatial comparison at the level of the judicial units superior to the courts of first instance (regional courts) shows that different regions use mediation in the civil agenda to quite different degrees (Figure 9.1). In this context, the example of Slovakia serves us well, where we find regions in which mediation was recommended for a quarter of all civil law disputes, while at the same time we find a region in which mediation was not recommended for any litigation in this agenda in the monitored 2017–2019 period (the region of Greater Bratislava). Of the three countries under study, mediation is most evenly used in Poland, as evidenced by the difference between the minimum (0.02 %) and maximum (0.39 %).

27. Filip Harzer, *Visegrádská čtyřka po 30 letech: funkční a silná, nebo rozdělená na dva bloky?*, https://www.seznamzpravy.cz/clanek/visegradska-ctyrka-po-30-letech-funcni-a-silna-nebo-rozdelena-na-2-bloky-142431.

28. *Ibid.*

Figure 9.1 Percentage of Civil Cases for Which Mediation Was Recommended or Used Out of the Total Number of Disputes per EU Country During 2017–2019

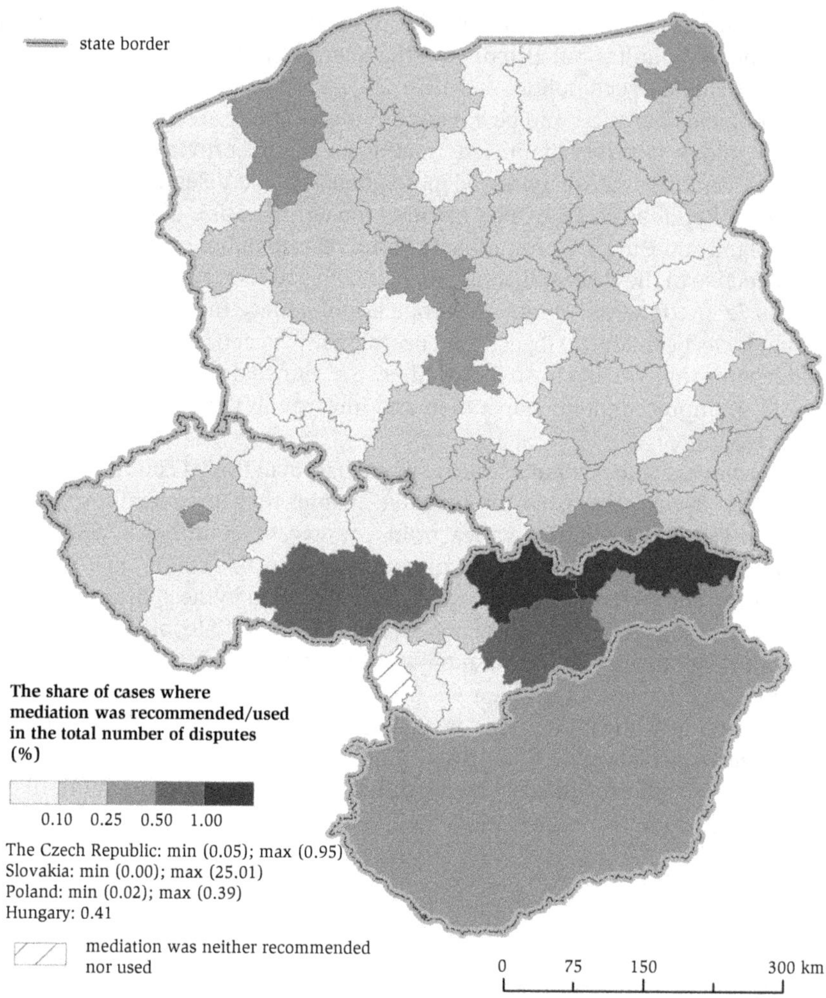

Slovakia is also a very special case in the family agenda. Although in the previous chapter Slovakia was in the same category of rates of recommendation or use of mediation in this agenda as Poland and Hungary, Figure 9.2 shows that the internal spatial concentration in certain territorial units is much higher than in the other countries mentioned. While three regions (out of eight) did not encounter mediation at all in the period under review,[29] the other two regions in the north/northeast of Slovakia show the highest rate of recommendation or use of mediation of all V4 regions (the maximum is even equal to 5.62%).

Figure 9.2 Percentage of Family Cases for Which Mediation Was Recommended or Used Out of the Total Number of Disputes per EU Country During 2017–2019

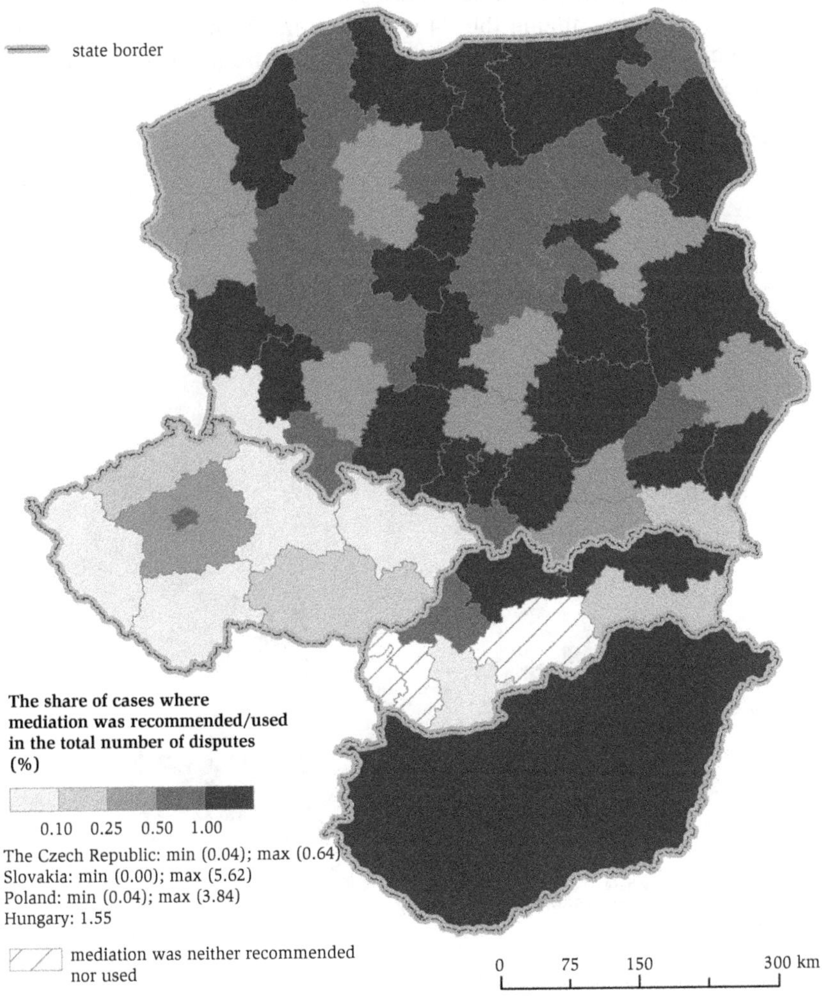

29. For Slovakia, unlike the other three countries, the rate of mediation use is based on an average of two years (2017 and 2018), not on a three-year period (2017–2019). However, this does not mean that the value for Slovakia should be higher or lower, but rather it may be more variable, which is confirmed.

As regards the criminal agenda, it should first be noted that Hungary does not use mediation in this area. Of the remaining three countries, the largest regional differences are again clearly in Slovakia. As in the agendas presented above, mediation in the criminal agenda is most used in the north and northeast of Slovakia, while it is least used in the southwest in the area of the capital Bratislava. Within the Czech Republic, the regions in the south of the country are again associated with the highest use of mediation, similarly to the previous agendas. In contrast to the two previous agendas (civil and family), mediation in the Czech Republic is relatively the most frequently used in the criminal area among the V4 countries. In Poland, an area with a lower proportion of mediated cases can be observed stretching from the north to the south in the west of the country (Figure 9.3).

Figure 9.3 Percentage of Criminal Cases for Which Mediation Was Recommended or Used Out of the Total Number of Disputes per EU Country During 2017–2019

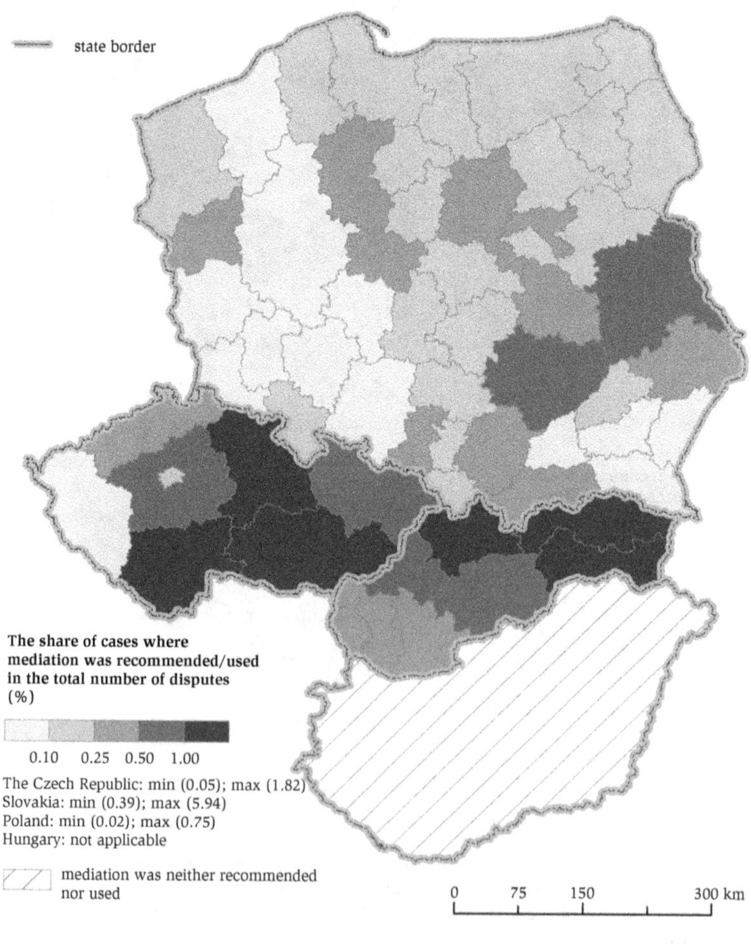

§9.05 THE CZECH REPUBLIC

The Czech Republic is the only one of the EU countries analysed where a gradual increase in the number and proportion of mediation use could be observed in all three years and in all three monitored agendas (*see* Chapter 8). This is of course partly due to the still relatively low rate of use of mediation compared to other EU countries. Moreover, it should be noted that the Czech Republic does not keep statistics on mediations carried out but on the number of cases in which an initial meeting with a registered mediator was ordered.[30] However, although in recent years there has clearly been an increase in the rate of use of the institution of the initial meeting with a registered mediator, this has not been uniform throughout the territory. There are courts where not a single initial meeting with a registered mediator has been ordered in the last three reporting years 2017–2019, even in both civil and family agendas[31] (Figures 9.4 and 9.5). These include the district courts in Benešov (BE), Děčín (DC), Jindřichův Hradec (JH), Prachatice (PT) and Rychnov nad Kněžnou (RK). In addition, there are another four district courts that have not ordered even one initial meeting with a registered mediator in the civil agenda (Figure 9.4) and another twenty-six district courts that have not ordered it in the family agenda (Figure 9.5). District courts in South Moravia then dominate the civil agenda (Figure 9.4). At the same time, the map in Figure 9.4 shows that there is not a single district court in Moravia that has not had experience with the institution of the initial meeting with a registered mediator in the civil agenda. In the case of custody disputes (Figure 9.5), Prague-East (PY) and some district courts of Prague (PHA: 1, 6 and 8) clearly dominate. In all of these courts, the proportion of disputes in which an initial meeting with a registered mediator was ordered exceeded 1% of all disputes. When comparing the two agendas (civil and family), it is clear that district courts use the institution of the initial meeting with a registered mediator to a greater extent in civil disputes than in custody proceedings. This dominance is mainly due to the non-use of the initial meeting with a registered mediator by all district courts. The use of the institution of the initial meeting with a registered mediator is much more spatially concentrated in custody disputes than in civil disputes. If we compare only those district courts that use the initial-meeting institution, we get twenty-five district courts using more initial meetings in civil disputes and, in contrast, twenty-seven district courts using more initial meetings in custody disputes. Thus, it is clear that the courts that use initial meetings with a

30. The purpose of the initial meeting with a registered mediator (pursuant to the provisions of s. 100(2) of Act No. 99/1963 Coll., Civil Procedure Code) is to provide the parties with the necessary information for them to decide whether to participate in mediation and to motivate them to resolve the dispute amicably by agreement. The initial meeting of three hours shall be ordered by the President of the Chamber. The mediation itself is only initiated by the conclusion of a mediation agreement (s. 4(1) of the Mediation Act). The parties therefore decide on the use of mediation voluntarily.
31. In the case of the Czech Republic and Slovakia, we also use the term 'family agenda' to maintain terminological consistency with Ch. 9. However, according to the court statistical sheets of both countries, only custody disputes are included. Other disputes arising from family-law relations are recorded under the civil agenda. This fact is probably one of the reasons for the lower rate of recommendation or use of mediation in the 'family agenda' in the two states.

registered mediator in both agendas being compared use the institution to a greater extent in custody disputes. Similarly, it is also evident that the maximum rate of use of the initial meeting is higher in the family agenda; specifically in Prague 1 (PHA 1) it is 5.09% of all custody disputes, while the maximum rate in the civil agenda is reached in Břeclav (BV; 2.48% of all civil disputes).

Figure 9.4 Percentage of Initial Meetings with a Registered Mediator in the Total Number of Disputes During 2017–2019 in the Civil Agenda

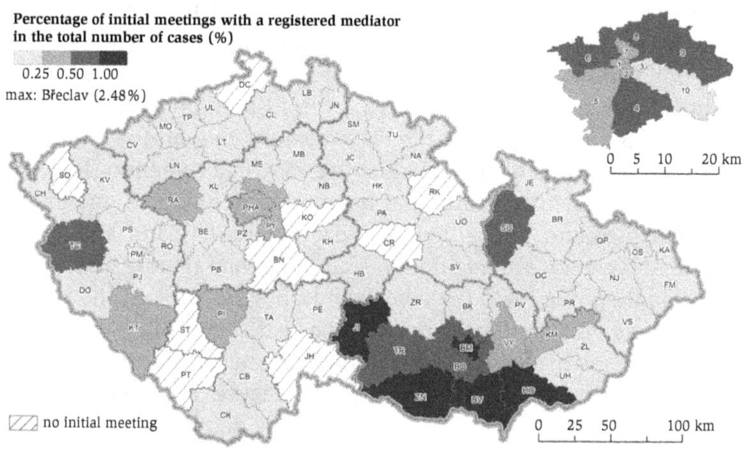

Figure 9.5 Percentage of Initial Meetings with a Registered Mediator in the Total Number of Disputes During 2017–2019 in the Family/Custodian Agenda

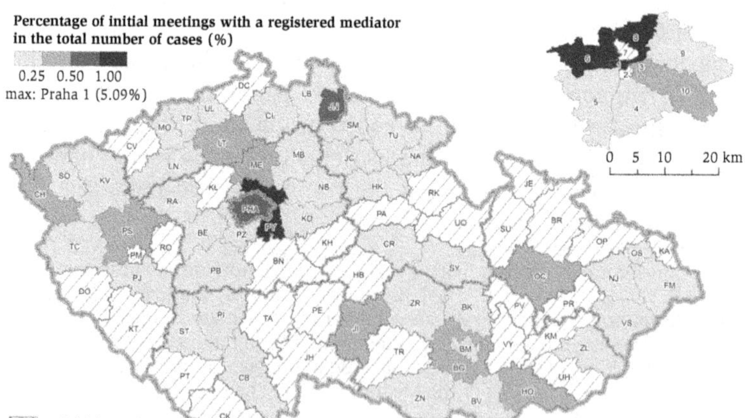

The percentage of mediated disputes in the criminal agenda is clearly higher in the Czech Republic than in the civil and family agenda. This is all the more so because the statistics of the Probation and Mediation Service of the Czech Republic report the number of mediations actually carried out, that is, not cases only recommended for mediation. Therefore, the scale selected in Figure 9.6 is different from the previous ones. In addition, all district courts applied mediation in the criminal area in the period under review. Part of the difference stems from the fact that there is no division of Prague (PHA) and that the urban districts of Brno = BM (Brno-město) + BO (Brno-venkov) and Pilsen = PJ (Plzeň-jih) + PM (Plzeň-město) + PS (Plzeň-sever) are combined. The reason for this is that mediation of criminal cases usually takes place at centres of the Probation and Mediation Service, which are established not only in individual district towns but also in other cities with large populations in the Czech Republic. When comparing the extent to which mediation in criminal law is used by individual district courts, it is clear that it is mainly used in more peripheral or border areas. In particular, districts involving population-sized cities fall below 1% of mediated cases: Prague (PHA), Brno (BM + BO), Ostrava (OS), Pilsen (PJ + PM + PS), Liberec (LB), Olomouc (OC) and others. Of the regional cities (the seat of higher territorial self-government units NUTS 3), of which there are fourteen, only Hradec Králové and Karlovy Vary are in the category of over 1% of mediated cases in the area of criminal agenda. Again, similarly to the civil and family cases, the district courts using mediation more are located in the area of South Moravia: BV, Hodonín (HO) and Vyškov (VY). Although this is not a periphery as in the case of Rakovník (RA) or Strakonice (ST), but rather an area with larger municipalities in terms of population, the rate of the use of mediation is relatively high, exceeding two or even 3%.

Figure 9.6 Percentage of Mediated Disputes During 2017–2019 in the Criminal Agenda

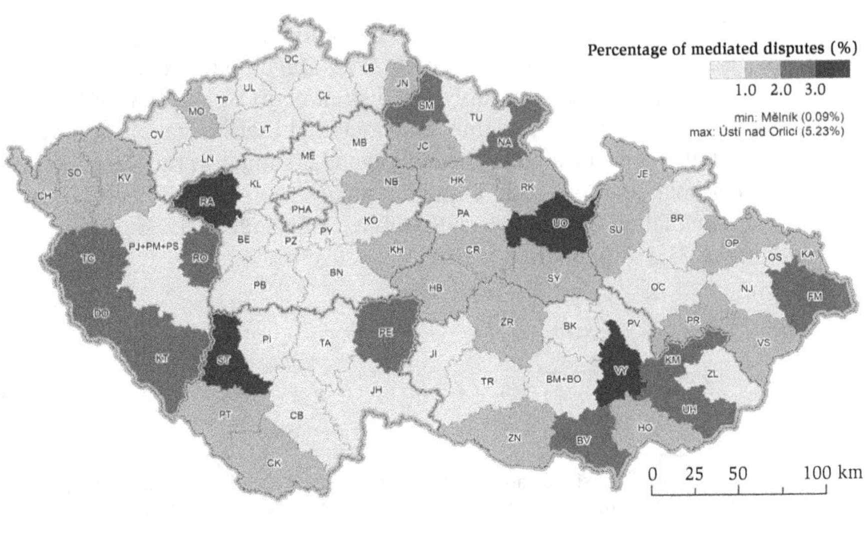

§9.06 SLOVAKIA

At first glance, it would seem that Slovakia, unlike the Czech Republic,[32] is one of the countries with a generally higher level of use of mediation in the resolution of court disputes. However, we believe that such a claim cannot be made. In the Czech Republic, the number of initial meetings with a registered mediator (not the number of cases actually mediated) is statistically reported and in Slovakia, the number of referrals to mediation is reported (also not the number of cases actually mediated). In terms of formality, organisation, personnel and time, referrals to mediation and initial meetings with a registered mediator cannot be compared. It is therefore problematic to compare the rate of use of mediation in the two countries. However, some indicative information on the use of mediation can be obtained. In addition to basic maps showing the relative rate of use of mediation (the proportion of disputes for which mediation has been recommended as a proportion of the total number of disputes), other map outputs will be presented in the case of Slovakia. The reason for the extended analysis carried out for Slovakia is the fact that in the comparison of the V4 countries at the level of regional courts, it was evident that Slovakia is characterised by a much higher degree of spatial concentration than the other countries. There are clearly visible areas where mediation recommendations are used to a much greater extent than elsewhere, across all the agendas monitored.

In the case of mediation in the civil agenda, there were only five district courts in the Czech Republic that used the institution of the initial meeting in more than 1% of civil court cases in the period under review. In comparison with Slovakia, we find thirteen such district courts, with even six of them reaching more than 5% (Figure 9.7). On the other hand, seventeen district courts did not recommend a single mediation. The spatial comparison then offers a clear answer to where mediation is most recommended. It is clearly linked to the Prešov judicial region in the east/north-east of Slovakia, which includes the territorial jurisdiction of the district courts of Poprad (PP), Kežmarok (KK), Stará Lubovňa (SL), Prešov (PO), Bardejov (BJ), Svidník (SK), Vranov nad Toplou (VT) and Humenné (HE). At the same time, this is the only judicial region in which all district courts have experience in recommending mediation in the civil agenda. Outside this judicial region, only the district court in Martina (MT) is in the highest category (above 5%). It can thus be concluded that mediation in Slovakia is significantly spatially concentrated in the civil agenda, similar to the Czech Republic. However, in contrast to the Czech Republic, many more district courts have no experience with mediation – in the Czech Republic, it is about 10.5% of district courts, in Slovakia, about 31.5% of district courts.

32. Considering the cultural proximity and the fact that the Czech and Slovak Republics were one state until 1993, we will compare the two countries more closely in the description.

Figure 9.7 Percentage of Civil Disputes for Which Mediation Was Recommended Out of the Total Disputes During 2017–2019

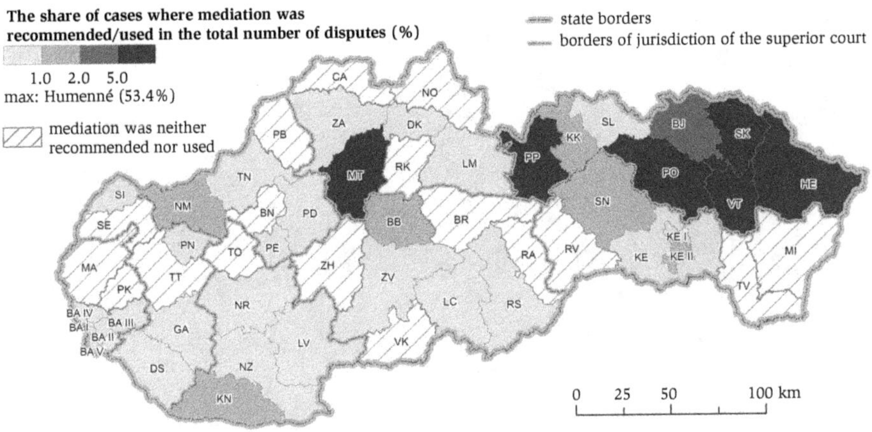

In addition to tracking referrals to mediation, the number of disputes in which at least one type of claim was settled by conciliation is also tracked (Figure 9.8). Here we get a much different picture than in the case of recommendations for mediation (Figure 9.7). The district courts in the east/north-east of Slovakia no longer dominate and are rather the 'Slovak average'. More than 3% of disputes with at least one claim that ended by amicable settlement are found in the district courts of Ružomberok (RK), Dolný Kubín (DK), Považská Bystrica (PB) and Piešt'any (PN). At the same time, this indicator is much more evenly distributed spatially and not as highly concentrated spatially as the proportion of disputes recommended for mediation. It is thus evident that these are two different approaches that are not very closely related. The correlation measured by Spearman's rank correlation coefficient shows a relatively low but direct relationship (the coefficient value is 0.22). Therefore, to some extent, the more disputes recommended for mediation, the more disputes in which at least one type of claim ended by amicable settlement.

Figure 9.8 Percentage of Civil Disputes in Which At Least One Type of Claim Ended by Amicable Settlement Out of the Total Number of Disputes During 2017–2019

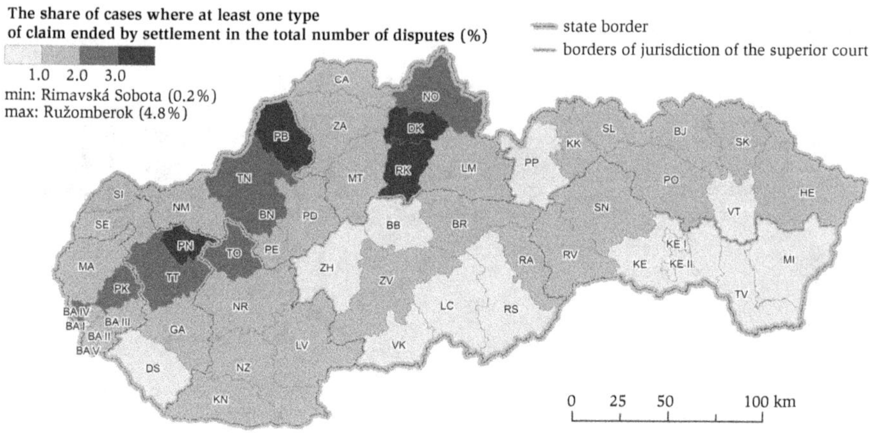

Even greater differences can be observed in the case of disputes falling under the family agenda. As mentioned above, the situation in Slovakia is similar to that in the Czech Republic, as only custody disputes are included in this agenda. First of all, what strikes us on the map (Figure 9.9) is the large number of district courts that did not recommend mediation for any custody dispute in 2017 and 2018[33] (forty district courts out of fifty-four in total). District courts in the three judicial districts have no experience recommending mediation in the two-year monitored period, which only contributes to the significant spatial concentration of this phenomenon.

33. Slovakia has not recorded the number of disputes for which mediation has been recommended in the family agenda since 2019. Instead, however, it started recording the number of family-law disputes in which a mediation agreement was approved by the court in full.

Figure 9.9 Percentage of Family/Custody Cases for Which Mediation Was Recommended or Used Out of the Total Number of Disputes During 2017–2018

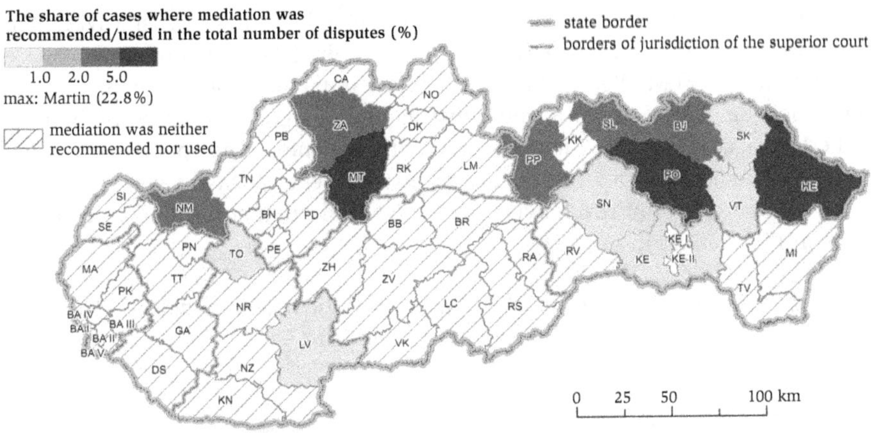

In 2019, every judicial district always had at least one district with experience approving a mediation agreement in custody disputes (Figure 9.10), yet a total of thirty-three district courts (out of fifty-four) did not record a single approved mediation agreement in custody disputes in 2019. In 2019, the district court in Humenné (HE) could boast a value of 2.5% of custody disputes that ended with the approval of a mediation agreement. Considering that only two other district courts (Žilina – ZA; Košice I – KE I) got over the 0.5% mark, this value is indeed significantly higher than is typical in Slovakia.

Figure 9.10 Percentage of Family/Custody Cases for Which a Mediation Agreement Was Approved by the Court Out of the Total Number of Disputes in 2019

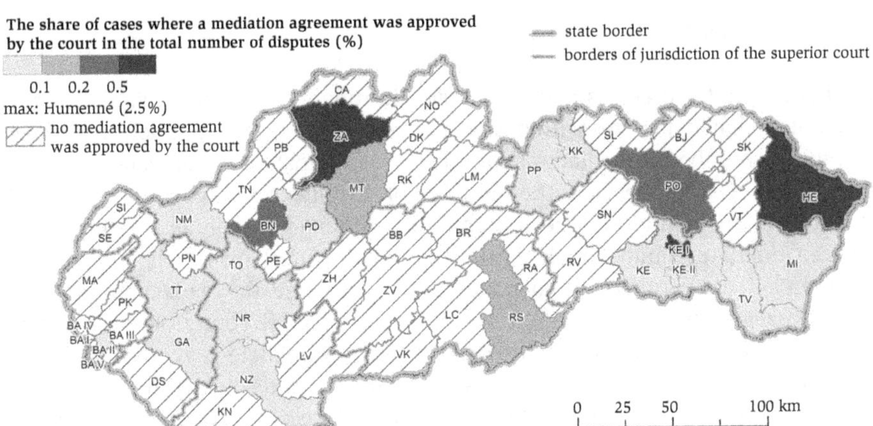

The similarity between the Czech Republic and Slovakia is also evident in the case of the criminal agenda. Only one district court in Slovakia (Pezinok – PK) had no experience with mediation in the period 2017–2019. While in the civil and partly also in the family agenda, the Prešov judicial district dominated in referring disputes to mediation, the Žilina judicial district with the judicial districts of Žilina (ZA), Čadca (CA), Námestovo (NO), Martin (MT), Dolný Kubín (DK), Ružomberok (RK) and Liptovský Mikuláš (LM) clearly dominated in the implementation of mediation in the criminal agenda. The majority of these district courts are characterised by more than 5% of criminal cases in which mediation was implemented. The opposite extreme can be observed in the district courts located in southern Slovakia, which practically without exception do not reach even 1% of the total number of criminal disputes in mediation (Figure 9.11).

Figure 9.11 Percentage of Criminal Disputes for Which Mediation Took Place Out of the Total Disputes During 2017–2019

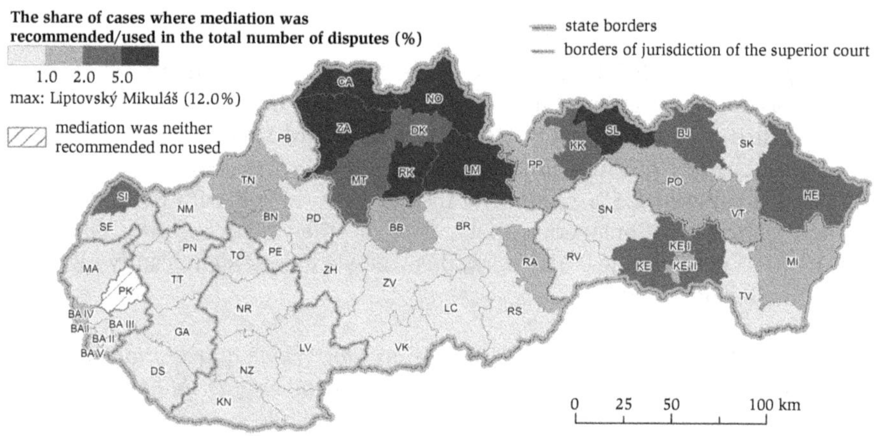

§9.07 POLAND

Poland is a country that has good and very thoroughly maintained statistics on the number of mediated disputes within each agenda. They are often publicly available; for example, the number of mediations for courts of first instance aggregated to the level of superior courts. As these are the numbers of disputes actually mediated, it is clear that comparisons with the Czech Republic (numbers of initial meetings with a registered mediator) and Slovakia (numbers of disputes for which mediation was recommended) are very difficult to make. At the same time, the reader should note that in some cases disputes resolved at the level of regional courts are first instance, although for the most part regional courts serve as appellate (i.e., second instance) courts. Therefore, some of these disputes can be (and are) resolved through mediation. In order to improve comparability, we have omitted cases handled by regional courts (albeit in the first instance) from the spatial analysis and focus only on district court statistics.

Within the civil agenda, it is clear that only 10 district courts (out of a total of 318) have no experience with mediation in the monitored period (Figure 9.12). It is of some interest, then, that these district courts are relatively close spatially and form clusters in space. As was already evident from the presented analysis at the level of regional courts (Figure 9.1), the spatial concentration in Poland is relatively small and individual district courts are very similar in the extent of use of mediation in civil law disputes. Only the Raciborz (1.10%) and Kościerzyna (1.09%) district courts have more than 1% of mediated disputes.

Figure 9.12 Percentage of Civil Disputes for Which Mediation Was Used Out of the Total Disputes During 2017–2019

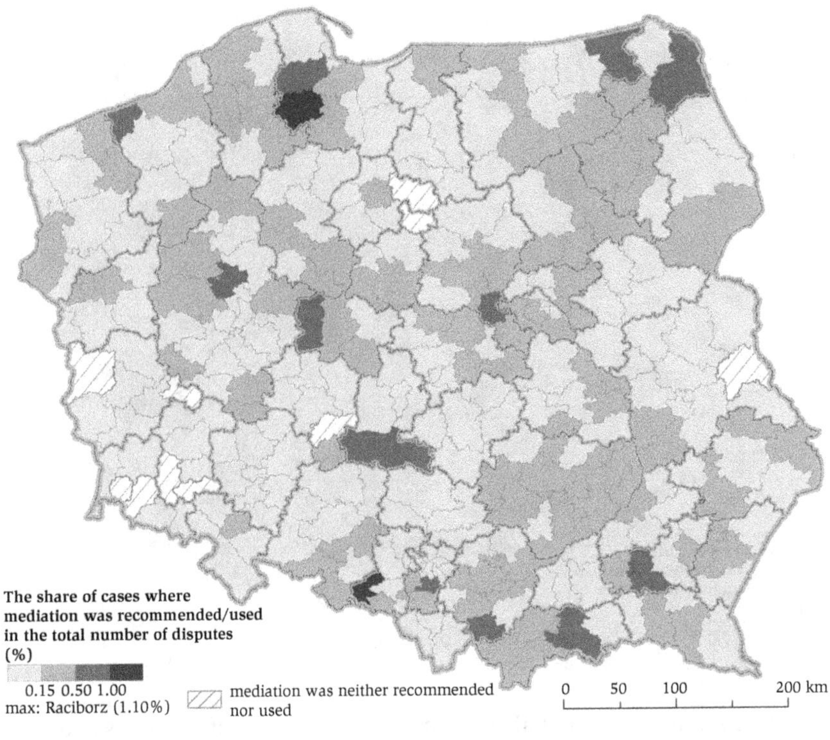

Poland is specific among the V4 countries in that it uses mediation in the family agenda, similarly to Hungary, to a greater extent than in the civil agenda. For the Czech Republic and Slovakia, we observe that the number of referrals to mediation (which may also be deemed to include orders of initial meetings with a registered mediator) is higher in these countries for the civil agenda. This may also be methodologically due to the observation of only custody disputes.

It is also necessary to draw attention to the fact that two district courts (Katowice-Wschód and Gdańsk-Północ) do not have resolution units for family-law disputes. Another ten district courts did not record any mediation in family cases in the period under review (Figure 9.13). In a total of twenty courts, the share of mediated family disputes is greater than 3 % (in eleven of them it is even greater than 5 %, and in the Szczytno District Court, it reaches 9.35 %). However, no obvious signs of spatial concentration can be observed, and thus we can only confirm the relatively even spatial distribution of the rate of use of mediation in the area of family law across the district courts in Poland.

Figure 9.13 Percentage of Family Disputes for Which Mediation Was Used Out of the Total Disputes During 2017–2019

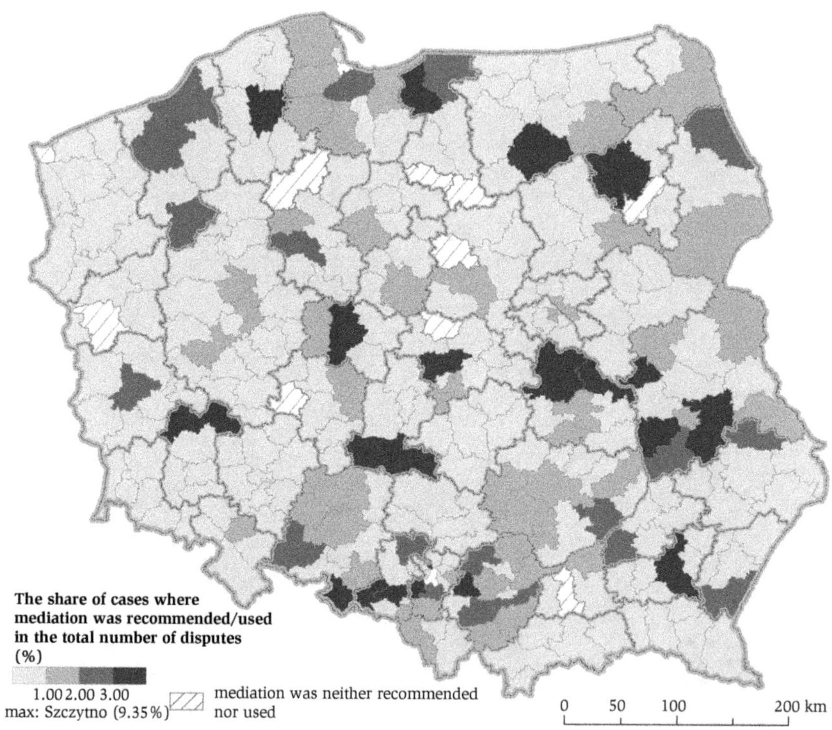

The highest degree of spatial concentration in the case of Poland is shown in the share of mediated cases in criminal law. A total of nine district courts did not use mediation in this area in the period under review. Looking at the map (Figure 9.14), it is evident that the use of mediation is higher in courts located in the southeast of Poland (the area between the cities of Kielce, Lublin and Radom). Eight courts are characterised by more than 1 % of mediated disputes with a maximum share equal to 1.79 % (Starachowice District Court).

Figure 9.14 Percentage of Criminal Disputes for Which Mediation Was Used Out of the Total Disputes During 2017–2019

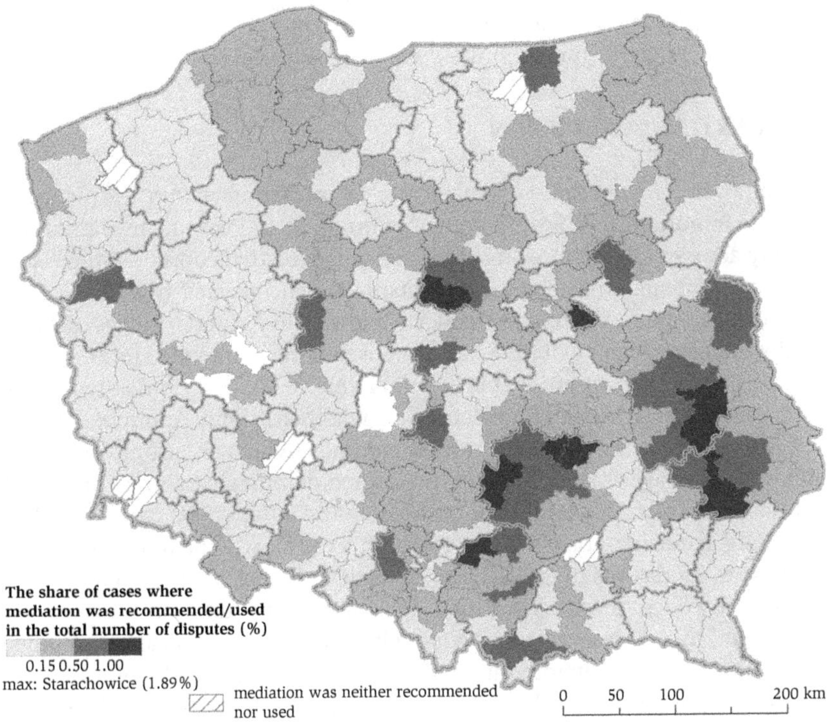

§9.08 HUNGARY

According to publicly available information, since 2013, parties have had the possibility 'in the bigger Hungarian courts to use mediation procedure in connection with pending civil, and non-judicial proceedings. The last 3 years prove that more and more citizens resort to the court mediation services. According to the statistics most of the court mediation proceedings end with the agreement of the parties'.[34]

For Hungary, the competent authority provided only basic data in the structure provided by the other EU countries, that is, only at the level of the whole country without distinguishing between individual courts of first instance. The intended spatiotemporal analysis of the rate of use of mediation for the years 2017–2019 at a more detailed level could thus not be carried out for Hungary due to the absence of data. We present the rate of use of mediation at the level of the whole country,

34. *Mediation in Europe and in Hungary – International conference on court annexed mediation*, Courts of Hungary (30 Apr. 2021), https://birosag.hu/en/international-conferences/mediation-europe-and-hungary-international-conference-court-annexed-mediation/.

compared to the other three V4 countries, in section §9.04 of this chapter. As can also be seen in Chapter 8, Hungary has significantly increased the proportion of mediated disputes in civil and family matters in recent years and mediation in this country seems to be developing in a desirable direction. The proportion of cases mediated is higher in family disputes, similar to Poland. On the other hand, mediation is not used in the criminal field in Hungary (unlike in the other V4 countries).

§9.09 PARTIAL CONCLUSION

A spatial analysis of the relative level of use of mediation within the V4 countries yielded quite important findings. In some countries (e.g., Poland), mediation is used more evenly across individual courts of first instance (district courts), while elsewhere its use or recommendation is significantly spatially concentrated (the Czech Republic and especially Slovakia). Therefore, thanks to a few 'active' courts/judges, the national share of disputes in which mediation has been used or recommended in some way may be increasing. It is thus questionable whether this really contributes to the overall increased use and awareness of mediation, or whether it 'only' improves the overall image of the state regarding the use of ADR methods, which are promoted by the EU.

Relevant data are essential to conduct a good empirical study. As already noted in the previous chapter, this is a major problem in the different EU countries. We have found the data-acquisition phase in our research to be clearly the most challenging. In some countries, no records of the number of mediated cases are kept at a central level at all. If a country does record certain data, such data are not uniform across the EU. To a certain extent, this corresponds to the models of mediation application and the form of incorporation of mediation into the legal systems of individual EU countries. Among the V4 countries, in the civil and family areas, the Czech Republic records the number of disputes in which the institution of the initial meeting with a registered mediator was applied (the purpose of which is to provide information about mediation and motivate the parties to amicably resolve their dispute), while Slovakia records the number of disputes in which the court recommended mediation to the parties. Only Poland and Hungary record the numbers of disputes in which mediation was actually carried out. In terms of data category, the situation is better in the criminal field, where, if mediation is possible, the number of cases actually mediated is usually recorded. We have almost no overview of the results of mediation, whether a mediation agreement was concluded and how the litigation was terminated as a result.

The situation is even more opaque when it comes to the categorisation of litigation for which the legal systems of EU countries allow mediation. For example, according to the court statistics sheets of the Czech Republic and Slovakia, only custody disputes are included in the family agenda. Other disputes arising from family-law relations are recorded under the civil agenda. This fact is probably one of the reasons for the lower rate of referral or use of mediation in the family agenda and the higher rate in the civil agenda in these two countries.

Although the V4 countries were able to provide us with detailed data (except Hungary, which probably does not have detailed data), comparability between them is very difficult due to the reasons mentioned above. On the one hand, the EU encourages Member States to create legal, personnel and other conditions for the application of mediation, and, on the other hand, there is a lack of greater support and assistance from the EU. Previous EU studies on mediation, as we mentioned at the beginning of Part IV of the book, have mainly been carried out through questionnaire surveys among national representatives, which is a limited way of obtaining relevant information on the development of mediation in the respective countries. There is therefore scope for methodological support from the EU to ensure uniform recording and management of statistical data in the field of mediation.

Part V

Prospects for the Development of Mediation in the EU

Jan Holas, David Fiedor & Lenka Holá

CHAPTER 10

Prospects for the Development of Mediation in the EU

Jan Holas, David Fiedor & Lenka Holá

The final chapter of the book aims to outline the authors' basic thoughts on the possible future course of development that mediation will take in the EU. This chapter is mainly based on the interweaving of the theoretical analysis of the systems of approach to mediation (Part III) and the results resulting from a spatiotemporal analysis of the rate of mediation use in individual EU countries (Part IV) and its success rate. The chapter is thus partly based on the results presented in these parts but, in addition, it discusses the success rate of mediation, which was addressed in the spatiotemporal analysis only marginally on the basis of the example of Slovakia.[1]

Although we are aware that the issue of assessing the success rate of mediation is not addressed in the literature unambiguously, given the focus of this book on the exercise of mediation in the context of judicial dispute resolution and the nature of the data collected for the spatiotemporal analysis of mediation in the EU countries, we rely on a formal approach to success rate.[2] Therefore, what we understand as success of mediation is the conclusion of a mediation agreement or a subsequent conclusion of a court settlement.[3] The theoretical background to our chosen methodological approach is discussed in the first part of this chapter. A more detailed description of the methodology is discussed in the first section of Chapter 8. At this point, we will only repeat that a total of twenty-three representatives of EU countries responded to our request for data, although four of these countries do not centrally record the requested data on mediation. This does not mean, however, that we have data for all the agendas examined (civil, family, criminal) for nineteen EU countries because some countries do

1. *See* Ch. 9, §9.06.
2. Cf. Klaus J. Hopt & Felix Steffek, *Mediation: Comparison of Laws, Regulatory Models, Fundamental Issues* 43–45, 103 (Klaus J. Hopt, Felix Steffek eds., Oxford University Press 2013).
3. *Ibid.*

not use mediation for some agendas or do not collect data (or do not distinguish between the civil and family agendas).

Given that the chapter is based on Parts III and IV of the book and thus has a different concept than the previous parts, it will not have the usual structure and will not contain a partial conclusion. This is because this chapter itself makes conclusions and formulates prospects for the further development of mediation on the basis of the previous parts of the book.

§10.01 SUCCESS RATE OF MEDIATION

A number of factors have been put forward as determinants of the success of mediation by which it can be judged.[4] A classic work by Kleiboer lists four sets of variables that influence the success of mediation, namely:

(1) the characteristics of the dispute;
(2) the parties and their relationship with each other;
(3) the characteristics of mediation; and
(4) context.[5]

Bercovitch and Houston[6] summarise these factors into only two main categories: contextual and procedural factors. Contextual variables refer to the characteristics of the disputes[7] or the mediator. Examples of contextual variables provided by the authors are the type of actors in the dispute, the relative power level between the disputants, and the nature of their prior relationship. The procedural component of this approach is illustrated by the approach to mediation (mediation model),[8] the choice of strategy and the mediation techniques used by the mediator.

With a great deal of generalisation, we could therefore say that the criteria for judging the success of mediation are its benefits which potential mediation actors consider when deciding to mediate and for which, after the mediation has ended, they

4. *See* Reina Zenelaj, Nimet Beriker & Emre Hatipoglu, *Determinants of Mediation Success in Post-Conflict Bosnia: A Focused Comparison,* 69 Australian Journal of International Affairs 414–437 (2015).
5. *See* Marieke Kleiboer, *Understanding Success and Failure of International Mediation,* 40 Journal of Conflict Resolution 360–389 (1996).
6. *See* Jacob Bercovitch & Allison Houston, *Why Do They Do It Like This? An Analysis of the Factors Influencing Mediation Behavior in International Conflicts,* 44 Journal of Conflict Resolution 170–202 (2000).
7. A very interesting study in this context was presented by Whiting. It deals with different success rates of mediation in cases where the dispute consists of only one issue and where there are several issues. On the basis of quantitative research on a sample of 111 cases, the author found, somewhat surprisingly, that in multiple-issue cases mediation was unsuccessful in only 15.63% of cases, while in single-issue cases the failure rate was 31.25%. What he considered failure was if the parties did not reach an agreement on the resolution of the dispute. Cf. Raymond A. Whiting, *The Single-Issue, Multiple-Issue Debate and the Effect of Issue Number on Mediated Outcomes,* 10 Mediation Quarterly 57–74 (1992).
8. *See* Ch. 6.

assess whether they have been fulfilled. Morineau summarises in this respect: 'Mediation ... provides a harmonizing structure to opposites. It enables the present to be rediscovered, whereas every conflict is only a repetition of the past. It allows us to embrace the future and not remain bound by our own suffering.'[9] In addition, Morineau considers the following to be advantages of mediation: high likelihood of resolution and termination of conflict; availability of mediation services without long waiting periods; lower cost; the parties to the dispute making their own decisions; opening of communication; preservation or renewal of relationships; confidentiality of information presented in mediation; and promotion of cooperation.

The definitions of mediation provide some answers to the question of what can be considered as criteria for the success of mediation, as we see in them the goal towards which mediation should aim. The problem, however, is that we do not find a consensus on this matter. As Vybíral notes, 'an exhaustive enumerative definition of interpersonal communication that includes all aspects (cognitive, philosophical, social, linguistic, cultural; all potential variables and possible levels of meaning and impact) is not possible'.[10] Therefore, we have essentially two options: to look for the goals of mediation in its legal definitions or in the literature. Given the formal approach to the success rate of mediation in this chapter, we will focus on the legal definitions.

Among the legal texts relevant to the conception of mediation in the European context, we can mention the EU Mediation Directive,[11] which states in its Article 3(a) that 'mediation means a structured process, however named or referred to, whereby two or more parties to a dispute attempt by themselves, on a voluntary basis, to reach an agreement on the settlement of their dispute with the assistance of a mediator. This process may be initiated by the parties or suggested or ordered by a court or prescribed by the law of a Member State'.

If we stay at the level of anchoring mediation in the legal systems of the EU Member States, we can cite as an example the Czech definition of mediation set out in Article 2 of the Mediation Act, where mediation is defined as 'a conflict resolution procedure involving one or more mediators who promote communication between the persons involved in the conflict ... so as to help them reach an amicable solution to their conflict by concluding a mediation agreement'. Under Article 2 of the Bulgarian Mediation Act, 'mediation is a voluntary and confidential procedure for out-of-court dispute resolution in which a third person – a mediator – helps the parties involved in the dispute to reach an agreement'.[12] Under Article 1 of the German Mediation Act, 'mediation is a confidential and structured procedure in which parties strive to resolve their conflict by mutual agreement on a voluntary basis and on their own authority, with the assistance of one or more mediators'.[13] Mediation is understood as a process

9. *See* Jacqueline Morineau, *Mediace řeší konflikty* 20–21 (Psychologie dnes 1999).
10. *See* Zbyněk Vybíral, *Psychologie komunikace* 30 (Portál, 2005).
11. Directive 2008/52/EC of the European Parliament and of the Council of 21 May 2008 on certain aspects of mediation in civil and commercial matters (hereinafter 'EU Mediation Directive').
12. *See* Evgeni Georgiev, *Chapter 4: Bulgaria* 98 (Nadja Alexander, Sabine Walsh, Martin Svatoš eds., Kluwer Law International 2017).
13. *See* Gustav Flecke-Giammarco & Kristina Osswald, *Chapter 13: Germany* 355 (Nadja Alexander, Sabine Walsh, Martin Svatoš eds., Kluwer Law International 2017).

of reaching an agreement or entering into a settlement also by some other national legal systems.[14]

All these legal definitions of mediation consider its objective to be 'reaching an agreement', 'resolving a dispute' or 'reaching an amicable solution (through a mediation agreement)'. However, even the fact that mediation has not reached a final agreement does not necessarily predict the failure of mediation. The question has been addressed by Aduda, who examined the effect of failed mediations (i.e., mediations in which no agreement was reached) on the possibility of future success (i.e., reaching an agreement). She sees limits in the voluntary nature of mediation, which leaves room for the parties to show (dis)interest in mediation and (not) reach a final agreement. Research suggests that previous mediation outcomes can both positively and negatively influence subsequent mediation efforts and the possibility of an agreement. The author emphasises that after a mediation in which no agreement was reached, disputants question the usefulness of mediation and the likelihood of reaching a mediated agreement decreases.[15] Other authors have reached similar conclusions.[16]

Legal definitions can also be evaluated in terms of the preferred mediation style. It can be said in agreement with Della Noce et al., Baruch Bush and Folger that any statutory definition is based on a particular vision of what mediation is and should be.[17] The experience of the United States Postal Service has shown that if there are political reasons that make one theoretical framework of mediation preferable, it is better to make that fact explicit. One guiding model of mediation tends to be selected (either explicitly or implicitly) in accordance with the prevailing conception and goals of mediation. This is of course reflected not only in the competency requirements of mediators but also in the expected outcomes of mediation.[18] A debated topic in the context of theoretical differences between frameworks, where standards developed for one framework are hardly applicable in a different framework, is how to ensure quality of mediation. In practice, the significant differences between the different approaches to mediation are then ignored.[19] This would, for example, be an interesting question for

14. *See*, e.g., Manuela Renáta Grosu, *Chapter 15: Hungary* 408 (Nadja Alexander, Sabine Walsh, Martin Svatoš eds., Kluwer Law International 2017); Mercedes Tarrazón & Marian Gili Saldaña, *Chapter 30: Spain* 744 (Nadja Alexander, Sabine Walsh, Martin Svatoš eds., Kluwer Law International 2017).
15. *See* Levke Aduda, *Failed Agreements and Their Impact on Subsequent Mediation Onset and Success in Intrastate Conflicts*, 45 International Interactions 893–916 (2019).
16. *See*, e.g., Govinda Clayton, *Relative Rebel Strength and the Onset and Outcome of Civil War Mediation*, 50 Journal of Peace Research 609–622 (2013); Constantin Ruhe, *Anticipating Mediated Talks: Predicting the Timing of Mediation with Disaggregated Conflict Dynamics*, 52 Journal of Peace Research 243–257(2015).
17. For example, the default mediation style in the Czech Republic, which is contained in the legal definition of mediation and thus also applied in judicial practice, is facilitative mediation. It is a solution-oriented model. Its primary objective is to reach an agreement on the dispute resolution and the settlement of relations between the parties. Both aspects – concluding a mediation agreement and reaching a settlement – are included in this legal definition of mediation.
18. *See* Dorothy J. Della Noce, Robert A. Baruch Bush & Joseph P. Folger, *Clarifying the Theoretical Underpinnings of Mediation: Implications for Practice and Policy*, 3 Pepperdine Dispute Resolution Law Journal 39 (2002).
19. *Ibid.*, 59.

further research, i.e., what models of mediation underlie the various statutory definitions of mediation.

A revision of efforts to categorise mediation was first brought about by the American lawyer and mediator Leonard Riskin. He noted that there was no widely shared comprehensive method for describing different approaches to mediation.[20] Subsequent literature on mediation styles has relied heavily on findings generated by social psychologists in the early 1970s.[21] Kressel's typology of three types of mediating roles (reflective, non-directive and directive)[22] paved the way for other similar taxonomies in the international context.[23] Further related categories of mediation strategies are offered by quantitative research.[24]

It can be concluded that the question of examining the success rate of mediation by the extent to which mediation agreements to resolve the dispute are reached is historically one of the most common in the empirical study of mediation. Foreign research conducted primarily from the 1990s to approximately the middle of the first decade of the twenty-first century focuses on the effectiveness of mediation as compared to standard court proceedings in particular. There has been an apparent effort to encourage wider application of mediation in practice through research findings.[25] In the subsequent part of this chapter, we will therefore examine the success rate of mediation in selected EU countries according to the extent to which a mediation agreement is reached.

§10.02 STATE OF USE AND SUCCESS RATES OF MEDIATION IN SELECTED EU COUNTRIES

In the previous sections of the present book, we reached two significant conclusions about the current state of use of mediation in the EU: we identified differences in the systems of approach to mediation and the low level of use of mediation across Member States.

20. *See* Leonard Riskin, *Understanding Mediators' Orientations, Strategies, and Techniques: A Grid for the Perplexed,* 7 Harvard Negotiation Law Review 7–51 (1996).
21. *See* Kenneth Kressel & James Wall, *Introduction to the Special Issue on Mediator Style,* 5 Negotiation and Conflict Management Research 334–339 (2012).
22. *See* Kenneth Kressel, Labor Mediation: An Exploratory Survey, 28 *Industrial and Labor Relations Review* 599–600 (1975).
23. *See* William I. Zartman & Saadia Touval, *International Mediation: Conflict Resolution and Power Politics,* 41 Journal of Social Issues 27–45 (1985).
24. *See, e.g.,* Kyle C. Beardsley et al., *Mediation Style and Crisis Outcomes,* 50 Journal of Conflict Resolution 58–86 (2006); Jacob Bercovitch & Scott Sigmund Gartner, *Is There Method in the Madness of Mediation? Some Lessons for Mediators from Quantitative Studies of Mediation,* 32 International Interactions 329–354 (2006); Scott Sigmund Gartner, *The Influence of Directive Strategies on Settlement Duration,* 19 International Negotiation 201–220 (2014).
25. *See* James A. Wall, Jr., John B. Stark & Rhetta L. Standifer, *Mediation: A Current Review and Theory Development,* 45 Journal of Conflict Resolution 370–391 (2001).

[A] Differences in Systems of Approach to Mediation in the Member States

The use of mediation in the Member States is continuously mapped by the EU. One of the important recent reports is the European Parliament's Resolution of 12 September 2017 on the implementation of the EU Mediation Directive.[26] It not only underlined the importance of the EU Mediation Directive for the use of mediation in the Member States but also noted that the functioning of mediation varies widely from one Member State to another.[27] The conclusion about the inconsistency of the systems of approach to mediation is confirmed by the findings in the previous sections of this book, where the basic models underlying the systems of approach to mediation in the Member States were presented (in particular, coercion-based models, motivation-based models and information-provision models).[28]

[B] Low Rate of Mediation Use

Despite the various measures used in the Member States to promote the use of mediation, the objective formulated in Article 1 of the EU Mediation Directive – to ensure a balanced relationship between mediation and court proceedings – has clearly not been achieved, as mediation is used in less than 1% of court cases on average in most Member States.[29] This is partly confirmed by the conclusions in Part IV of this book. The relative rate of mediation use varies considerably from one EU country to another. As can be seen in Chapter 8, also our spatiotemporal analysis confirmed that mediation is used in less than 1% of all disputes in most countries. However, large variations can be observed across court agendas (for the civil agenda, ten out of the fourteen EU countries for which we have data[30] have a relative share of less than 1%; for the family agenda, it is only five out of fourteen;[31] for the criminal agenda, four out of six[32]). It is thus clear that, at least for the family agenda, there is generally a greater use of mediation. An extreme case in this context is Malta, where mediation was used in 62.9% (over the last three years) of family-law disputes. The opposite extreme of the countries we have analysed is the Czech Republic, where the proportion in the last three years ranged from 0.14% to 0.21% in the area of family law. As will be shown below, in the case of the family agenda in Malta, this is mainly due to the concept of mandatory mediation where court proceedings take place only if the parties fail to reach agreement in mediation.

---

26. *See* European Parliament, *Resolution on the Implementation of Directive 2008/52/EC of the European Parliament and of the Council on certain aspects of mediation in civil and commercial matters* (2016/2066(INI)), https://eur-lex.europa.eu/legal-content/EN/TXT/HTML/?uri=CELEX:52017IP0321&qid=1614194030734&from=CS.
27. *See* European Parliament, paras A and C.
28. *See* Ch. 6, §6.04.
29. *See* European Parliament, para. F.
30. *See* Ch. 8, §8.02, Table 8.1.
31. *See* Ch. 8, §8.03, Table 8.2.
32. *See* Ch. 8, §8.04, Table 8.3.

It appears that there is a relationship between the set-up of the system of access to mediation and the recorded rate of mediation use. Clearly, and this has already been mentioned in Chapter 9 by means of an interpretation of Spearman's rank correlation coefficient, it is true to some extent that the more mediation is recommended or used in the context of judicial dispute resolution, the higher the proportion of disputes that end in conciliation. It is reasonable to assume that mediation agreements were certainly a prerequisite for court conciliation. In order to assess the prospects of further development of mediation in individual EU Member States, it is necessary to rely not only on the data already presented on the relative use of mediation to resolve court disputes but also on the success rate of mediation. In section §8.01, the process of obtaining data from individual EU countries was presented, with some countries providing data beyond what we had requested (or reporting different data than we had originally intended). Therefore, for the following countries, we have not only the number of mediations carried out but also the number of disputes in which a mediation agreement was concluded or mediation led to a settlement: Bulgaria, Finland, Italy,[33] the Netherlands, Slovenia and Spain. Thanks to good statistical records, it is also possible to look up data for Lithuania.[34]

Of the seven countries mentioned above, Finland clearly has the highest success rate and is also one of the countries with a relatively high proportion of cases that have been mediated. In the last three years under review (2017–2019), the success rate was 77.4% for the civil agenda and 67.1% for the family agenda. This is probably also due to the system applied in mediation in Finland. Commenting on the information provided, the Finnish source adds: 'The court decides whether mediation is to be undertaken. If the case is pending also as a regular adjudicative matter, the court proceedings are interrupted for the duration of the mediation. A judge sitting in the court where the case is pending serves as the mediator. Thus, no one else but a judge can mediate in court mediation in Finland.'[35] The Netherlands also has a high relative success rate, although there are relatively large differences between the different agendas. While mediation has a success rate of 'only' 49.9% in the civil agenda, it is 57.0% in the family agenda and even 73.7% in the criminal agenda. For the criminal agenda, it should be added that 'the public prosecutor and the court may still continue the prosecution and conviction. However, they typically take the agreement into consideration in their decisions'.

Of the countries mentioned, Lithuania and Slovenia follow in terms of mediation success rates, with success rates slightly below 50% (Lithuania 47% – civil and family together, Slovenia 45.5% – civil only). When looking at the number of disputes in which mediation has been used,[36] it is clear that Lithuania uses mediation to resolve

33. Ministero della Giustizia, *Civil Mediation Legislative Decree 28/2010, Statistics for the Period January 1st – December 31st 2019*, https://webstat.giustizia.it/Analisi%20e%20ricerche/Civil%20mediation%20in%20Italy%20-%20Year%202019%20(ENG).pdf.
34. National Courts Administration, *The Courts of Lithuania. Activity Results 2019*, https://www.teismai.lt/data/public/uploads/2020/04/trumpa-ataskaita-lapai-en-04-14.pdf.
35. We obtained the information from the Department of Development at the National Courts Administration.
36. *See* Ch. 8, Tables 8.1–8.3.

court disputes much less than Slovenia. Although we do not know the total number of disputes for Slovenia, when comparing the size of the two countries by population, it is clear that mediation is used much more in Slovenia. This country has a smaller population (by about a quarter), and the total number of mediations in the civil and family agenda was four times higher in Slovenia than in Lithuania.

Bulgaria, Italy and Spain have the lowest mediation success rates. Nevertheless, there are also clear differences between them. While Spain has a mediation success rate of over 30% in both civil and criminal matters, the success rate in family matters is only less than 12%. Bulgaria has the lowest success rate in the civil agenda (27.2%), where it is quite comparable to Italy (about 27%). In the other agendas, Bulgaria has a success rate of over 30% (32.0% in the family agenda and 37.0% in the criminal agenda). The reasons for the relatively low success rate are probably different. Currently, of those disputes for which mediation is recommended in Italy, the parties decide to participate in mediation in 49% of cases. If we look at the success rate of mediation in disputes where the parties decide to use mediation after an informative meeting with the mediator, the success rate of mediation in Italy (during 2017–2019, it was in the range of 42.2–48.5%[37]) is comparable to the levels achieved in Lithuania and Slovenia.

§10.03 PROSPECTS OF THE FUNCTIONING OF MEDIATION IN THE EU

Despite numerous efforts and incentives by the EU, Member States and other stakeholders, the desired mediation culture is not yet established in most EU countries.[38] As Member States often have different systems of approach to mediation,[39] the impact on the general public and professionals may be different. In a general sense, it is evident that efforts to use mediation led from above (by the authorities) are not sufficient if there is no primary interest from below (the public). The question of setting up the right system of mediation so that the public is interested in using mediation to resolve disputes seems all the more crucial at present.

When considering how to set up a system of approach to mediation, one is confronted with a wide range of possibilities. As outlined at a basic level earlier, one can consider:

- the specific degree of coercion into mediation;
- the use of motivational tools; and
- the system of providing and obtaining information about mediation and the possibility of dispute resolution within the framework of mediation.[40]

We consider it very promising to set up a system using tools based on the provision of information about mediation and motivation-based tools (with a lower

37. Ministero della Giustizia, *supra* n. 33.
38. *See* European Parliament, para. 2. *See also* Chs 8, 9 and §10.02.
39. *See* Ch. 6.
40. *Ibid.*

level of indirect coercion).[41] However, these must be effective tools that will actually be able to bring the disputants to mediation voluntarily.

Promoting greater awareness of mediation seems to be crucial. This is in line with the recommendation of the European Parliament, which calls on the Member States to increase their efforts to promote the use of mediation. It recommends that they do so through appropriate information campaigns providing comprehensive information on the nature of the procedure and its advantages in terms of time and cost savings. Such information should then be disseminated to citizens and legal entities, that is, to the potential parties to the dispute.[42]

We see the need to promote, first and foremost, raising of awareness about mediation because it appears that in some Member States the promotion of ADR is still relatively low.[43] This is illustrated by a public questionnaire survey conducted in the Czech Republic in November 2018 on a sample representing the Czech population. When asked 'What is mediation in your opinion?', only 33.6% of respondents selected the correct answer 'A way of out-of-court conflict solving'.[44] The finding that only a third of respondents were able to select the correct answer, with even this group not fully indicating whether they knew more detailed information about mediation, demonstrates the very low awareness of mediation and only supports the reflection on the need to provide more information.

If we look at the level of use of mediation within the selected Central European (V4) countries, it is evident that some countries are characterised by a much higher concentration of mediation. In other words, it is clear that mediation is recommended in some courts to a much greater extent than in others, which is problematic from our perspective. This is particularly the case in Slovakia and partly also in the Czech Republic because there are large differences in the rates of recommendation of mediation (Slovakia) or in the use of the institution of the initial meeting with a registered mediator (the Czech Republic). Some courts there practically do not recommend mediation at all, while others strongly recommend it. In Poland, on the other hand, we did not see this spatial differentiation. Individual courts are characterised by only minor differences in the extent to which mediation is used to resolve court disputes. The reasons for this are probably complex, but it is possible that the level of awareness of mediation may have some influence on the consistency of the recommendation of mediation. According to the 2020 EU Justice Scoreboard,[45] Poland ranks significantly better than the Czech Republic and Slovakia in the evaluation of methods of promotion of and incentives for using ADR.

The process of learning about mediation or, more generally, amicable dispute resolution procedures can ideally begin in primary school. From an early age, pupils

---

41. Cf. European Parliament, para. 11.
42. *See* European Parliament, para. 11.
43. *See* European Commission, *The 2020 EU Justice Scoreboard,* Publications Office of the European Union 28 (2020), https://ec.europa.eu/info/sites/info/files/justice_scoreboard_2020_en.pdf.
44. Martina Urbanová, Lenka Holá & Martin Lakomý, *Mediation in the Context of Law Acquaintance,* 11 DANUBE 9 (2020).
45. *See* European Commission, *The 2020 EU Justice Scoreboard,* Publications Office of the European Union 28 (2020), https://ec.europa.eu/info/sites/info/files/justice_scoreboard_2020_en.pdf.

should be taught to resolve their disputes amicably. They should adopt this method and see it as natural. A suggested measure could therefore be to include mediation in the school curriculum. However, this does not rule out information campaigns and further education among adults. Lawyers may also have a duty to inform their clients before bringing legal proceedings and should also try to settle disputes with the parties primarily out of court.[46]

It may also be appropriate to provide for tools of an incentive nature, in particular with a low level of indirect coercion. As a result, an environment may be created in which it is highly advantageous for the parties to the dispute to favour mediation over judicial resolution. However, from a comparative perspective, a fully suitable model that provides the desired environment has not been found. Refunding court fees already paid or not awarding costs to the successful party because mediation has not been used may not always fulfil this role to the extent required.[47] In the future, it therefore seems appropriate to consider other options, which may be linked, for example, to better accessibility of mediation services (in the court building, etc.) or price advantages (free mediation system, etc.).

As far as coercion is concerned, the use of a mandatory mediation model, in which the parties to a dispute are obliged to attend an informational meeting with a mediator or a voluntary model could be considered.[48] In the context of these considerations, it is also useful to confront the proposed models with the limits of coercion in mediation.[49]

It is precisely in the light of the limits of coercion to mediation that we do not see the introduction of systems of approach to mediation based on the mandatory mediation model, especially those using across-the-board coercion (a general obligation to initiate mediation), as promising in contemporary Europe. Taking into account the specific systems, this level of coercion may already severely limit the principle of voluntariness and consequently have a negative impact on the whole concept of mediation.[50] Similarly, it may also have a negative impact in terms of fundamental guaranteed rights (in particular, the right of access to court or the right to property may be affected[51]) and in terms of civil procedure (here the court's obligation to proceed ex officio in proceedings, the disposition principle, and the principle of procedural economy may be undermined).[52]

Models based on a general obligation to attend an informational meeting with a mediator may also have similar consequences in terms of guaranteed fundamental rights and the civil procedure. In this context, we can point to the Italian system based on a general obligation to attend an informational meeting with a mediator. It has been

46. Cf. Ch. 6, §6.07.
47. *See* Ch. 8. For example, in Bulgaria and Romania, where the court fee or a part of it is refunded when the case is settled in mediation, this circumstance is not reflected in the use of mediation.
48. *See* Ch. 6, §6.05.
49. *See* Ch. 7.
50. *See* Ch. 7, §7.01.
51. *See* Ch. 7, §7.02.
52. *See* Ch. 7, §7.03.

noted above that the success rate of mediation in Italy is 27%.[53] One may then ask for how large a proportion of the remaining 73% of disputes this obligation is rather a burden and an obstacle to the dispute resolution.

In addition to the risk of exceeding the fundamental limits of coercion into mediation, the motive for which mandatory mediation or informational meetings with a mediator have often been introduced in the Member States, namely, the decongestion of the courts, is also becoming less relevant.[54] According to recent data from the European Commission published in the 2020 EU Justice Scoreboard, there has been a positive development in the efficiency of Member States' judicial systems.[55] In particular, the length of first-instance proceedings has decreased or remained stable in many Member States and a high clearance rate has been recorded, meaning that courts are able to keep up with incoming cases while being able to deal with backlogs.[56] For this reason, the need to decongest courts could be lower at least in most states.

Traditionally, European civil procedure has been built on the guarantee that a litigant seeking justice as dispensed by the court will not be pushed against its will to settle the case amicably.[57] In the event that elements of coercive mediation are incorporated, they should be introduced into legal systems with great caution. If the parties to a dispute are forced to initiate mediation, it is of the utmost importance to ensure that refusal to resolve the dispute in this way does not incur additional costs and delay the resolution of the dispute.[58] This can be helped at least to some extent by ensuring that mediation or informational meetings with a mediator are not imposed across the board but on the basis of predetermined referral criteria. Such criteria should not be set vaguely and should be applied contextually.[59] In the system introduced, the difference between the number of cases in which parties are ordered mediation or an informational meeting with a mediator and the number of cases in which an out-of-court settlement or court settlement is subsequently reached should be as small as possible.

Rather than designing systems of approach to mediation based on high levels of coercion, it may be very interesting to explore the possibilities of conciliation and the

53. *See* §10.02.
54. *See* Ch. 6, §6.05 [A], [1].
55. *See* European Commission, *The 2020 EU Justice Scoreboard,* Publications Office of the European Union 6–13, 19–20 (2020), https://ec.europa.eu/info/sites/info/files/justice_scoreboard_2020_en.pdf. *See also* European Commission, *EU Justice Scoreboard 2020: Continued improvements in efficiency and accessibility of EU justice systems, coupled with decline in the perception of judicial independence in some Member States* (10 Jul. 2020), https://ec.europa.eu/commission/presscorner/detail/en/ip_20_1316.
56. *Ibid.*
57. Peter L. Murray & Rolf Stürner, *German Civil Justice* 488 (Carolina Academic Press 2004).
58. *See* Stella Vettori, *Mandatory Mediation: An Obstacle to Access to Justice?,* 15 African Human Rights Law Journal 357 (2015). *See also,* e.g., Edward F. Sherman, *Court-Mandated Alternative Dispute Resolution: What Form of Participation Should Be Required,* 46 SMU Law Review 2111–2112 (1993); Shahla F. Ali, *Nudging Civil Justice: Examining Voluntary and Mandatory Court Mediation User Experience in Twelve Regions,* 19 Cardozo Journal of Conflict Resolution 287 (2018).
59. *See,* e.g., Nadja Alexander, *International and Comparative Mediation: Definitions and Developments* 167 (Nadja Alexander ed., Kluwer Law International 2009).

use of mediation within the courtroom.[60] Mediation sometimes substitutes for the conciliatory role of the judge.[61] In European civil procedure, the judge can act actively[62] and usually has certain tools at his or her disposal to reconcile the parties. The judge can order a preparatory hearing and make the parties sit down face to face and communicate their interests, which can help to eliminate communication difficulties between the parties.[63] The judge may also provide the parties with preliminary evaluative feedback, in which the parties receive a preliminary factual and legal assessment of the case. This may be helpful to the parties in considering the possibility of a court settlement and its form.[64] Last but not least, the judge may set a 'cooling-off period' as part of conducting the proceedings, which may serve to allow the parties to reconsider an amicable resolution of the dispute.[65] Such a system then need not go beyond the defined limits of coercion into mediation. The Finnish system may be mentioned here as an example of good practice.[66]

In trying to analyse systems of approach to mediation in relation to its success rate, we find it problematic to respond to the data available on the success rate of mediation. Here we have concluded that Italy and Finland have specific systems of mediation. These are then also taken into account in §10.02 and conclusions are drawn in relation to them. However, the other countries for which we have mediation success rates are based on voluntary mediation with the possibility for the court to recommend mediation. Therefore, the differences in mediation success rates cannot be justified based on the system of approach to mediation in those states. Although there are some nuances in these states (the obligation to inform the parties about mediation is the duty of lawyers, the court fee is reimbursed if the dispute is resolved in mediation, etc.), we have not found support for the extent to which these can be attributed to the observed success rate. Moreover, other aspects, including non-legal ones, may also play a role. Therefore, based on the data presented here, we cannot draw generalised conclusions in relation to systems of approach to mediation. In order to do so, data from all EU Member States would be needed, which, however, appears to be a problem given the lack of records.[67]

It can therefore be summarised that what has been identified as the main promising approach of the functioning of mediation in the EU is the strengthening of the model of provision of information on mediation. Acting to reduce the information deficit on mediation appears to be a priority in many Member States. This goes hand in hand with efforts to ensure that the parties to a dispute are appropriately (especially positively) motivated to use mediation. On the other hand, the use of tools based on an across-the-board direct coercion to use mediation is not seen as promising for further development of the approach to mediation.

60. Alexander, *supra* n. 59, at 130–139.
61. Murray & Stürner, *supra* n. 57, at 489.
62. *Ibid.*, 496.
63. *Ibid.*, 489.
64. *Ibid.*, 489–490.
65. *Ibid.*, 491.
66. *See* §10.02.
67. *See* §9.09.

Summary

The main aim of the book was to analyse the legal, cultural, social, systemic and spatial aspects of implementation of mediation into the legal practice of European countries by applying various methodological and conceptual approaches and, based on a spatiotemporal analysis and models of mediation in the EU, to identify the reasons for the fragmentation of its legal regulation and the possible impact on the low level of its use in practice.

Although the focus has been on Europe, the topic of sociolegal, cultural and value resources in a general sense is not geographically bound. On the other hand, models of mediation and systems of its operation are analysed in the context of the EU. The EU is heterogeneous enough for this analysis as it includes both the developed states of Western Europe and the post-socialist countries of Central and Eastern Europe. This allowed us to see the application of mediation in different contexts. The topic is gaining in relevance with the search for the place and identity of mediation in Europe and its individual countries, also in the context of European processes of cultural integration. Despite European harmonisation tendencies, which provide legislative and organisational frameworks for mediation systems at the national level, each country approaches the issue individually. We can say that the different forms of mediation use vary from country to country, namely, in the following aspects:

- Organisational arrangement: This depends on the justice system in question and the way mediation is integrated into the legal system of the country.
- The level of institutionalisation: For example, how the mediation system is organised, the extent to which state and non-state organisations are involved, and how and to what extent their performance is standardised.
- Qualifications of professionals: This refers in particular to the qualifications of mediators and the related requirements for their competences, the organisation of training or the conditions for certification.
- Method of work: This refers to the forms of mediation, for example, according to the mediation style, the area of application or the degree of cooperation with other institutions and experts.

The conclusions reached in the individual parts of the book can be summarised in the following text. The causes and effects of law acting as an instrument of social change are increasingly difficult to identify, as economic, ideological, political and legal elements form a tight conglomerate of interacting and intertwining relationships. The process of globalisation and europeanisation of law adds to this lack of clarity and gives a new quantitative and qualitative dimension to the ongoing social change. It is very difficult to identify the sources of social change, the purposes that the change in law is intended to serve, and the breadth of the consequences of legal regulation. The postmodern situation means increasing demands on law, from the part of both society and the state. As this postmodernisation progresses, law not only reflects and confirms social change in society but also in itself becomes an increasingly important tool for social change.

The relationship between law and social change takes the form of a number of possible variations expressing mutual influence as well as negation and ignoration, which is also evident in the changing relationship between mediation and law. The introduction of mediation can be seen as a societal change in the national dimension, which should be reflected in appropriate legislation. In the case of mediation, a change in law is accompanied by an expected social change, particularly in terms of the beneficial effects in the area of the practical use of mediation.

The question of the gradual introduction of mediation into legal theory and practice is analysed in the second part of the book from a sociocultural and legal-theoretical perspective, in which the two approaches are interconnected by a discussion of the question of values in culture, society and law. If mediation is to create the reciprocity that conditions cooperative relations, there must be shared values to which individual societies subscribe, including through their legal norms.

Social functioning in mediation refers to people's efforts to resolve the particular conflict situation in which they find themselves. This enables them to perceive both their own problem and the issues of the social context in which they seek resolution. The empowerment approach applied in mediation is the strengthening of individuals, groups and communities in their ability to manage or constructively create their life situation through their own activities. We come to the conclusion that in the context of the social sciences, mediation is aimed at improving the social functioning of individuals through their mutual participation and empowerment.

Finally, in anchoring mediation in law, we draw on ideas from legal philosophy and legal theory, where the typical value argument is the argument of the principle of justice. In this context, mediation can be seen from three perspectives: as a means of improving citizens' access to justice, as a means of applying social justice in society and as a means of restorative justice. Therefore, if mediation builds on the above values and has become part of the legal system of a given country, then the above values of mediation should also be confirmed, guaranteed, highlighted and protected by specific laws.

In Part III of the book, it was pointed out that the form of mediation systems in the EU is very diversified. The different settings in the individual Member States were certainly influenced by the different processes of incorporating mediation into their legal systems, which took place without a strong unifying element. The contribution of the EU Mediation Directive can be seen as positive. It has undoubtedly had an influence on the incorporation of mediation into legislation in some Member States and on the wider awareness of at least governments and legislators. Nevertheless, the mediation culture in the EU is still far from becoming mainstream.

In terms of the design of systems of access to mediation in the Member States, three basic models have been distinguished in a comparative perspective: the coercion-based model, the motivation-based model and the model based on the provision of information about mediation. These models are generally applied in different forms in different Member States. What is proving problematic is exceeding a certain degree of coercion of the parties to the dispute to use mediation. This can undermine the principles and values on which mediation is built, the concept of guaranteed fundamental rights and civil procedure, and these concepts may not then be able to achieve their desired goal as a result of such coercion. Therefore, the limits of coercing parties to a dispute towards mediation were further explored. These limits were identified in terms of mediation, in terms of fundamental rights (right of access to court), and in terms of civil procedure.

Based on an analysis of national data on mediation in various legal systems, we conducted a spatiotemporal analysis of the rate of mediation use. It shows to what extent mediation is used in each country and how this phenomenon changes over time. In most countries, the rate of use of mediation was less than 1% of all disputes resolved, confirming the conclusions of previously published studies. On the other hand, due to the impact of established mediation systems, the experience in some countries is significantly greater. Within the civil agenda, mediation is most widely used in Belgium, followed by Slovakia, although the fact that the reported disputes are those in which mediation was only recommended plays a role here. In the family agenda, the case of Malta dominates, where more than 60% of family agenda disputes are mediated, mainly because the parties are obliged to first try to resolve the dispute through mediation. Mediation is then least used in the Czech Republic in the context of family law. Data for the criminal agenda were obtained from only seven EU countries, and complete data from only five EU countries. In the following chapter, we focused on a more detailed analysis of the extent to which mediation is used at the level of courts of first instance in the Visegrad Four (V4) countries, mainly because of their geographical, historical and cultural-political proximity. Here we found, *inter alia*, a strong spatial concentration of mediation use in the case of the Czech Republic and Slovakia. In Poland, on the other hand, the rate of use of mediation is relatively evenly distributed spatially; that is, individual district courts apply it to a very similar extent. The research will provide one of the first comprehensive insights into the use of mediation in litigation in individual EU states. A spatiotemporal analysis of the extent of use of mediation in a region as spatially large and at the same time diverse as the EU has never been carried out before.

The last chapter of the book aims to outline the perspectives for the further development of mediation in the EU. The chapter is mainly based on the interweaving of the theoretical analysis of the systems of approach to mediation and the results of a spatiotemporal analysis of the rate of mediation use in individual EU countries, which is examined especially in relation to the mediation success rate. We were able to conduct the analysis using comprehensive data from seven EU countries, namely, Bulgaria, Finland, Italy, the Netherlands, Slovenia, Spain and Lithuania. It is clear that to some extent, the more mediation is recommended or used in the context of judicial dispute resolution, the higher the proportion of disputes that end in conciliation. Of the seven countries mentioned above, Finland clearly has the highest success rate and is also one of the countries with a relatively high proportion of cases that have been mediated. Bulgaria, Italy and Spain have the lowest mediation success rates.

What can be said in conclusion? We believe that the determinants of mediation discussed in the book provide a starting point for its institutionalisation, legitimacy and legislative set-up in the different EU countries. It will be useful to coordinate these with the CEPEJ (2019) 9 (European Handbook for Mediation Lawmaking), developed during the term of the second GT-MED-CEPEJ working group and adopted on 14 June 2019, and with other European documents. In our view, the great diversity of systems for the practice of mediation in the EU is also due to the absence of a strong unifying element.

By looking at the different systems of mediation in the EU, we thought it would be possible to identify and draw inspiration from significantly better functioning systems. However, by conducting a spatiotemporal analysis, it became clear that there are no significant differences in the rates of use of mediation across countries. Rather, they are generally very low. The reasons for this may be many and are suggested in the theoretical parts of this book. It is these aspects that need to be addressed in the future if we are to create the conditions for a wider use of mediation in line with the aims of the European society. At the same time, greater EU support and assistance to Member States in their mediation efforts seems to us to be urgently needed.

Relevant (uniform) data are needed to conduct high-quality empirical studies. Obtaining such data has proved to be a major limitation for us. Therefore, it can be suggested that the EU should ensure uniform recording and management of statistical data for Member States in the field of mediation. Furthermore, we propose the implementation of a high-quality European information campaign on mediation, and the possibility of methodological recommendations and expert consultations. If the EU is perceived as a driving force in the field of mediation and at the same time mediation is still so little used by the Member States, these would be specific actions to help Member States with greater application.

This book has sought to contribute new topics to the scholarly discourse on mediation and to stimulate further scholarly discussion and elaboration. The book may also serve as a theoretical underpinning in legislative efforts to regulate mediation, particularly in EU Member States, and thus support EU efforts to make wider use of mediation in dispute resolution.

Lenka Holá et al.

Index

D

E

F

G

H

I

J

L

M

N

O

P

Q

R

S

GLOBAL TRENDS IN DISPUTE RESOLUTION

1. Nadja Alexander (ed.), *Global Trends in Mediation,* Second Edition, 2006 (ISBN 978-90-411-2571-2).
2. Giuseppe De Palo and Mary B. Trevor (eds), *Arbitration and Mediation in the Southern Mediterranean Countries*, 2007 (ISBN 978-90-411-2684-9).
3. Lars Kirchhoff, *Constructive Interventions – Paradigms, Process and Practice of International Mediation*, 2008 (ISBN 978-90-411-2685-6).
4. Nadja Alexander, *International and Comparative Mediation: Legal Perspectives*, 2009 (ISBN 978-90-411-2684-9).
5. Ewald A. Filler, *Commercial Mediation in Europe: An Empirical Study of the User Experience*, 2012 (ISBN 978-90-411-3116-4).
6. Ian Macduff (ed.), *Essays on Mediation: Dealing with Disputes in the 21st Century*, 2016 (ISBN 978-90-411-8366-8).
7. Nadja Alexander, Sabine Walsh and Martin Svatos (eds), *EU Mediation Law Handbook: Regulatory Robustness Ratings for Mediation Regimes*, 2017 (ISBN 978-90-411-5859-8).
8. Nadja Alexander and Shouyu Chong, *The Singapore Convention on Mediation: A Commentary*, 2019 (ISBN 978-94-035-1481-9).
9. Anna Howard, *EU Cross-Border Commercial Mediation: Listening to Disputants – Changing the Frame; Framing the Changes*, 2021 (ISBN 978-94-035-1753-7).
10. Lenka Holá, Martina Urbanová, Miloš Večeřa, David Fiedor & Jan Holas, *Mediation in the Reflection of Law and Society: European Perspectives*, 2022 (ISBN 978-94-035-4214-0).

www.ingramcontent.com/pod-product-compliance
Lightning Source LLC
LaVergne TN
LVHW020641300926
849161LV00004B/767
9789403542140